Mark Z. Danielewski

Contemporary American and Canadian Writers

Series editors
Nahem Yousaf and Sharon Monteith

Also available

Louise Erdrich   David Stirrup
Passing into the present: contemporary American fiction of racial and gender passing   Sinéad Moynihan
Paul Auster   Mark Brown
Douglas Coupland   Andrew Tate
Philip Roth   David Brauner

Mark Z. Danielewski

Edited by **Joe Bray and Alison Gibbons**

Manchester University Press

Copyright © Manchester University Press 2011

While copyright in the volume as a whole is vested in Manchester University Press, copyright in individual chapters belongs to their respective authors, and no chapter may be reproduced wholly or in part without the express permission in writing of both author and publisher.

Published by Manchester University Press
Altrincham Street, Manchester M1 7JA, UK
www.manchesteruniversitypress.co.uk

British Library Cataloguing-in-Publication Data is available

Library of Congress Cataloging-in-Publication Data is available

ISBN 978 0 7190 9933 5 *paperback*

First published by Manchester University Press in hardback 2011

This paperback edition first published 2015

The publisher has no responsibility for the persistence or accuracy of URLs for any external or third-party internet websites referred to in this book, and does not guarantee that any content on such websites is, or will remain, accurate or appropriate.

Printed by Lightning Source

Contents

List of illustrations	*page* vii
Series editors' foreword	ix
Acknowledgements	xi

Introduction   1
Joe Bray and Alison Gibbons

I. *House of Leaves*

1. This is not for you   17
   Alison Gibbons

2. Katabasis in Danielewski's *House of Leaves* and two other recent American novels   33
   Finn Fordham

3. Houses of leaves, cinema and the new affordances of old media   52
   Paul McCormick

4. This haunted house: intertextuality and interpretation in Mark Danielewski's *House of Leaves* (2000) and Poe's *Haunted* (2000)   68
   Mel Evans

5. Trickster authors and tricky readers on the MZD forums   86
   Bronwen Thomas

II. *The Fifty Year Sword*

6   Reading the graphic surface of Mark Z. Danielewski's
The Fifty Year Sword   105
Glyn White

III. *Only Revolutions*

7   Only evolutions: Joyce's and Danielewski's works in
progress   123
Dirk Van Hulle

8   *Only Revolutions,* or, The most typical poem in world
literature   141
Brian McHale

9   Mapping time, charting data: the spatial aesthetic of
Mark Z. Danielewski's *Only Revolutions*   159
N. Katherine Hayles

10   Print interface to time: *Only Revolutions* at the crossroads
of narrative and history   178
Mark B. N. Hansen

11   *Only Revolutions* and the drug of rereading   200
Joe Bray

    Contributors   216
    Index   219

Illustrations

1 Text-world and negative text-world in 'This is not for you' 21
2 Reinterpretation of originating text-world 25
3 M. Z. Danielewski (2000) *House of Leaves by Zampanò with Introduction and Notes by Johnny Truant*, London; New York: Doubleday, p. 141 47
4 M. Z. Danielewski (2000) *House of Leaves by Zampanò with Introduction and Notes by Johnny Truant*, London; New York: Doubleday, p. 142 48
5 M. Z. Danielewski (2002) *Only Revolutions*, page 179, Take tt7 – December 3, 2002 188
6 M. Z. Danielewski (2004) *Only Revolutions*, page 181, Annotated Rim-Through Dailies – March 14, 2004 189

Series editors' foreword

This innovative series reflects the breadth and diversity of writing over the last thirty years, and provides critical evaluations of established, emerging and critically neglected writers – mixing the canonical with the unexpected. It explores notions of the contemporary and analyses current and developing modes of representation with a focus on individual writers and their work. The series seeks to reflect both the growing body of academic research in the field, and the increasing prevalence of contemporary American and Canadian fiction on programmes of study in institutions of higher education around the world. Central to the series is a concern that each book should argue a stimulating thesis, rather than provide an introductory survey, and that each contemporary writer will be examined across the trajectory of their literary production. A variety of critical tools and literary and interdisciplinary approaches are encouraged to illuminate the ways in which a particular writer contributes to, and helps readers rethink, the North American literary and cultural landscape in a global context.

Central to debates about the field of contemporary fiction is its role in interrogating ideas of national exceptionalism and transnationalism. This series matches the multivocality of contemporary writing with wide-ranging and detailed analysis. Contributors examine the drama of the nation from the perspectives of writers who are members of established and new immigrant groups, writers who consider themselves on the nation's margins as well as those who chronicle middle America. National labels are the subject of vociferous debate and including American and Canadian writers in the same series is not to flatten the differences between them but to acknowledge that literary traditions and tensions are cross-cultural and that North American writers often explore and expose precisely these tensions. The series recognises that situating a writer in a cultural context involves a multiplicity of influences, social and geo-political, artistic and theoretical, and that contemporary fiction defies easy categorisation. For example, it examines writers who invigorate the genres in which they have made their mark alongside writers whose aesthetic goal is to subvert the idea of genre altogether. The challenge of defining the roles of writers and assessing their reception by reading communities is central to the aims of the series.

Overall, *Contemporary American and Canadian Writers* aims to begin to represent something of the diversity of contemporary writing and seeks to engage students and scholars in stimulating debates about the contemporary and about fiction.

Nahem Yousaf
Sharon Monteith

Acknowledgements

This project, originally conceived in 2007, has been a long journey. On the way, we have inevitably been helped by a number of people who deserve thanks and acknowledgement for their contributions and support.

The team at Manchester University Press, including Deborah Smith, Reena Jugnarain and Kim Walker, have made this book possible. Matthew Frost has been with the project from the start and we owe a great deal to his guidance and vision. We are also indebted to the initial reviewers of the proposal for their enthusiastic words, to the series editors Sharon Monteith and Nahem Yousaf for their support, and to the reader of the completed manuscript for his or her fervent recommendation and suggestions. The striking cover design is a product of the creativity and imagination of Wayne Christian and Mike Tierney at Studio View Design Agency; we are particularly grateful to them for all their hard work and for the considerable patience and persistence they have shown throughout the process.

We have been continually impressed by the talent and precise critical thinking of our contributors who, without exception, have been diligent and a pleasure to work with. We would also like to thank others who have expressed an interest in the volume, especially Anita Nell Albertsen, Simon Barton, and Michael Hemmingson. Larry McCaffery's encouragement was also most welcome and timely.

Finally, our greatest thanks go to Mark Z. Danielewski himself. His work continues to inspire and mystify us in equal measure. Mark's agent Warren Frazier has also been a valuable and charismatic intermediary. Their joint support and enthusiasm from the margins has spurred us on and helped us bring the text to the point where we are ready to announce it to the world.

This edition of *Mark Z. Danielewski* contains 11 chapters and an introduction. It is a critical work and every effort has been made to provide appropriate translations and accurately credit all sources. If we have failed in this endeavour, we apologise in advance. Now, read.

– The Editors

Here you are.

Introduction

Joe Bray and Alison Gibbons

> – Do you have the time?
> – We are the time.
> *Only Revolutions* (H243)

The turn of the millennium was preceded by Y2K anxiety: the fear of the millennium bug which threatened to crash computer systems; a concern, and in some cases a celebration, that books as material objects were 'on the way out' in favour of the hypertextual and the cybernetic; and an unnerving sense that our cultural and personal lives, from entertainment to surveillance, would become increasingly visual and technologically mediated. Such predictions did not immediately come to fruition. Yet as we begin the second decade of the twenty-first century, it is clear that they were not far from the mark: we can read literature on the internet, on interfaces such as the Sony Reader or the Amazon Kindle; our mobile phones, such as Apple's iPhone, can facilitate almost every aspect of our twenty-first-century lives, from playing video games to cooking from a recipe or using GPS navigation. Whatever we want in this day and age, 'there's an app for that' as the Apple slogan goes. Yet Y2K anxiety, and certainly the fear of the millennium bug, was misguided. Instead, we can take a positive attitude: the rapid technological changes of the last decade have not made older forms obsolete but, in many cases, released anew their potential for creativity.

Published in the year 2000, Mark Z. Danielewski's *House of Leaves* seemed to break the mould of the book. It challenged what a book was and is. This did inspire a number of comparisons to technological media such as Hansen's (2004; 2006) work on the novel's 'digital topography' and Hayles' (2002a; 2002b) on the book's remediation of media. Hayles (2002b: 780) suggests that the textuality of the book is manipulated in such as way as to create a 'represented world on astonishingly diverse media ... The inscription technologies include film, video, photography, tattoos, typewriters, telegraphy, handwriting, and digital computers'. Of these, film and the cinematic is perhaps the most significant, since *House of Leaves*' thematic centre is a fictional video, 'The Navidson Record' (see McCormick, this volume). Furthermore, the novel enacts the formal properties of the filmic medium itself through intermedial evocation (see Gibbons forthcoming 2011). Ultimately though, Hayles still has to acknowledge that many of the book's textual effects are 'specific to the print book; they could not operate in the same way in any other medium' (2002b: 793). Indeed, it is precisely *House of Leaves*' material body, its bookishness, that is one of its most beguiling features. Although the 700-page novel was ten years in the making, it seemed to readers and critics alike that Danielewski had burst onto the literary scene with a book unrivalled in its innovation. Speaking of his own work, Danielewski suggests that he is 'creating something that goes beyond books' (qtd in Miller 2006), exploring the formal and imaginative properties of the novel and its textual space.

Yet this innovation was not present at every stage of the book's creation. When asked by Larry McCaffery about the rise of computer technologies in recent book production and in particular on the writing of *House of Leaves*, Danielewski remarked with glee: 'I say "*HA!*" here because I didn't write *House of Leaves* on a word processor. In fact, I wrote out the entire thing in pencil!' (McCaffery and Gregory 2003: 119). As such, *House of Leaves*, as well as Danielewski's other novels, can be seen as negotiating a fine balance between the medial and the material. This balance is not only evident in the book as a textual artefact, but in its reading experience as well.

In speaking of *House of Leaves* as a 'networked novel', Pressman (2006) suggests that reading the book involves a 'feedback loop' with other media entities. These include those technological forms mentioned above as well as intertextual references made in the novel (which further complicate and enrich its narrative) to additional multimedia instantiations such as the *House of Leaves* website (www.houseofleaves.com) and Danielewski's sister Poe's musical album *Haunted* (for a discussion of *House of Leaves*' relationship with the latter see Evans, this volume). The MZD forums (see Thomas, this volume) are another instantiation of the *House of Leaves* network, and one which is not unfamiliar territory to the

Introduction

author himself. Although the forum fans can only speculate as to whether Danielewski himself frequents these virtual spaces under a shadow persona, they are certainly monitored closely by his associates (his agent Warren Frazier, for example, has pointed us towards what he sees as particularly astute posts). From a medial perspective then, reading *House of Leaves* involves both experiencing its remediation of technologies as well as tracing its narrative across real-world media objects. Gibbons (forthcoming 2010) suggests that the extensive narrative web of *House of Leaves* is part of its appeal to fans; it means that 'putting this book down is not an easy task'.

As a 700-page novel, however, picking up *House of Leaves* is not an easy task either, at least when compared to reading what we consider to be the 'normal', traditionally sized book. *House of Leaves* is a 'door-stop' of a book that is heavy in a reader's hands, instantly foregrounding its materiality. This is also true of Danielewski's other works, *The Fifty Year Sword* (2005) and *Only Revolutions* (2006). *The Fifty Year Sword*, despite being a short 100-page novella, exceeds A4 paper size in height, while *Only Revolutions* presents a contemporary take on the dos-à-dos format, meaning that the narrative is read from both sides (front and back cover if either of these exist in this case), with a note from 'the publisher' suggesting 'alternating between Hailey & Sam, reading eight pages at a time'. As such, reading Danielewski's work is always a corporeal encounter, a heightened awareness of our embodied relationship to the book, and often to the narrative too (see Gibbons forthcoming 2010), that intensifies the reading experience.

House of Leaves may have been published in the year 2000, but Danielewski's fascination with writing started as early as 1976: At the age of ten, he was already experimenting with fiction. *Publisher's Weekly*'s (2000) introduction to the author at the time of his first novel cites the following autobiographical reflection:

> 'I wrote a book about a New York kid who becomes a cocaine addict, beats up a cop and goes to prison,' he says. 'My parents were shocked. My father thought it was immoral. And a teacher of mine in Utah called it a dirty book [it had the "f" word in it]. After that it took me a long while before I would show my work around.'

Danielewski's ability to shock, to present the unexpected, in his literary works has not diminished, though of course his narratives have grown in intricacy and sophistication. Indeed, the author's nonconformist approach to fiction may well be the cause behind his rejection from every writing seminar he applied for on his English Literature programme at Yale. It perhaps also explains the unique ground-breaking nature of his literary opus, and why *House of Leaves* caused such a stir in the literary world when it burst onto the scene in 2000, achieving 'bestseller' status soon after its publication, and amassing both huge critical success and a cult following for the author.

More recently, in 2006, the equally daring and innovative *Only Revolutions* was shortlisted for the prestigious National Book Award, confirming Danielewski as a significant presence in the American literary landscape. The judges' citation praised the novel for 'rais[ing] the level of American literature to a new height of experimentation', and Danielewski is indeed increasingly bracketed with the foremost experimental American novelists. In a somewhat grudging review of *Only Revolutions* in *The Observer*, for example, Sean O'Hagan puts Danielewski alongside Dave Eggers and David Foster Wallace as 'a writer whose cleverness is writ large for all to see and for whom the traditional narrative is a hopelessly old-fashioned form.' Yet the thematic scope of his novels to date suggests that Danielewski may come to be placed in the company of an older generation of great American writers. In her study of the 'epic novels' of John Updike, Philip Roth and Don DeLillo, Catherine Morley argues:

> the instinct to find the epic in the everyday, to weave grand narratives from ordinary actions or through the collation of apparently inconsequential ephemera and press jottings, is, I argue, part of the American literary tradition, from the transcendentalists through postmodernism to the contemporary epic. (2009: 4)

Danielewski certainly shares with Updike, Roth and DeLillo a fascination with reworking traditional 'epic' tropes, such as the journey to the underworld in *House of Leaves*, and the building of the nation state in *Only Revolutions* (for more on *House of Leaves*' use of the epic in particular, see Fordham, this volume). Like all three of his predecessors, Danielewski underscores his 'grand narratives' with a playful attention to the everyday and the quotidian, even in the case of *Only Revolutions* inviting his online audience to send him the names of 'an animal you admire', 'a plant you pause for' and 'your favourite car', and then including such 'apparently inconsequential ephemera' in the text.

As Morley notes, the works of Emerson and Melville (especially

Introduction

Moby Dick) are crucial precursors for the contemporary American epic, particularly in their tendency to 'discover the grand and consequential in the apparently mundane' (2009: 3). Nabokov's *Pale Fire* (1962) and Pynchon's *Gravity's Rainbow* (1973) are inheritors of this tradition and their breadth of concerns and narrative complexity have clearly influenced Danielewski's works too. More specifically, his novels draw on *Gravity's Rainbow* for its assimilation of pop culture and the technologies of other media, especially film, and on *Pale Fire* for its self-reflexive meta-commentary and its experimentation with paratext (for a discussion of the 'editor' Charles Kinbote's Index in relation to that of *House of Leaves*, see Hayles 2002b: 780 and Fletcher 2007).

Yet for all Danielewski's obvious debt to his American forefathers, his novels also reach out, like those of Updike, Roth and DeLillo, to European traditions. Morley explores the 'literary transnationalism' of these three writers, focusing on their complex engagement with Joyce. The polyphony of narrative voices in Danielewski's 'epic novels', coupled with their constant reflections on their own medium, also encourages comparisons with both *Ulysses* and *Finnegans Wake* (see Van Hulle, this volume). Other European presences are felt too in his work, from Shakespeare to Borges, from Milton to Milorad Pavić. Pavić's novels, for instance, similarly tackle the material form of the book, and play with narrativity, linearity and intertextuality. Pavić's *The Inner Side of the Wind* (1993 [1990]), a retelling of the story of Hero and Leander with two front covers, one on each side associated with each of the protagonists, in particular bears remarkable formal similarities to *Only Revolutions*.

The range of literary allusions in Danielewski's work is at times bewildering; to Larry McCaffery's comment that '*House of Leaves* seems incredibly self-conscious about the influences it has absorbed', Danielewski cheerfully replies 'It is probably fortunate that I live in an age in which "self-consciousness" isn't a bad thing for an author' (McCaffery and Gregory 2003: 106). However, as McCaffery and Gregory observe of *House of Leaves*, 'even an exhaustive citation of possible influences ultimately seems beside the point'. Drawing attention to 'the rich array of idiosyncratic voices and idioms that Danielewski enters into, reconstructs, and projects with such startling ease and joyfulness', they urge sceptics to read *House of Leaves* 'to see where the novel has been and where it is heading' (McCaffery and Gregory 2003: 102, 103). *Only Revolutions* similarly opens new directions for the novel, American and otherwise, playfully and joyfully transforming great literary voices by mixing them with the register of the everyday.

While scholarly articles on Danielewski are appearing with growing frequency in leading journals, this volume is the first booklength study on the author, presenting essays on all three of his major works. It is thus, like his texts themselves, urgently to-the-moment. The volume opens with five essays on *House of Leaves*. In 'This is not for you', Alison Gibbons attends to the novel's remarkable opening. While these opening words are mentioned in other critical essays (such as Slocombe 2005), her approach and detailed focus are unique. Although a small piece of text, Gibbons suggests that the opening five words to *House of Leaves* have dramatic impact on readers in terms of how they enter into their reading experience of the novel. Taking a cognitive approach, she demonstrates the effects of Danielewski's use of the second-person pronoun, negation, and visual presentation on the literary experience. In doing so, Gibbons introduces two cognitive psychological concepts; cognitive dissonance and reactance. These, she argues, are part of an experiential journey, generated by Danielewski's precise opening and contributing to 'a sense of discomfort for the reader'. It is this very sense of discomfort which Gibbons sees as crucial for readers as they enter the *House of Leaves*.

In interview, Danielewski has suggested 'there are many ways to enter *House of Leaves*' (McCaffery and Gregory 2003). Some of these are character-based, yet the substantial caverns of footnotes in the novel are also entry-points in themselves. Finn Fordham muses on the footnotes of *House of Leaves* as part of the text's 'architextural underworld'. In doing so, Fordham situates *House of Leaves* alongside two other recent American novels, David Foster Wallace's (1996) *Infinite Jest* and Don DeLillo's (1997) *Underworld*. These works, Fordham suggests, share two common features: Firstly, the 'clandestine productions and samizdat disseminations of filmed sequences' and secondly, the 'epic convention of *katabasis*', a literary descent into underground structures and underworlds. When discussing *House of Leaves*, Fordham focuses upon the complex textuality of Chapter IX, noted for its labyrinthine interweaving of footnotes. He concludes with a philosophical rumination on language itself as underworld, whereby Danielewski is seen to perform 'a gothic horror spin take on language as an unencompassable labyrinth'.

Introduction

The remaining three essays on *House of Leaves* are interested in the novel's connections to other media forms. While Fordham mentions the filmed sequences that feature in Danielewski's novel, Paul McCormick takes a narratological approach in examining the cinematic qualities of *House of Leaves* as part of the book's 'media interface'. Borrowing the term 'affordance' from ecological psychologist J. J. Gibson, which signifies both the inherent properties of an artefact and its perceived usage, McCormick proposes that Danielewski transposes the media affordances of cinema into the book medium in four central ways: 'a video diary, the perceptual frame of a surveillance camera, the concept of cinematic montage, and a documentary film'. Such properties work in *House of Leaves* on both a narrative and a formal level, creating what McCormick calls a 'postmodern uncertainty' and a 'level of indeterminacy' which ultimately render the novel eternally incomplete and firmly situated within the media environment of 1990s America.

The media network of *House of Leaves* is also explored by Mel Evans, whose particular focus rests upon the intersection between Danielewski's novel and his sister Poe's musical album *Haunted*, also released in the year 2000. Evans advocates the album as yet another entry-point into the multilayered narrative of *House of Leaves*. As such, her essay presents a fresh perspective on the novel, illuminating both *House of Leaves* and *Haunted* through a reading of their intertextual relationships. Evans rightly concludes that the 'effect of the intertext to foreground previously marginalised or unnoticed themes, events, or objects within the novel cannot be underestimated'.

Like Evans, Bronwen Thomas investigates new ground in Danielewski studies in the final essay on *House of Leaves*. Thomas considers the online communities of the MZD fan forum websites. Such sites are generated by, and work to sustain and develop, the novel's cult following, with the popular *House of Leaves* forum boasting a staggering number of active members. Thomas' thought-provoking discussion of the behaviour of 'fans' who use the site is supported by email interviews conducted with prominent forum members, allowing 'inside-access', or at least critical and personal insight, into this virtual culture. Ultimately, Thomas' essay reveals the value of forums in 'mapping the journeys of readers of Danielewski's work, and in illustrating the ways in which these journeys are endlessly unpredictable and enriching'.

Since *House of Leaves*, Mark Z. Danielewski has published two other fictional works, *The Fifty Year Sword* (2005) and *Only Revolutions* (2006). *The Fifty Year Sword* is a novella (only available in limited print-run through Dutch publisher De Bezige Bij) that, like *House of Leaves*, borders the horror genre. In this case, however, it is also in part a children's book. Certainly it is marketed as such – the blurb claims, 'Read aloud *The Fifty Year Sword* will captivate any child'. Like most children's books, Danielewski's novella is accompanied by drawings (12 in total). Illustrated by Dutch artist Peter van Sambeek, these images take sole occupation of either a single page or a double spread. The novella also uses coloured quotation marks with each of five colours used to signify a different speaker, yet in the telling of what is essentially a ghost story the five voices complete each other's sentences, creating a unified yet dislocated narrative voice.

Glyn White's essay focuses on this unusual novella, exploring the ways in which typography and visual design are utilised to create a narrative that is intertextual and, above all, fragile. White has two central interests: he first considers the coloured quotation marks and polyvocal narration of *The Fifty Year Sword*, and secondly, studies the novella's unusual page design. Consideration of the latter prompts White to remark that 'the layout of the text looks somewhat like poetry', an observation which links *The Fifty Year Sword* with *Only Revolutions* (see McHale, this volume, for a discussion of *Only Revolutions* as poetic text). White is not only interested in the formal and structural properties of *The Fifty Year Sword*, but how these properties engender the reading experience. Through recourse to Derrida's thoughts on textual white space or what he calls the 'blank' (*blanc/blank*), White speaks of the graphic surface of *The Fifty Year Sword* as essentially disruptive. It is this disruption to the textual flow, and thus to immersion in the sense used by Marie-Laure Ryan (2001), that makes the novella so fragile and endows it with a particular texture, what White calls 'the texture of fabric(ation)'.

As several essays in the volume note, Danielewski's most recent work, *Only Revolutions* (2006), seems to have been designed, at least in part, as an inversion of *House of Leaves*. In a 2007 interview with Kiki Benzon, the author argues that while his first novel 'is what I would call a centripetal book', concerning itself with 'interiorities', *Only Revolutions* is 'pointedly a centrifugal novel. It was about getting outside' (Benzon 2007). The essays on this text in this volume address the different ways in which it seeks to 'get outside', from its interaction with the online community, to its complex engagement with sources of inspiration, whether these be literary, cultural or technological. Dirk Van Hulle's essay, for example, explores the relationship between *Only Revolutions* and Joyce's *Finnegans Wake* (1939), through the lens of two concepts employed by the situationists: *récupération* and *détournement*. Outlining both authors' indebtedness to Darwin's theories of evolution, Van Hulle shows how Danielewski's engagement with Joyce's last novel is poised between the exploitative reductivism of *récupération* and the more 'revolutionary orientation' of *détournement*. He concludes that while from a situationist point of view, *Only Revolutions* could be thought of as 'a case of neo-experimental *récupération*', from a more positive perspective, the text 'could be regarded as a functional re-employment of *Finnegans Wake*'s circular bends and swerves'.

While Van Hulle's essay locates *Only Revolutions* in the history of the twentieth-century novel, and Danielewski himself describes his work as a 'novel' in the Benzon interview (see above), other essays in the volume are more cautious about applying this generic label, given the text's verse form. Brian McHale notes that 'novel or not, *Only Revolutions* is certainly a *narrative* text' and claims that this 'aligns it with the mainstream of poetry world-wide, if we take the long view'. Indeed, following Victor Shklovsky's claim that *Tristram Shandy* is the most typical novel in world literature, McHale provocatively puts the case for *Only Revolutions* as 'the most typical poem in world literature', in the sense that it 'lays bare the poetics of poetry in something like the way that *Tristram Shandy* (according to Shklovsky) laid bare the poetics of the novel'. This argument is developed through attention to two particular definitions of poetry: segmentivity (as proposed by the poet Rachel Blau DuPlessis) and parallelism (which develops from Roman Jakobson's definition of 'the poetic function' of language). McHale demonstrates both that *Only Revolutions* is 'segmented on multiple scales, in units ranging in size from the isolated word up to the whole book', and that it takes to extremes Jakobson's observation that 'the poetic function . . . projects the principle of equivalence from the axis of selection into the axis of combination', such that it 'is organised as a single, complex parallelistic structure on a massive scale'. This makes *Only Revolutions*, for McHale, 'not merely . . . a *typical* poem, but something like a *hyper*-typical one, if that were possible'.

The transposition of the paradigmatic onto the syntagmatic in *Only Revolutions*, or, as she puts it, 'the overlaying of alternative choices onto the linear order of narrative', is also examined in N. Katherine Hayles' essay. Pointing to the proliferation of different kinds of data in the text, Hayles claims that it manifests a 'deterritorialized spatial dynamic': 'Among the transformations and deformations the text implements is a profound shift from narrative as a temporal trajectory to an element of a topographic plane upon which a wide variety of interactions and permutations are staged.' She highlights 'four different kinds of data arrangements relevant to *Only Revolutions*', each of which interacts with narrative and affects the 'topography of the page and page spread'. This distinctive topography is only made possible by the use of sophisticated computer software; though technology is absent from the narrative of *Only Revolutions*, this is an absence, Hayles notes, 'that would be almost impossible to achieve without the calculative and data-searching capabilities of networked and programmable machines'. Thus in her view digital technology permeates the text: 'nowhere present within the narrative diegesis, digital technologies are everywhere apparent when we consider the writing-down system as a whole'.

Mark B. N. Hansen agrees that *Only Revolutions* is 'thoroughly if indirectly permeated' by digital technology, 'both through the history of its composition and in the infrastructure underlying its appearance'. He claims that the text exemplifies Hayles' pronouncement, at the end of *Electronic Literature: New Horizons for the Literary*, that 'More than a mode of material production (although it is that), digitality has become the textual condition of twenty-first-century literature' (Hayles 2008: 186). Recalling McCormick's argument about how *House of Leaves* uses cinema as an 'interface' to interact with 'the 1990s American media environment', Hansen claims that *Only Revolutions* affirms 'the print book's power not so much to absorb and imitate other (analogue *and* digital) media as to mediate for its readers a new digital world of information'. He claims in particular that as a physical object Danielewski's book offers 'a singular interface to time and to history', showing how it imbricates A-series time (lived, subjective and phenomenological) with B-series time (objective, subject-independent, historical) through such features as the historical sidebar of 'Chronomosaics', the result of Danielewski's invitation to his fanbase to post suggestions for significant historical events online. This 'collective-personal self-reference' signifies, for Hansen, the lack of a clear demarcation between A-series and B-series time, marking 'a continuity and a

Introduction

personal, living connection to the past – a sense that the past is not simply past, but remains part of our present'.

Underlying both Hayles' and Hansen's essays is a sense of the new, creative ways of reading opened up by the text's distinctive integration of print and digital technology. This is an explicit theme of Joe Bray's essay, which argues that the highly constrained form of the book of *Only Revolutions* 'paradoxically dictates that the ways in which it can be read, and crucially, reread, are without limit'. Like Gibbons in the first essay in the volume, Bray adopts a cognitive perspective, drawing in particular on the concepts of figure and ground as used in cognitive poetics, in order to illuminate the dynamic experience of reading Danielewski's text. As the reader switches between Sam's and Hailey's narratives, rotating the book 180 degrees each time, new linguistic features are foregrounded. Bray shows how passages from the two narratives contain subtle interplays of sound and sense which encourage a constant rereading, as though the reader were, in Roland Barthes' terms, 'under the effect of a drug (that of recommencement, of difference)'. This drug is often so strong that on reaching the apparent end of the book, the reader is compelled to rotate it and start again, an experience reported by Hayles in her essay. Bray argues that the formal symmetries of *Only Revolutions* thus challenge the notion of a first, innocent reading and a second, more sophisticated one, inviting instead 'only continual, illimitable rereadings'.

Only Revolutions' demand to be reread represents a further way in which, for all its technological innovation, the text is inscribed in literary history, and the history of the novel in particular. In two recent essays, Deidre Lynch has traced 'the slow emergence' in the late eighteenth and early nineteenth centuries of 'an idea of "literature" as that which we are always rereading and never reading for the first time' (2009a: 89). She gives Samuel Richardson as an example of an author who sought 'to elude the consequences of [his works'] sequentiality', noting how he 'always arranged for his novels in their concluding volumes to begin replaying themselves and to begin staging their own rereadings' (2009b: 215). This recalls how the final words of Sam's and Hailey's narratives, 'I could never walk away from you,' both echo and anticipate their third and fourth lines ('I can walk away / from anything') and encourage the reader to rotate the book and begin each narrative again. *Only Revolutions*' resistance to ending links it with many canonical texts in the history of the novel. Lynch shows, for example, how Jane Austen's novels were a particularly fruitful source for nineteenth-century readers in search of 'the inexhaustibly rereadable novels that would sponsor their steady adherence to routine' (2009b: 210). Insisting that 'linear reading is no more natural than any other ritual we perform with books' (2009b: 216), Lynch seeks to remind 'academic readers' in particular 'how our own reading practices, semester in, semester out, take us in circles' (2009a: 102).

Throughout his career to date, Danielewski has shown himself to be fully aware of such academic reading practices. *House of Leaves*, as many critics have noted, is laden to the point of parody with many of the familiar techniques of literary criticism, including sometimes bafflingly obscure footnotes (see Fordham, this volume). In his interview with Kiki Benzon, Danielewski argues that, in contrast with his first novel, *Only Revolutions* 'goes beyond what you can anticipate in academia. It requires a new kind of nomenclature, I think, to address it' (Benzon 2007). Whether this complex, challenging text has defied the efforts of academics to address it is for readers of this volume (including Danielewski himself) to judge. Certainly it demands a new critical vocabulary, and perhaps a new way of doing criticism. Yet the ways of reading it inspires are, like those generated by *House of Leaves* and *The Fifty Year Sword*, 'revolutionary' in both senses of the word: deeply rooted in literary traditions at the same time as they are ground-breaking and innovative. Danielewski delights in taking his readers 'in circles' while simultaneously pointing the way forward for the twenty-first-century novel. To return to the quotation which opened this introduction, his works are not simply conscious of their position in time and literary history, they are also of the moment: '*We are the time*' (S243, H243) / 'We are at once' (S320, H320).

Works cited

Benzon, K. (2007) 'Revolutions 2' [Interview with Mark Z. Danielewski]. *Electronic Book Review* (no pagination). www.electronicbookreview.com/thread/wuc/regulated.

Danielewski, M. Z. (2006) *Only Revolutions*, New York: Pantheon Books.

Fletcher, R. (2007) Presentation at the Project Narrative workshop on *House of Leaves*, held in the Ohio State University Department of English on 20 September 2007. http://projectnarrative.osu.edu/events/video.cfm.

Gibbons, A. (forthcoming 2010) *Multimodality, Cognition, and Experimental Literature*, London; New York: Routledge.

Gibbons, A. (forthcoming 2011) 'Narrative worlds and multimodal figures in *House of Leaves*: "-find your own words; I have no more" ', in Grishakova, M. and Ryan, M-L. (eds) *Intermediality and Storytelling*, Berlin: Walter de Gruyter.

Hansen, M. B. N. (2004) 'The digital topography of Mark Z. Danielewski's *House of Leaves*', *Contemporary Literature* 45(4): 597–636.

Hansen, M. B. (2006) *Bodies in Code: Interfaces with Digital Media*, New York; London: Routledge.

Hayles, N. K. (2002a) *Writing Machines*, Cambridge, MA: MIT Press.

Hayles, N. K. (2002b) 'Saving the subject: remediation in *House of Leaves*', *American Literature* 74(4): 779–806.

Hayles, N. K. (2008) *Electronic Literature: New Horizons for the Literary*, Notre Dame, IN: University of Notre Dame Press.

Lynch, D. (2009a) 'Canons' clockwork, novels for everyday use', in Ferris, I. and Keen, P. (eds) *Bookish Histories*, London: Palgrave, pp. 87–110.

Lynch, D. (2009b) 'On going steady with novels', *The Eighteenth Century: Theory and Interpretation* 50(2–3) [Special Issue on 'Technologies of Emotion']: 207–218.

McCaffery, L. and Gregory, S. (2003) 'Haunted house – an interview with Mark Z. Danielewski', *Critique* 44(2): 99–135.

Miller, A. (2006) 'Revolutionary: *House of Leaves* author Mark Z. Danielewski returns with an epic poem/novel that travels across the American landscape', *Los Angeles City Beat*, 21 September 2006 (no pagination). www.onlyrevolutions.com.

Morley, C. (2009) *The Quest for Epic in Contemporary American Fiction: John Updike, Philip Roth and Don DeLillo*, New York; London: Routledge.

O'Hagan, S. (2006) 'I wouldn't say this is unreadable . . .', Review of *Only Revolutions* in *The Observer*, 24 September.

Pavić, M. (1993 [1990]) *The Inner Side of the Wind*, London: Penguin.

Poe (2000) *Haunted*, Atlantic Records.

Pressman, J. (2006) '*House of Leaves*: reading the networked novel', *Studies in American Fiction* 34(1): 107–122.

Publisher's Weekly, 'PW: a budding crop of first fiction', *Publisher's Weekly*, 1 October 2000 (no pagination). www.publishersweekly.com/article/418253-PW_A_Budding_Crop_of_First_Fiction.php.

Ryan, Marie-Laure (2001) *Narrative as Virtual Reality: Immersion and Interactivity in Literature and Electronic Media*, Baltimore: The Johns Hopkins University Press.

Slocombe, W. (2005) '"This is not for you": nihilism and the house that Jacques built', *Modern Fiction Studies* 51(1): 88–109.

I
House of Leaves

1

This is not for you

Alison Gibbons, De Montfort University, Leicester

Mark Z. Danielewski's debut novel *House of Leaves* opens with the extraordinary admonition, 'This is not for you' (Danielewski 2000: ix). This caution initially appears to be a strange tactic by the author designed to deter readers. The present chapter investigates the opening to *House of Leaves* through close textual analysis, which is divided into five parts. The first three consider the linguistic significations of 'This is not for you' and their cognitive effect on the reader. Specifically: section one begins a dialogue on the pronoun usage and introduces the cognitive framework of Text World Theory; section two focuses on linguistic negation and its effect on cognitive process and text-world creation; section three focuses on the signification of the second-person pronoun. Subsequently in the fourth part of the chapter, the presentation of the text itself is brought to bear on the analysis. In conclusion, I connect such features to the aesthetic texture of *House of Leaves*' opening, suggesting that the inferred meaning(s) and related experience of the opening play an important role in establishing the unsettling atmosphere for the 'mood' of the novel.

I. Open the door

If 'This is not for you' is interpreted as a warning to the reader, the demonstrative pronoun 'this' refers to the novel, the object of the book itself as well as the reading experience it entails. Similarly, the perceptual deictic 'you' functions as an address to the reader of the novel. Fludernik states, '*You*, even if it turns out to refer to a fictional protagonist, initially always seems to involve the actual reader' (1995: 106). Her observation of readers' initial reactions to *you* is apposite to Danielewski's provocative opening, endorsing a reading of it as a direct address.

It is likely, however, that a reader might search for other referents that the 'you' may signal. If the reader chooses to search overleaf for the referent of the address, s/he would merely uncover a seeming dead-end, running up against the 'Introduction' heading which signals a textual shift into another narrative episode. This new episode is written in first-person narration: 'I still get nightmares. In fact I get them so often I should be used to them by now. I'm not. No one ever really gets used to nightmares' (Danielewski 2000: xi). The 'I' being used here denotes the central character of the novel, who can later be identified as Johnny Truant, an unreliable narrator and 'club-kid going nowhere fast', according to the book's publisher Random House. Evidently, the obscurity of the initial second-person reference cannot be resolved by looking at its proximal narrative context, creating the impression that this non-character-specific use of 'you' is an isolated or rare occurrence. Thus, the second-person pronoun functions to set up an inferred dialogue between implied author and actual reader (Booth 1983).

In order to understand the full impact of the opening sentence, further consideration of both readerly cognitive process and multimodal design is required. Examination of linguistic negation, pronoun usage, and the effects of these on text-world creation (all introduced below), leads to a more intricate understanding of the meaning-making layers encapsulated in this aperture.

Text World Theory (see Werth 1999; Gavins 2007a) is a discourse framework, focusing on how linguistic structures trigger different and various text-worlds. The theory uses the powerful TEXT AS WORLD conceptual metaphor to articulate the way in which readers comprehend any given discourse by producing a cognitive realisation of it, an imaginative construct which may appear so vivid as to take on a world-like quality. A text-world is therefore a mental construct which is the joint production of producer and recipient. Moreover, there are a number of conceptual levels within which these worlds operate. The preliminary level is the context in which the communicative event takes place. This is called the 'discourse-world', referring to the external and immediate situation of the participants. The second level is the 'text-world' itself which, as mentioned, is the cognitive representation of the communication.

The entrance to any storyworld is an important boundary. In Text World Theory, written communication usually incurs a split discourse-world (Gavins 2007a; 2007b), as participants involved in the communication normally occupy different spatio-temporal locations. Gavins explains, 'the vast majority of readers are separated from the writers communicating with them' (2007b: 137). In 'bridging this gap', as Gavins (2007b: 137) puts it, readers utilise their knowledge frames to create a text-world in which the communication takes place. These knowledge frames vary from our knowledge of a location or an author to our familiarity with the convention of reading. For example, paratextual features aid in setting expectations as to the genre of a book, such as horror or romance, and thus the type of text-world generated, even before the reading experience begins. Building upon Young's (1987) concept of 'edgework', which refers to the boundaries between narrative worlds, Segal states:

> When the first sentence of the first chapter of a novel or short story is being read (or the curtain opens on a play, or the words 'feature presentation' are replaced by a scene at the movies), a reader usually responds by anticipating that what comes next will represent a new entity. The objects and events represented by the discourse following the boundary are to be instantiated in the space made available. (1995: 75)

The first sentence in *House of Leaves* challenges the customary creation of and shift into the text-world. Since the first sentence does not seem to be anchored in any narrative or storyworld, the words are attributed to the author and it has been shown that the personal pronoun 'you' functions as a mode of direct address, engaging the actual reader. Despite familiarity between participants being established by direct address, the negative adverb 'not' works to alienate the actual reader. In 'This is not for you', with 'this' signalling the novel, Danielewski performs an act of prohibition, suggesting that the reader should not read the book. The effect is that 'This is not for you' appears to traverse the discourse-world divide in an effort to obstruct the reader's entrance into the text-world of the novel.

Danielewski's prohibiting aperture is intriguing. It is a radical move for an author to deny the reader access into the narrative world, especially before the novel has even begun. Of course, in making the latter statement I am being somewhat crude. Danielewski is not simply denying access to the narrative as his use of direct address works antithetically by inviting reader engagement. This paradox is a deliberate strategy, the motivation for which will be revealed in the course of my consideration of 'This is not for you.' At present, the paradox presented to the reader suffices to demonstrate that Danielewski does not write escapist fiction. Rather, with the opening sentence to *House of Leaves*, he issues readers a number of complex cognitive challenges.

II. Do not enter

'This is not for you' is a negative proposition. Negation, the linguistic and conceptual denial, absence or non-being of something, is signalled in this sentence through its essential reliance upon the explicitly negative word 'not'. As Hidalgo Downing explains, words such as 'not' 'are negative in meaning, they are marked morphologically for negation and they follow co-occurrence restrictions that single them out as syntactically negative' (2000a: 42).

Linguistic negation necessarily demands complex cognitive operations. Hidalgo Downing states that 'negation as a structure involves the formation of a complex structure with regard to the corresponding affirmative' (2000a: 36). Clark and Clark (1977: 108, 110) in their book on psycholinguistics cite empirical studies to show that negative assertions take longer to process precisely because they involve this conception of a supposition first at its affirmative pole followed by the cancellation of it. The title of Lakoff's (2004) book on cognitive framing provides an excellent demonstration of the accentuating power of negation: *Don't Think of an Elephant*. Of course, despite the negative imperative, this phrase demonstrates the inherent impossibility. The linguistic mention of an elephant triggers its conceptualisation, before it can be 'erased' from one's mind. As Lakoff phrases it, cognitively 'when we negate a frame, we evoke the frame' (2004: 3). That is, negative polarity can only be comprehended through reference to its opposing affirmative. Cognising 'This is not for you,' therefore, is only possible by interpreting it alongside and in comparison with 'This is for you.'

In text-world terms, Werth (1999: 249–257) classifies negation as a foregrounding process that creates a subworld. Both Hidalgo Downing (2000a; 2000b; 2002) and Gavins (2007a) have developed Werth's ideas on negation in Text World Theory. Although Hidalgo Downing follows Werth in classifying negation as a subworld, she finds that negation in poetry 'evokes two complementary conceptual spaces or worlds' and, rather than seeing one foregrounded over another, speaks of the negation in question as bringing 'forward

This is not for you 21

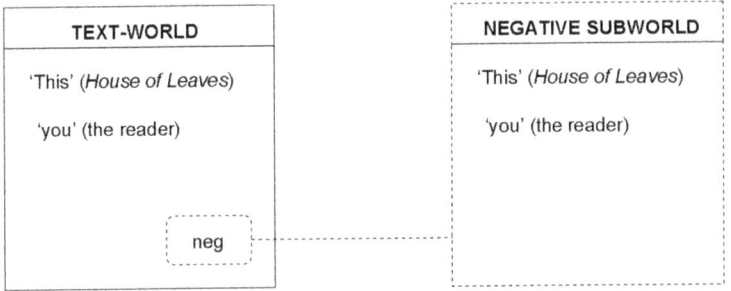

1 Text-world and negative text-world in 'This is not for you'

the relation between both' (2002: 127). Even though she reaches a similar conclusion, Gavins' (2007a: 102) description of negation differs slightly in that she asserts that negation produces a negative text-world whose contents must be conceptualised before they can be translated into an exclusion in and from the separate positive text-world. For Gavins, then, while this negative world can impact upon the positive world, there is an implication that the negative world is part of a conceptual route rather than a simultaneous and equally realised domain as envisaged by Hidalgo Downing. This study accords with Gavins' model since, despite being inclined to acknowledge an ontological tension between positive and negative worlds, I do not perceive these worlds as ever existing in a state of concurrent stability.

The text-worlds involved in processing 'This is not for you' can be identified and represented by Figure 1. The negation in the opening to *House of Leaves* serves to create a fleeting negative text-world in which 'This is for you' is foregrounded in the reader's mind. In Werth's words, 'to deny the existence or presence of an entity, you have to mention it. The very act of denying it brings it into focus' (1999: 251). This process enables the negation in the originating text-world to be conceptualised (Gavins 2007a: 102).

Nørgaard claims that a negated proposition, like 'negatives in general, ultimately entails two (incompatible) viewpoints' (2007: 39), albeit perceived consecutively – the positive presence of a thing followed by its absence. Danielewski takes cognitive incompatibility beyond the complex cognitive operations demanded by the cerebral processing of linguistic negation. The author also generates cognitive dissonance for the reader. Cognitive dissonance, as formulated by Festinger (1957), is 'the experience of nonfitting relations among cognitions' (1957: 3). Individuals experiencing cognitive dissonance will be actuated to seek resolution or, as Festinger posits, 'The existence of dissonance, being psychologically uncomfortable, will motivate a person to try to reduce the dissonance and achieve consonance' (1957: 3). Cognitive dissonance can occur not just between conflicting knowledges, but also between a held belief and a behaviour or action. Festinger's original example is that of the smoker who continues the habit despite knowing that smoking is bad for one's health. When behaviour and belief are in conflict like this, the forces inducing desire to diminish dissonance are considerable.

In relation to the opening of Danielewski's *House of Leaves*, a reader encountering this sentence has presumably bought or borrowed the book and therefore decided that it is a novel s/he wants to read. Effectively, readers hold the belief that 'this is for them'. In consequence, 'This is not for you' takes on a great magnitude of dissonance since incongruity arises between the primary narrative statement and the reader's preceding actions and belief. Furthermore, the inference communicated is dissonant with a reader's impulse and intent to read on. Readers must therefore find a means with which to reconcile the dissonance between their habits in the practice of reading and the semantic implication of the sentence.

Related to cognitive dissonance is another cognitive behaviour, cognitive reactance. Theorised by Brehm (1966), this social-psychological behaviour plays a significant part in a reader's cognitive experience of 'This is not for you' as well as in his or her response to it. Crawford et al. define reactance in the following way:

> Reactance theory holds that there exists a set of free behaviors from which an individual can potentially choose. When any of these free behaviors is eliminated or threatened with elimination, the individual experiences psychological reactance, a motivational state directed toward the reestablishment of the free behavior. (2002: 56)

In other words, we react against overt attempts to persuade us or to delimit our choices. Thus, the popular concept of reverse psychology relies upon reactance as by insisting upon the implementation of a particular behaviour or course of action, it aims to induce a person to perform the opposite. What distinguishes reactance from reverse psychology is its emphasis upon choice and behavioural freedom, thus making reactance a more subtle and sophisticated psychological model. Notably, the new trend in marketing known as reverse psychology or anti-marketing (Sinha and Foscht 2007) is implicitly informed by the notion of reactance. Its efficacy relies not upon 'push' marketing strategies, which are likely to cause reactance and resistance on the part of the consumer, but through an understated 'pull' dynamic, often making products seem unreachable in order to heighten their allure.

Baron and Byrne (2003) relate the theory of reactance in accessible terms, explaining that, when we are persistently asked or told to do a particular thing, we are more likely to resist. In their words, we 'change our attitudes (or behaviour) in a direction exactly opposite to that being urged of us' (Baron and Byrne 2003: 140). For this reason, being issued with the negative statement 'This is not for you' is likely to provoke an adversative effect; the reader becomes more adamant that the experience of reading *House of Leaves* will be something s/he welcomes and expects to appreciate.

Considering schematic meaning adds weight to this assertion. Discussing prepositional phrases formed through the combination of preposition and noun phrase such as 'to me' and 'on the floor', Evans and Green (2006) suggest that constructions of this kind are underwritten by the 'highly schematic meaning, DIRECTION OR LOCATION WITH RESPECT TO SOME PHYSICAL ENTITY' (2006: 117). As 'for you' is a prepositional phrase of this format, it is evident that this schema is highly applicable. Since in order to understand the negated meaning, a reader must initially cognise that which it negates, directional schematic meaning is both valid and pertinent in regard to constructing any conclusions of a cognitive nature. Acknowledging this meaning also enables comparison with the negative variation.

'Not' has a noticeable impact upon both the semantic and schematic content of the sentence. 'Not' almost appears to reverse the oriented movement suggested by the preposition. Admittedly, such reversal would be an oversimplification, yet when we imagine the phrase in use it is often accompanied not by giving as in the unnegated form but with taking away. Indeed, it is somewhat reminiscent of the forbidding words of a parent to their child as they move a potentially exciting object away from the child and out of reach. Since negation involves the foregrounding of the content of the negative text-world followed by its exclusion in the positive text-world, one could argue that Danielewski is linguistically presenting the reader with a gift, the book, tantalising the reader before forbidding him or her to read it. This gives rise to a tension between the reader as the intended recipient of the book (signalled by the second-person direct address) and as a persona non grata, thus contributing to readerly cognitive reactance. As such, the schematic meaning and reactance triggered by Danielewski's opening strengthens the paradox of 'This is not for you' as both invitation and prohibition, increasing the tension it entails, both in terms of meaning and psychological affect.

III. Negotiate the lock

In order for a reader to reduce the dissonance that 'This is not for you' creates, the meaning of the perceptual deictic personal pronoun 'you' can be negotiated. In the English language, the second-person pronoun can be used to indicate a number of referents. Wales (1996) describes personal pronouns in general as 'multi-functional in their roles in different contexts, which is tantamount to a kind of polysemy' (1996: 7). Herman (1994; 2002), in his exploration of 'textual *you*' in fictional second-person narrative, points to at least five functional types of textual *you* which he terms as: (1) generalised *you*, (2) fictional reference, (3) fictionalised (=horizontal) address, (4) apostrophic (=vertical) address and (5) doubly deictic *you* (1994: 381; 2001: 345). As I interpret these categories, type two, fictional reference, signifies a protagonist in the storyworld through what Herman, drawing on Margolin (1984; 1986–7), calls 'deictic transfer' in which the narrative *you* is 'convertible to the first or third person' (Herman 1994: 382).

While generalised *you* seems rather self-explanatory in referring to the indefinite plural form of the second-person pronoun, Herman cites it as 'another species' of deictic transfer (1994: 380), this time shifting from the individualised participant to this impersonal form. The third category, fictionalised address, diverges from fictional reference since although it still functions within the storyworld, it involves address to and/or by fictional characters in much the same way direct address functions in real-world conversation. Apostrophic address, in comparison, transcends the boundaries of the fiction and 'directly designates the audience comprising readers of (or listeners to) a fiction' (Herman 1994: 387).

This is not for you

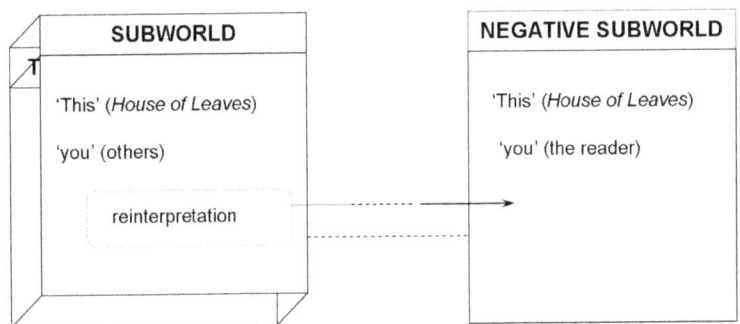

2 Reinterpretation of originating text-world and subsequent foregrounding of negative text-world in 'This is not for you'

Before considering Herman's final type of textual *you*, it is useful to pause and consider 'This is not for you' in light of the pronoun's polysemy. Thus far, this analysis has defined the use of second-person pronoun in 'This is not for you' as direct address, emphasising its apostrophic sense. However, *you* is a polysemous pronominal and can also be reinterpreted as a generalised *you* for dissonance-reducing purposes. This would enable manipulation of the referential ambiguity of 'you' to reason that it does not in fact involve the reader. Instead, the reader can actively disassociate, perceiving 'you' to refer to a group of 'others', perhaps unworthy readers, from which s/he is exclusively omitted. As a result, the text-world in which the absence of the reader exists is re-established. As depicted in Figure 2, it can now be seen to contain 'others'. Such reinterpretation causes the enhanced foregrounding of the negated text-world in which the reader and novel are synchronised. As demonstrated by the shift from dotted to solid boundary lines, the negative text-world, in which 'This is for you' is conceptually realised, evolves from the fleeting negative world usually triggered by negation into a more stable conceptual space.

Herman's final functional type of *you* is the doubly deictic *you*. For Herman, this signifies that 'on some occasions *you* functions as a cue for superimposing two or more deictic roles, one internal to the discourse situation represented in and/or through the diegesis and the other(s) external to that discourse situation' (1994: 381). As Herman himself acknowledges, a doubly deictic *you*, conflating virtual (storyworld) and actual (real world) reference, is often difficult to pinpoint. I would be quick to concede that Danielewski's 'you' is not of this order since both construals are positioned in the actualised domain. Nevertheless, Herman's concept is valuable. Although Danielewski points to two meanings of 'you' both of which are modes of what Herman calls vertical address, there is a recognisable capacity for interpretive movement between them. In Herman's terms, this subtle perceptual shift can be seen as a case of oscillating deictic transfer between apostrophic and generalised you.

Discussing the second-person pronoun from a cognitive linguistic and discourse analysis perspective, Lee (2001) suggests that the potential ambiguity of 'you' can be manipulated by speakers, and utilised for rhetorical purposes (2001: 177). Wales also notes:

> The fact that standard (English) English does not formalise the distinction between singular and plural sometimes has an advantage. In advertising language, for example, where *you* occurs so frequently in direct if simulated 'personal' address, empathy is heightened by ambivalence: a mass-consumer relationship is simultaneously an individual singled out. (1996: 74)

Danielewski's employment of 'you' also utilises the pronoun's referential multiplicity, creating a slippage between its individualised and generalised meanings. In short, he exploits two senses in the semantic network of *you* for literary effect. However, Danielewski's skilled usage of the pronoun differs from the examples given by Lee and Wales above. Instead of heightening subjective affinity through a blurring of the individual and the plural, Danielewski creates distance and desirability.

As a result of reinterpreting 'you' to signal its generalised meaning and then disassociating from this grouping, the reader now appears to occupy a unique subject position (as embodied in the text-world of 'This is for you'). This subject position takes on an uncharacteristic quality of exclusivity, such as that promoted by anti-marketing strategies (Sinha and Foscht 2007). In such marketing campaigns, the desirability of a product is enhanced as a direct consequence of its limited availability. Therefore, an implicit conclusion that can be drawn from Danielewski's crafted employment of the second-person pronoun is that the referential slippage it facilitates creates an appealing subject position for the reader to adopt, one distinct from those encapsulated by the now interpreted generalised *you* in 'This is not for you.' If generalised *you* here refers to unworthy readers, this would make this desirable subject position that of an ideal reader. Self-implication (Kuiken, Miall and Sikora 2004) of actual reader with ideal reader leads to two related effects. Firstly it promotes readerly projection into the foregrounded negative text-world of 'This is for you', thereby intensifying a reader's reactance to the proposition 'This is not for you.'

IV. Choose to trespass

The multimodal dimension of 'This is not for you' also has a part to play in the intricacies of the novel's initial statement. It is therefore worth considering the positioning of the sentence upon the page. As mentioned, these five words are the only imprint upon a single page – in fact, upon a double-page spread. A reader who experiences reactance to this negated assertion must turn the page in order to encounter succeeding text in the form of the (fictional) introduction. While this is not exactly a demanding task, proceeding to read *House of Leaves* would be easier if further linguistic content appeared upon the same page. Had this been the case, the 'choice' either to continue or stop reading would have been rather less noticeable or significant, since most readers are likely to proceed out of habit. As a result, the white space of the page takes on a less innocent façade. This 'emptiness' of the remainder of the page transforms the normally unremarkable operation of turning the page into a defiant performance of reactance, one which works to reassert the reader's free behaviour.

Another multimodal consideration affecting the meaning of 'This is not for you' is its positioning, not just upon the page but within the book more generally. Since it is placed between the foreword and introduction, we are able to read it as the opening of the narrative, and thus experience the effects described above. However, an additional knowledge frame that could apply is that of the dedication. In his work on paratextual features, Genette states, 'the canonical site of the dedication has obviously been at the head of the book, and today, more precisely, on the first right hand page after the title page' (1997: 126). In *House of Leaves*, the preceding foreword complicates this, enabling 'This is not for you' to be read as both opening sentence and dedication. Dedications usually occur in the ellipted form, '[ ] For [proper noun/noun phrase]'. Reversing the ellipsis, we would arrive at something not dissimilar to 'This is for [proper noun].' The resulting implication is that Danielewski's 'This is not for you' is a form of negative dedication.

As a brief aside, 'This is not for you' can be perceived not just as paratext but intertext too, echoing the title to Jane Rule's (1970) novel. While this is an obscure link which not all readers will be aware of, it is significant as Rule's novel is a second-person fiction, albeit one which employs fictional reference in Herman's terms, *you* signifying a specific character. The title of Rule's novel *This is Not for You*, which is also the final line of the novel, executes doubly deictic address, at once signifying the character to whom the narrative is written but will never be read by and the reader (who is not said character). In this way, it bears relevance to *House of Leaves*. As Kacandes says about Rule's novel but equally applicably to Danielewski's, it 'seemingly initiates contact to shut it down; it calls, but paradoxically it claims not to address the one it calls – *this is not for you*' (2001: 142).

Returning to paratext, Genette's discussion of dedicatees can be used to enhance an understanding of the subversive potential of Danielewski's negation. Within what Genette considers a 'no doubt playful set' of dedicatory subjects, he lists self-dedication, dedication to the hero and dedication to the reader – 'that is, to the real addressee of the work' (1997: 133). The dissident nature of a dedication of this sort can be seen from two examples. Firstly and briefly, Marge Percy's (1972) *Small Changes*, which utilises the personal pronouns for feminist goals: 'For me. For you. For us. Even for them.' As Pearce explains, 'them' refers to men who are positioned 'outside the boundaries of an inclusive address' (1997: 69), and therefore not included in an ideal reading audience. Secondly, consider the following dedication from Neil Gaiman's (2005) *Anansi Boys*:

> You know how it is. You pick up a book, flip to the dedication, and find that, once again, the author has dedicated a book to someone else and not to you.
> Not this time.
> Because we haven't yet met/have only a glancing acquaintance/are just crazy about each other/haven't seen each other in much too long/are in some way related/will never meet, but will I trust, despite that, always think fondly of each other . . .
> This one's for you.
> With you know what, and you probably know why. (Gaiman 2005)

Clearly, Gaiman is toying with the conventional boundaries of the dedication format. The first sentences, reminiscent of the opening to Italo Calvino's (1979) *If On a Winter's Night A Traveller*, employ *you* in an active voice using simple present tense. Combined with the generic descriptions, this creates a *you* that embraces both a definite and indefinite audience, encouraging the reader to feel that he or she is in some form being addressed by the text. Gavins (2007a: 85–6) discusses this form of transcendental address in which a connection is made between an implied author (or author-enactor) and an apostrophically addressed reader, commenting that the 'closer the resemblance between the life of the text-world enactor and the life of the real world reader, the more likely it is that the reader will comfortably inhabit the new projected text-world persona' (2007a: 86). Gaiman cleverly avoids readerly disengagement by making his dedication maximally applicable, as evident in the semantic alternatives punctuated by the use of the '/' punctuation mark. What I find most interesting in Gaiman's dedication is his explicit mention of a book dedicated 'to someone else and not to you', shortly succeeded by the unembedded 'This one's for you' which is foregrounded as a result of the semantic contrast. Gaiman's concluding sentence is also remarkable in its proximal and repeated use of interrogatives functioning as ambiguous pronouns.

Gaiman's dedication is a fitting contrast to Danielewski's negated adaptation. Unfortunately, Genette does not consider the possibility of a negative dedication, but he does speak of the author's choice not to include a dedication: 'the absence of dedication, in a system that includes the possibility of one, is significant as degree zero. "This book is not dedicated to anyone" – isn't such an implied message loaded with meaning?' (1997: 135). Genette's rhetorical question assumes an affirmative response, though I would argue that this is only the case when the absence is noticed by the reader. Danielewski, in exposing his subversive intent, exhibits the agency of his intention and harnesses the potency of such literary insurgence.

As an explicit negated dedication, 'This is not for you' is without question charged with semantic value. By using negation to create dissonance and reactance, alongside the referential slippage of the pronoun *you*, Danielewski heightens readerly desire to read the novel. While multimodality is restricted in this extract, its importance must be acknowledged in enhancing the psychological intensity and complexity evoked by the opening sentence.

Genette speaks of paratextual features as 'thresholds', that is 'the literary and printerly conventions that mediate between the world of publishing and the world of the text' (1997: xvii). Danielewski's literary (-linguistic and -multimodal) manoeuvres entice readers inwards. His use of direct address brings semi-permeability into effect, working not to alienate the reader through ontological distancing, but engage them in an active performance.

V. Conclusion

The creative aperture that has focused the analysis acts as a threshold to the novel, a door into the *House of Leaves*. Yet, paradoxically, it is an entrance into a place we are being forbidden to enter. By both inviting and prohibiting the reader, the opening possesses a tension of meaning that Danielewski employs to create a sense of discomfort for the reader to take with them as they turn the page. The paradox and feeling of discomfort are crucial for a novel often cited by critics as belonging to the horror or gothic genre. In *The Mysteries of Udolpho*, a foundational gothic novel, Radcliffe writes of imaginatively evoked fear: 'a terror of this nature, as it occupies and expands the mind, and elevates it to high expectation, is purely sublime, and leads us, by a kind of fascination, to seek even the object, from which we appear to shrink' (1966: 248). Danielewski's 'This is not for you' tempts us to trespass, luring us inside the *House of Leaves*.

Works cited

Baron, R. A. and Byrne, D. (2003) *Social Psychology*, 10th edn, Boston; London: Allyn and Bacon.
Booth, W. C. (1983) *The Rhetoric of Fiction*, Chicago: University of Chicago Press.
Brehm, J. W. (1966) *A Theory of Psychological Reactance*, New York; London: Academic Press.
Calvino, I. (1998 [1979]) *If On A Winter's Night A Traveller*, trans. William Weaver, London: Vintage.
Clark, H. H. and Clark, E. V. (1977) *Psychology and Language: An Introduction to Psycholinguistics*, New York: Harcourt Brace Jovanovich.
Crawford, M. T., McConnell, A. R., Lewis, A. C. and Sherman, S. J. (2002) 'Reactance, compliance, and anticipated regret', *Journal of Experimental Social Psychology* 38: 56–63.

Danielewski, M. Z. (2000) *House of Leaves by Zampanò with Introduction and Notes by Johnny Truant*, London; New York: Doubleday.

Evans, V. and Green, M. (2006) *Cognitive Linguistics: An Introduction*, Edinburgh: Edinburgh University Press.

Festinger, L. (1957) *A Theory of Cognitive Dissonance*, Stanford: Stanford University Press.

Fludernik, M. (1995) 'Pronouns of address and "odd" third person forms: the mechanics of involvement in fiction', in Green, K. (ed.) *New Essays in Deixis: Discourse, Narrative, Literature*, Amsterdam: Rodopi, 1995, pp. 99–129.

Gaiman, N. (2005) *Anansi Boys*, London: Headline Book Publishing.

Gavins, J. (2007a) *Text World Theory: An Introduction*, Edinburgh: Edinburgh University Press.

Gavins, J. (2007b) '"And everyone and I stopped breathing": familiarity and ambiguity in the text world of "The day lady died"', in Lambrou, M. and Stockwell, P. (eds.) *Contemporary Stylistics*, London; New York: Continuum.

Genette, G. (1997 [1987]) *Paratexts: Thresholds of Interpretation*, trans. Jane E. Lewin, Cambridge: Cambridge University Press.

Herman, D. (1994) 'Textual you and double deixis in Edna O'Brien's *A Pagan Place*', *Style* 28(3): 378–410.

Herman, D. (2002) *Story Logic: Problems and Possibilities of Narrative*, Lincoln; London: University of Nebraska Press.

Hidalgo Downing, L. (2000a) *Negation, Text Worlds, and Discourse: The Pragmatics of Fiction*, Stamford: Ablex Publishing Corporation.

Hidalgo Downing, L. (2000b) 'Negation in discourse: a text world approach to Joseph Heller's *Catch-22*', *Language and Literature* 9(3): 215–239.

Hidalgo Downing, L. (2002) 'Creating things that are not: the role of negation in the poetry of Wislawa Szymborska', *Journal of Literary Semantics* 31: 113–132.

Kacandes, I. (2001) *Talk Fiction: Literature and the Talk Explosion*, Lincoln; London: University of Nebraska Press.

Kuiken, D., Miall, D. S. and Sikora, S. (2004) 'Forms of self-implication in literary reading', *Poetics Today* 25(2): 53–74.

Lakoff, G. (2004) *Don't Think of an Elephant*, Vermont: Chelsea Green Publishing.

Lee, D. (2001) *Cognitive Linguistics: An Introduction*, Oxford: Oxford University Press.

Margolin, U. (1984) 'Narrative and indexicality: a tentative framework', *Journal of Literary Semantics* 13: 181–204.

Margolin, U. (1986-7) 'Dispersing/voiding the subject: a narratological perspective', *Texte* 5/6: 181–210.

Nørgaard, N. (2007) 'Disordered collarettes and uncovered tables: negative

polarity as a stylistic device in Joyce's "Two gallants"', *Journal of Literary Semantics* 36: 35–52.
Pearce, L. (1997) *Feminism and the Politics of Reading*, London; New York: Arnold.
Percy, M. (1972) *Small Changes*, London: Penguin Books.
Radcliffe, A. (1966 [1794]) *The Mysteries of Udolpho*, ed. Dobree, B., Oxford: Oxford University Press.
Rule, J. (1970) *This is Not for You*, London: Pandora.
Segal, E. M. (1995) 'A cognitive-phenomenological theory of fictional narrative', in Duchan, J. F., Bruder, G. A. and Hewitt, L. E. (eds) *Deixis in Narrative: A Cognitive Science Perspective*, Hillsdale, NJ: Lawrence Erlbaum, pp. 61–78.
Sinha, I. and Foscht, T. (2007) *Reverse Psychology Marketing: The Death of Traditional Marketing and the Rise of the New 'Pull' Game*, Basingstoke; New York: Palgrave Macmillan.
Stockwell, P. (2002) *Cognitive Poetics: An Introduction*, London: Routledge.
Wales, K. (1996) *Personal Pronouns in Present-Day English*, Cambridge: Cambridge University Press.
Werth, P. (1999) *Text Worlds: Representing Conceptual Space in Discourse*, London: Longman.
Young, K. G. (1987) *Taleworlds and Storyrealms: The Phenomenology of Narrative*, Hingham, MA: Kluwer.

2

Katabasis in Danielewski's *House of Leaves* and two other recent American novels

Finn Fordham, Royal Holloway, University of London

It is intriguing and remarkable that *House of Leaves*, in its structural complexity and in certain thematic preoccupations, overlaps with at least two other recent American novels – David Foster Wallace's 1996 *Infinite Jest* and Don DeLillo's 1997 *Underworld*. All three display energies of narrative and of characters swirling through topological, social and discursive planes. The stock-in-trade of ambitious complex novels can be found in abundance and in sparkling form: multiple strands of narrative, families oscillating between unity and fragmentation, individuals and gangs on quests, investigations of secret histories, counter-cultural depths which conventional history conceals, mixed styles and registers, sentiment complicated by layers of irony. Such features, while not unexpected, are combined with more idiosyncratic particularities of content, two of which are particularly striking: first, the clandestine productions and samizdat disseminations of filmed sequences which prove central to all three novels, and second, powerful allusions to underground structures, to underworlds and *katabasis* – the epic convention of descending into such structures.

In this chapter, while I will mention film, I wish to compare the deployment of underworlds, using Wallace's and DeLillo's coincident and correlated novels as context for Danielewski's in order to highlight certain issues. I will examine three aspects of the underworld: first, the way katabasis relates the novel to the epic; secondly, the adolescent cultural politics associated with *de profundis* narratives; thirdly, the relation between text and architecture and how, in *House of Leaves* above all, underworld narratives work alongside spatial aspects of the book in ways which reinvigorate meanings of the book, thus dissolving concerns about perceived threats to the book's status from the cinema and visual and digitized media more generally. In conclusion, I suggest a parallel between the underworlds and language in terms of them being incomprehensible systems.

I. Novel vs epic

The features mentioned above locate each novel in the context of different media and different genres: the cinematic and the epic. The presence of clandestine film reflects a historical realisation that the present is saturated, from the mainstream to the margins, by visual representations and narratives; it also illustrates literary fiction's ongoing critical reflections on how its roles are differentiated from the cinematic, develop in response to it, and are threatened by and compete with it.

Literary fiction cannot help picturing itself in a cultural world that is dominated by the cinematic and visual media: it might distance itself from, critique or ignore, pay homage or condescend to its younger and more popular sister art. I will read the deployment in these novels of katabasis in part alongside this ambivalence in the novel's relations to cinema. And while it is a sign of other things too, these can be related back to cinema. Katabasis, for instance, marks the novel's exploratory stretching out towards its encyclopaedic potential, straining towards a cosmological imaginary and a rerooting back in its epic sources. In the context of American political history, this straining of the 1990's novel through the conventions of katabasis, conflict and quest, reveals an attempt to hold together the contradictions in America's self-perception: the one single superpower in the 1990s when, as an Empire, it was reluctantly relinquishing whatever illusions it had ever entertained of being non-interventionist or not being interventionist. Epic is the imperial genre and katabasis an extreme sport for imperial superheroes. Danielewski's Holloway is a satirical version of such a hero and he is consistent with those American versions of the narrative, especially in such Vietnam movies as *The Deer Hunter*, *Apocalypse Now*, *Full Metal Jacket* and *Platoon*, which are scored through with trauma rather than triumphalism.

This exploration, strain and contradiction is superegotistical, both self-critical and critical of other genres. The novel, in its ambitions,

Bakhtin once contended, has a competitive relation to the epic genre and has internal contradictions for this very reason:

> Here the novel ... emerges consciously and unambiguously as a genre that is both critical and self-critical, one fated to revise the fundamental concepts of literariness and poeticalness dominant at the time. On the one hand, the contrast of novel with epic (and the novel's opposition to the epic) is but one moment in the criticism of other literary genres (in particular, a criticism of epic heroization); but on the other hand, this contrast aims to elevate the significance of the novel, making of it the dominant genre in contemporary literature. (Bakhtin 2002: 10–11)

The novel's continuous aim to be the 'dominant genre' in literature by surpassing epic helps explain the deployment of such epic conventions as katabasis. But the novel is also, as Bakhtin suggests, critical of epic, of its heroisation for example, and it may be so through parodic mockery of katabasis.

Bakhtin's Darwinian view of a struggle for generic dominance can be applied to the cinema, though Bakhtin does not himself do this. His deep and rich historical knowledge of European narrative tended to universalise the condition of the novel, subsequent to its emergence, in ways that could not always be alive to particular events or conditions in the history of culture. Examples of such transformative events would include the emergence of cinema which had a large and immediate impact on the forms and goals of the novel. This gap in Bakhtin's theories is a sign of the predominance of formalism over a focused historicism, within an oeuvre that had to be wary of direct allusions to contemporary political and cultural history. Insofar as cinema can be thought to threaten the dominant status of the literary novel in the general field of culture, literature will attempt to defend its status in several ways: by producing narratives which enclose film, and by exploiting aspects of books which films do not have. The aspects Danielewski exploits, supremely well, include the space of the book and the flexible manipulability of its status as an object. Katabasis helps here: the expansive exploration of the minimal space of the book as an object is laid alongside the narrative katabasis with its exploration of unfamiliar, innovative, defamiliarising underground and maximal space. This layering is central to Danielewski's homage to the manipulable and tactile space which the book as an object inhabits and which differentiates it from the space of cinema. As I will show, literary fiction occupies an underground space in relation to film. Our readings are descents into the worlds of the undead: reading is a katabasis.

II. Regressive underworlds

Novels – and narratives generally – are lured to the underworld and the underground for several reasons. As the films *Brazil*, *Subway*, *Delicatessen* and *The Matrix III* indicate, both are spaces associated with repressed forces, the services, the servile, the mechanical and human servants, out-of-sight downstairs. Such spaces are arenas or pits offering structure to counter-cultures in which strategies of liberation are planned, and from which eruptive hell-like powers will one day belch forth the dead to judge the living. They are thick with political symbolism: incubating undiscovered segments of secret narratives, they are locations for sub-plots, subversive plots and subversions of plots. History conceals a multiplicity of tunnels: in the fluid sequences of historical events, some narrative sequences flow out of sight, underground, so that events on the surface then unfold in a manner that cannot be explained by what is on the surface. Novelists like getting hold of these alternative moments that have become 'lost' to history, and yet have changed the course of events. They have an appeal to the Gothic sensibility, evoked in writing from Coleridge's evocation of 'caverns measureless to man' leading to 'a sunless sea' to Tom Waits' declaration, on *Swordfishtrombone*, that 'there's a world going on underground'. These spaces contain mysterious alternatives, repressed or unencompassable by rationality. Their rhizomatic spread in unpredictable directions is the negative image of that tidy nuclear household which the Navidsons, in retiring to the country house, had been hoping to embody.

Many of our narratives project worlds going on underground, where they do not exist. David Pike's enthusiasm in *Subterranean Cities* lists the fantasies to which Danielewski contributes:

> Contemporary Western culture seems obsessed by all things underground. The sewers and catacombs are among the most visited attractions in Paris. London's biggest draw is the disused railway arches that house the shopping counterculture-themed Camden Town; . . . No action movie is complete without a sensational climax in a metropolitan subway, utility tunnel, or sewer, or a showdown in the arch-villain's subterranean stronghold. The image of the late twentieth and early twenty-first-century city is dominated by underworld beings:

prostitutes and pimps, dealers and addicts, sexual deviants, mafiosos, terrorists, illegal aliens, slum dwellers . . . How did so many disparate phenomena . . . become so closely identified with the same space? . . . It all began with the nineteenth century. (Pike 2005: 7–8)

Pike's enthusiasm exaggerates: parts of the vast market of Camden Town house themselves under arches of an overground railway but at no point is any of it actually underground. The identification of the nineteenth century as an origin, moreover, even of the specifically urban underground, is strategic hyperbole used to posit a period as an origin. The lure of the underground in narrative and the functions of the underground in reality (present as caves, quarries, crypts and the necropolis) are ancient, perhaps prehistoric in myth. The nineteenth century alone will not provide an explanation for katabasis narratives. Rejecting a particular historical origin does not necessarily mean we must explain it through universally archetypal psychic forces, projections of some psychic battle. One explanation Danielewski indirectly provides for the lure and fetishisation of the underworld and its discourses is that they are regressively superstitious. They follow on from an exhaustion with the empirical, a defeat of realism, a surrendering of rationality, which in turn lead to commodifications of narcissistic *mises en abîme* and to entertainments from which flow feelings of terror always limited by relief. Languishing from a *nostalgie de la tombe*, the Gothic critic seeks terror for its enervated state, in the spectral, the ghostly, the uncanny and the vampiric, by unsealing an apparently terrifying double of our world, seething just under the ground, on which, he or she believes, it is impossible to build anything anyway. The underworld provides the Gothic imagination with a space back over which it can look so it may believe in a world that contains more than just materiality – as if it needed more. Orpheus looked back not to check that Eurydice was there, but in the hope of having confirmed the miracle of the existence of spirit in matter, of life within and after death. Irrationality feeds off irrational fear: in such narratives, irrational phobias (of the dead, of spirits, of ghosts) are given rational grounds through the perceived necessity of overcoming them and the manner in which certain heroic qualities (bravery, strength, unity, intelligence, loyalty) are employed to that end.

Bret Easton Ellis in his influential review of *House of Leaves* registered this attraction for phantasmagoric underground terror, claiming that the novel is 'sublimely creepy, distressingly scary' (Danielewski 2000: cover). Ellis' reading thus associated Danielewski with the cult of soft terror whose page-turning prophet is Stephen King, whose high-priestess is Buffy, whose theory is 'the uncanny', and for which *Twilight* offers the most recent propaganda. Danielewski may deploy but he also qualifies and subverts this genre which is predominantly adolescent. The adolescent is impatient for, frightened by and exaggerates the imminent transformations that are stages on the road to adulthood. There is a series of more or less formalised initiation ceremonies especially for males – the first long journey away from the family home, the loss of virginity, the experimentation with various substances, encounters with foreign authorities – which provides context for these transformations and builds up pressure around them. The katabasis is an expression of such ceremonies. Mircea Eliade speaks about how 'descending into Hades means to undergo "initiatory death", the experience of which can establish a new mode of being' (Edmonds 2004: 18). The katabasis is a narrative of machismo and masochistic initiation, for adolescents of all ages. The mid-life crisis, as evident in Navidson, attempts to relive the openness and suppleness of adolescence. The dramatic thrill of adolescent cultures makes katabasis a regressive journey. Navidson's wish to explore the house is regressive with respect to Karen who wishes him to be a responsible *pater familias* and stay above ground and within the conventional bounds of the family home she wishes them to build and embody. The adolescent aspect may seem to be qualified by social responsibility: Navidson's return to help Jed and Wax, a version of the Vietnam recovery narratives mentioned above, seems responsible, but such a return to a primitivist space is clearly associated with the adolescent initiatory katabasis, since the return hopes to recapture and reinhabit that part of one's self that got stuck in adolescent fantasies, to live the experience of a white man taking risks under the gaze of a jungle people or atavistic force.

III. Architectural underworlds: Wallace and DeLillo

Of the three novels that focus this essay, Wallace's (1996) treatment of katabasis is most rationalised, satirical and marginal. Early on in his book, Wallace seductively introduces the reader to an underground space which is described with fetishistic obsession. Later on, however, any such fascination is uncovered as regressive, even

Katabasis in *House of Leaves, Infinite Jest* and *Underworld* 39

infantile: 'small U.S. boys seem to have this fetish for getting down in the enclosed fundaments underneath things – tunnels, caves, ventilator-shafts' (Wallace 1996: 666). There is no room for the supernatural or cosmological in Wallace's satire of a rationalised corporate world in which the underground is thoroughly artificial, materialist, architectural. Wallace's early description of his underworld is elaborate and long but deserves inclusion not only for its remarkable implicit qualities but also because Wallace has been cited as an antecedent of Danielewski and a point of intertextual reference for Danielewski's elaborate and textualised sense of space (Ponicsanyi 2001):

> E.T.A's hilltop grounds are traversable by tunnel. Avril I., for example, who never leaves the grounds anymore, rarely travels above ground, willing to hunch to take the off-tunnels between Headmaster's House and her office next to Charles Tavis's in the Community and Administration Bldg., a pink bricked white-pillared neo-Georgian thing that Hal's brother Mario says looks like a cube that has swallowed a ball too big for its stomach.[3] Two sets of elevators and one of stairs run between the lobby, reception area, and administrative office on Comm.-Ad.'s first floor and the weight room, sauna, and locker/shower areas on the sublevel below it. One large tunnel of elephant-colored cement leads from just off the boys' showers to the mammoth laundry room below the West Courts, and two smaller tunnels radiate from the sauna area south and east to the subbasements of the smaller, spherocubular, proto-Georgian buildings (housing classrooms and subdormitories B and D); these two basements and smaller tunnels often serve as student storage space and hallways between various prorectors'[4] private rooms. Then two even smaller tunnels, navigable by any adult willing to assume a kind of knuckle-dragging simian posture, in turn connect each of the subbasements to the former optical and film-development facilities of Leith and Ogilvie and the late Dr. James O. Incandenza (now deceased) below and just west of the Headmaster's House (from which facilities there's also a fair-diametered tunnel that goes straight to the lowest level of the Community and Administrations Bldg., but its functions have gradually changed over four years, and it's now too full of exposed wiring and hot-water pipes and heating ducts to be really passable) and to the offices of the Physical Plant, which offices and custodial lounge are in turn connected to E.T.A.'s Lung-Storage and -Pump Rooms via a pargeted tunnel hastily constructed by the TesTar All-Weather Inflatable Structures Corp., . . . The crude little rough-sided tunnel between Plant and Pump is traversable only via all-fours-type crawling and is

essentially unknown to staff and Administration, popular only with the Academy's smaller kids' Tunnel Club, as well as with certain adolescents with strong incentive to crawl on all fours . . .
   When the court's Lung is down and stored, Hal will descend . . . and crawl to the [Pump Room . . .] and get secretly high. (Wallace 1996: 51–52)

While a plan or map would make this structure more easily understood, it would fail to express the comic display of effort in the strenuous description, like the comic amazement at a man removing his vest without taking off his suit (as described in an annotation to this very passage). Here the writing is both weapon and target, as the potential in textual expression chooses to compete with visual media for consumers' imaginations. The description aims at pinning down a structure in its entirety, compulsively pursuing every tunnel and its relations to other spaces. But it describes these relations in terms of things whose relations to each other have not been described so that no cognitive map of the tunnel series that opens up during the description can be easily plotted. This early passage about passages (which contains, moreover, a textual passage down to an endnote on page 983) raises apprehensions and teases our expectations about both the door-stopping novel's likely complexity and also the unpredictability of how its elements will or will not interconnect.

The syntagmatic structure of the excerpt's style, with its convoluted sub-clausal sentences, invites comparisons with the architectural structure of the convoluted tunnels it describes. The passage energetically packs the page so it seems to bulge awkwardly with its own information, like the anthropomorphised building itself, which resembles 'a cube that has swallowed a ball too big for its stomach'. It mocks corporate economies, taking up time to save space, using acronyms and abbreviations ('Bldg., ATHSCME'), as if short of space, leaving unremarked the ironic coincidence of an air intake fan whose name sounds like 'asthma', which normally limits air intake. The structure is finally not pinned down, but leaves loose threads leading away from it, trailing, as it were, off underground, beyond the labyrinth described, setting up a strong expectation that they will surface later (as the subterranean 'film-development facilities' indeed will). As the reader struggles for space to breathe through this dense matter, there is a further demand made through the annotation marks after the word 'stomach' and 'prorectors'' which oblige him or her to burrow down through the body of the book where eventually we begin to familiarise ourselves with the 'End Notes and Errata' finding, on page 983, the following:

> 3. E.T.A. is laid out as a cardioid, with the four main inward-facing bldgs. convexly rounded at the back and sides to yield a cardioid's curve, with the tennis courts and pavillions at the center and the staff and students' parking lots in back of Comm.-Ad. forming the little bashed-in dent that the air gives the whole facility the Valentine-heart aspect that still bulges all derived from arcs of the same r, a staggering feat given the uneven ground and wildly different electrical-and-plumbing-conduit wallspace required by dormitories, administrative offices, and polyresinous Lung, pull-offable probably by on the whole East Coast one guy, E.T.A.'s original architect, Avril's old and very dear friend, the topology world's closed-curve-mapping-Ubermensch A.Y. ('Vector-Field') Rickey of Brandeis U., now deceased, who used to wow Hal and Mario in Weston by taking off his vest without removing his suit jacket, which M. Pemulis years later exposed as a cheap parlor-trick-exploitation of certain basic features of continuous functions, which revelation Hal mourned in a Santa's-not-real type of secret way, and which Mario simply ignored, preferring to see the vest thing as plain magic. (Wallace 1996: 983)

Having journeyed down to this endnote, we find there an allusion to a semi-divine designer ('Ubermensch Rickey') of the system in its mathematically complex entirety, combining the god-as-builder and author-as-god myths. The reader moves through all these signs at two defamiliarising levels: through the signifiers, arranged in complex syntactic structures, and through the signifieds of weird architectural structures. Just as 'Avril I.' (short for Avril Incandenza, the mother of the characters here named Hal and Mario, but also carrying the subversive association of Fool's Day submerged within it) is 'willing to hunch to take the off-tunnels', so the reader is invited to think of the narrative and its digressions as tunnels and off-tunnels, and given a model for uncomfortable readjustment, a precedent for the disruptions of flow and the tracing of the many arms of this serially bifurcating narrative.

In DeLillo's *Underworld* tunnels similarly provide a schematic paradigm for the relation of different narrative streams. It is becoming increasingly clear that DeLillo, for Wallace, was a master in whom he must have found a model of tone in which comedy, complexity, satire and pathos were brought together (Streitfeld

2008). The influence of DeLillo on Danielewski is not so clear, but his shadow over the contemporary American novel is unavoidable. Underground spaces in DeLillo's *Underworld* (H-bomb-test sites and the New York subway) are, like Wallace's, artificial. Yet in his reconstruction of Eisenstein's *Unterwelt*, a mythical film about mythical underground spaces, DeLillo prefigures Danielewski. DeLillo (born in 1927) is agnostic but steeped, one senses, in Catholic narratives of sin and redemption. His narratives are expansive and complex, but nonetheless relatively conventional. The Underworld, for DeLillo, is, romantically, the womb of fresh counter-cultural ideas conceived in the depths of its members' adversity. Its under-class will return to judge those above ground. In a world of disconnection, he has a nostalgia for an intuited connection and equal communion between the upper- and the under-worlds. Architectural man-made structures organise hierarchy and disconnection, but art and the supernatural can transcend these and resolve the problematic desires for connection.

The novel presents us with two artists: an avant-garde conceptual artist Klara Max and a graffiti artist Ismael Munoz, whose tag is *Moonman 157*. Through these characters, DeLillo codes the romantic idea that art is made underground by exiles, that it emerges above ground proclaiming the existence of the artist and the transformative power of the artist's vision. In the third chapter of part IV, at a crossroads and the middle of the novel, an elite screening of Eisenstein's *Unterwelt* takes place, a copy of which had emerged out of a post-Warsaw-Block East Germany. The film

> deals with people living in the shadows . . . Figures move through some underground space. They are victims or prisoners, perhaps experimental subjects. A glimpse of a prisoner's face shows he is badly deformed and it is less shocking than funny. He has the sloped head, shallow jaw and protuberant lips of an earthworm . . . – but a worm with a human pathos about him. (DeLillo 1997: 429)

The film has an intermission, and Klara Max, the focaliser, stands outside with friends:

> They heard a rumble. They felt something shaking under their feet and Klara studied the white parchment wall, listening carefully.
> Then she took a drag and said, 'S'Okay, friend. Only the subway. The IND plowing under Sixth Avenue with its cargo of human souls.' (DeLillo 1997: 432)

Although an attempt is made to rationalise the potentially frightening sensations, the myth of the underworld land of the dead is inescapable, as this moment near a cargo of souls introduces, briefly, with a Virgilian reassurance, a Dantean katabasis. A few lines later they hear again 'the rattle of another subway run'. The narrative jumps levels, switches track, to the 'subway artist' Munoz as DeLillo is lured by the romantic counter-cultural discourses of the underworld:

> The train was one of his, Moonman's, he had a dozen pieces running through the system, top-to-bottom burners, and it just so happens he was aboard tonight, under the water mains and waste pipes, under the gas and steam and electric, between the storm sewers and telephone lines, and he moved from car to car . . . checked out the people with their retractable subway faces . . . (DeLillo 1997: 433)

Munoz, an undercover artist at his own opening, with a 'dozen pieces running', is like DeLillo sending multiple narratives coursing through *Underworld*'s hidden structural subway system. The main event occurs is when the train comes out of the tunnel:

> [Y]ou have to stand on a platform and see it coming or you can't know the feeling a writer gets, how the number 5 train comes roaring down the rat alleys and slams out of the tunnel, going whop-pop onto the high tracks, and suddenly there it is, Moonman riding the sky in the heart of the Bronx, over the whole burnt and rusted country, . . . you can't *not* see us anymore, you can't *not* know who we are, . . . this is the art that can't stand still, it climbs across your eyeballs night and day, the flickery jumping art of the slums and dumpsters, flashing those colors in your face – like I'm your movie, motherfucker. (DeLillo 1997: 440–441)

A spiritual telepathic connection is being forced between Munoz and Klara: as she returns to the second half of *Unterwelt*, his work is – or should in fact be – her movie. What she watches harmonises, is in synchrony with, Moonman's narrative.

> It seems you are witnessing an escape. Figures moving upward through gouged tunnels into a dark rainy night . . . Yes, the film has climbed to the surface, to a landscape shocked by light, pervasive and overexposed. The escaped prisoners move across flat terrain. (DeLillo 1997: 441–442)

As indicated earlier, underground structures provide a schematic paradigm for the relation of different narrative streams in all the novels. DeLillo's novel provides a place where the hierarchies are not inverted but lifted up and laid on their side, where the different levels are brought into equivalent status. Danielewski keeps his artists separate: Johnny Truant's beat-style narrative, as he moves into depression and paranoia, is a katabasis which may be analogous to the katabasis of the Navidson Record. But there is little chance of any joining or resolution between them. Though *Underworld* was described as 'post-paranoid' by Michael Wood, the novel is a continuation of a compulsion for connectivity of which paranoia is a symptom (Wood 1998: 3). It is Danielewski who, not sharing DeLillo's nostalgia for connection, is 'post-paranoid'.

Underworld also plays none of the textual games in which the other two novels revel. Although it is not clear what, if anything, Danielewski might owe to DeLillo, the former's connection to Wallace has been emphasised: Danielewski's 'glee in footnotes', as John Ponicsanyi's Amazon review mentions, bears a 'similarity to David Foster Wallace that is almost too obvious to mention' (Ponicsanyi 2001). Indeed, one crucial point of resemblance is the coincidence of architectural and textual structure which, in both novels, creates a sense of the expansive potential in the internal space of books. In what follows, I call this coincidence 'architextural'.

IV. Architextural underworlds: *House of Leaves*

Danielewski builds on the architextural much more elaborately than Wallace did and, in this area at least, is more innovative. Chapter IX, considered by the author to be 'the most complex section of the book', illustrates many such innovations (Wittmershaus 2000). Its elaborate systems of annotations and the 'duct note', running from page 119 to 142, in particular, help create a labyrinth of interconnecting routes. Whether readers find their way through all the material or not, and whatever routes through the maze readers choose to construct for themselves, one definite effect is an experience of the book as a three-dimensional object, beyond the usual experience of textual flow as continuously mono-linear. Each illustration prompts me to make two suggestions: one, that the space of language can be imagined as resembling the ideal underground space of *House of Leaves* (in that its structure has no outside) and, second, that Danielewski reveals the limitations of the cinematic which the book – in its tactility and manipulability – manages to transcend.

One of Chapter IX's inventive games is to play with the formalist practice of a loop narrative, by which a text, in some manner, returns to its beginning. After three epigrams, the chapter begins, on page 109, by introducing the need to 'address the more complex ideation of convolution, interference, confusion, and even decentric ideas of design and construction'. But this is not in fact the beginning of the chapter, as just before the first letter a small 'K' sign pokes up its head, an annotation mark which does not seem to refer to any visible footnote. The K sign however crops up again a few pages later at the *end* of footnote number 136 on page 114 and *also* at the end of footnote 183 (itself a footnote to a footnote and in 'mirror hand') on page 144. Twice therefore we are directed back to the beginning of the chapter. It turns out that the text following the first 'K' is in fact an annotation to these subsequent footnotes, placing the text in a secondary rather than primary relation. Centre and periphery seem to have swapped places. The formal game of the loop narrative has been complicated, moreover, into a knotted narrative since the 'K' indicates two means of re-entering the start point of the maze. The reader, as in a maze, finds him or herself retreading similar ground, unable to move forward.

Another sequence which contributes to this labyrinthine quality begins on page 134, where some text introducing the idea of 'what distinguishes documentaries from Hollywood releases' is annotated with the number 166, directing us to a footnote that is squinched and upside down, to read which we have to turn the pages back, one by one, to page 130. At its end, it is annotated with the number 167, the footnote to which, lying on its side, starts on page 131 and reads now *forwards* to page 135, so the reader retraces steps and returns the pages. At the end of note 167, there is another mark – 168 – whose three-page-long note is internally annotated many times, one of which, note 171, itself leads to four other notes, while yet another, 177, starts us on a chain that takes us eventually to 'Appendix II./B./ The Pelican Poems' (573–580), seemingly beyond the chapter and even the main text's conclusion. This might momentarily feel like an escape out of Chapter IX, but these poems relate, in a style reminiscent of Beat poetry, another circuitous and fragmentary journey round Europe (beginning in Warsaw, ending in Greece) with a series of obscure personal references, an extension, therefore, of the maze connected to it by a tenuous textual tunnel. As a conscientious reader you still in fact have a way to go in the original chapter, and so must retrace your steps back to footnote 166 on page 134, not forgetting to check the other footnotes which you had not penetrated on the way.

This textual labyrinth is clearly an experiment in mimetic form where the narrative content of three men exploring a series of dark interlinked labyrinthine rooms, and a discussion of labyrinths, is being represented through the text's appearance and thence projected into the reader's experience of the text. A reader who drives him or herself to follow those routes (which of course, he or she does not have to do) is subversively made to identify with the several obsessive questers in the film's and book's narratives and with the parodied academics whose prolix works are quoted to an extent that clearly mocks the entire Humanities Industry (of which this collection, is, of course, a part). Danielewski takes his mimesis even further. The narrative in which the shape-shifting cavernous corridor is explored describes physically demanding (and macho) activities. While the physical demands of reading *House of Leaves* are in no way equivalent, they are so different from the usual reading experience, so unfamiliar – perhaps, excitingly so – especially in the aspects of tactility and manipulation of the book, that in this unfamiliarity, lie parallels to tangible reminders of the physically demanding and unfamiliar exploration. Readers handle and manipulate the physical object that contains the text: turning it over and round and upside down, thumbing backwards, riffling through to other disparate sections. The reader manoeuvres through it, operates it, explores and chases up the notes the book has made to itself, in a series of activities that may come to feel eccentric, even obsessive. Such a foregrounding of tactility and manipulability, moreover, contributes to the debate which the book opens up about the different competing phenomenological nature and values of the cinematic, the photographic and the literary. Visual media make few demands on the body of the viewer or consumer – there is no handling of the object which is being consumed. *House of Leaves* suggests the potential intensity of the direct involvement of the body in an interface with the object of reading. The point is not new, nor is it unproblematic, but Danielewski's way of highlighting it is ingenious and invigorating.

Mirroring the increasing frustration which comes from getting lost in a maze, the complexity of the chapter as it progresses – or digresses – creeps dramatically upwards into the text. One early

Currently, the greatest threat comes from the area of digital manipulation.

In 1990 in *The New York Times*, Andy Grundberg wrote:

modillions, or even trefoil, Tudor, stilted, horseshoe, ogee, lancet, or equilateral arches, most probably resembling basket handle though without any sign of a keystone, pier, spandrel, voussoir, springer, or import.

Picture that. In your dreams.

"In the future, readers of newspapers and magazines will probably view news pictures more as illustrations than as reportage, since they will be well aware that they can no longer distinguish between a genuine image and one that has been manipulated. Even if news photographers and editors resist the temptations of electronic manipulation, as they are likely to do, the credibility of all reproduced images will be diminished by a climate of reduced expectations. In short, photographs will not seem as real as they once did."[184]

[184] Andy Grundberg, "Ask It No Questions: The Camera Can Lie," *The New York Times*, August 12, 1990, Section 2, 1, 29. All of which reiterates in many ways what Marshall McLuhan already anticipated when he wrote: "To say 'the camera cannot lie' is merely to underline the multiple deceits that are now practiced in its name."

141

3 M. Z. Danielewski (2000) *House of Leaves by Zampanò with Introduction and Notes by Johnny Truant*, London; New York: Doubleday, p. 141

Also in 1990, Associated Press executive, Vincent Alabiso, acknowledged the power of digital technology and condemned its use to falsify images:

> "The electronic darkroom is a highly sophisticated photo editing tool. It takes us out of a chemical darkroom where subtle printing techniques such as burning and dodging have long been accepted as journalistically sound. Today these terms are replaced by 'image manipulation' and 'enhancement.' In a time when such broad terms could be misconstrued we need to set limits and restate some basic tenets.

"The content of photographs will NEVER be changed or manipulated in any way."

A year later, the NPPA (National Press Photographers Association) also recognized the power of electronic imaging techniques:

> "As journalists we believe the guiding principle of our profession is accuracy: therefore, we believe it is wrong to alter the content of a photograph in a way that deceives the public.

4 M. Z. Danielewski (2000) *House of Leaves by Zampanò with Introduction and Notes by Johnny Truant*, London; New York: Doubleday, p. 142

instance of these complications, beginning on page 119, is note 144 which we might name a 'ductnote', lined off in a box running through the middle of the book until page 141. Writing in the recto side appears the right way round, but the verso is exactly that – a reversed version of the page before, as if we are looking at a cross-section through a stick of rock, and seeing the letters right-way-round on one side, reversed on the other (Figures 3 and 4).

The note occupies a kind of shaft which has been drilled through the central text. It is appended to and expands on the following words in the 'central text': 'not one object, let alone fixture or other manner of finished work has ever been discovered there.[144]' So it comprises a list of features that do *not* appear in the mysterious underground structure. These invisible features are all man-made things:

> [144] Not only are there no hot-air registers, return air vents, or radiators, cast iron or other, or coiling systems – condenser, reheat coils, heating convector, damper, . . . (Danielewski 2000: 119)

The content of the ductnote describes a space of emptiness and negation, while its form evokes the subterranean tunnelling nature of the labyrinth, like some vast abandoned termite's nest. The surrounding text, the sense of whose already compromised status as central is now further undermined by the location of the ductnote, can be imagined as either the aggregated matter which surrounds tunnels, or a further series of adjacent differently designed tunnels. The ductnote serves to indicate a simple opposition between the underground spaces of Wallace which we have encountered and those of Danielewski. Where the former set are artificial and man-made, the latter are at once natural and supernatural.

V. Conclusion: language as underworld

What the mimetic form of Chapter IX's underground textual labyrinth suggests is that there might be an analogy between the imagined space Danielewski takes us through and language itself. Language is a system of great complexity, whose grammatical laws allow an infinite arrangement of a finite number of objects; the hermeneutic circle is a closed maze with no way out; following inter-textual relations is like entering an endless rabbit-warren. Like the underground structure in *House of Leaves*, language both changes shape and reveals vast tracts of unexplored space. But what is particular to Danielewski's abyss is that it reveals no outside or externality from which or by which an analytical observer might sense, measure, limit or comprehend that structure. We can map a maze or a house and represent it from outside in a plan, but we cannot see language whole from the outside, nor comprehend it through another medium.

Heidegger famously provided a metaphor for our relation to language as a structure which is relevant here:

> Die Sprache ist das Haus des Seins. In ihrer Behausung wohnt der Mensch. Die Denkenden und Dichtenden sind die Wächter dieser Behausung. (Heidegger 2002: 313)
> [Language is the house of Being. In its home man dwells. Those who think and those who create with words are the guardians of this home.] (Heidegger 1993: 217)

At the risk of taking metaphors literally, while we might well dwell, as Heidegger claims, within language, this cosy metaphor of language being a house, or a home (which needs guardians, therefore), implies both that we can see language whole from outside and that this makes clear certain borders that require guarding. Yet we cannot do this. There is not an edge to language where some other medium begins which can be used to designate the limits of language or the structure of its totality. Where only language can describe language, it produces more of what it is that is trying to be comprehended. Part of the meaning of a house or a home is that it is recognisable from the outside. The familiarity of a building's shape is vital to our experience of it, especially as a home, just as it is crucial to any experience of homecoming. The kind of dwelling which you cannot see from the outside might be more like an underground structure. Language is, metaphorically, at least, a subterranean sprawling, interlinking and unencompassable structure, and thus resembles the space which the editors, academics, war-vets, war-photographers and explorers in Danielewski's epic get caught up in exploring. Danielewski spins a mock-Gothic narrative around such a figuring of language as an unencompassable labyrinth. Insofar as language is something which we simply cannot see whole and in the round, above-ground structures – such as a city, or the world itself – might just as effectively provide material for metaphors to communicate the sense of unencompassable totalities. But these would not have served Danielewski's purpose of writing a thrilling, sinister and intellectually challenging page-turner.

Through the visionary deployment of space by all these authors, the novel manages subversively to emphasize the limitations of dominant cinematic and visual media. The novel can thus seem to occupy, in relation to the 'above ground' of such media, an 'underground' status, out of which continue to emerge fresh ideas and narratives – seemingly subordinate but in fact subversive. Danielewski shows that the potential for the novel to transform itself, descending into its expandable internal structures and digging down deep into realities that get overlooked and buried, remains without limits. With such novels, we can turn from the lights and surfaces of cinema to make journeys into the underworlds of language. Reading imagines and offers all the thrill and excitement of a katabasis, as it enters the tactile labyrinth of texts which are fully aware of the unencompassability of language.

Works cited

Bakhtin, M. (2002) *The Dialogic Imagination: Four Essays*, trans. Emerson, C. and Holquist, M., Austin: University of Texas Press.
Danielewski, M. Z. (2000) *House of Leaves*, London: Anchor.
DeLillo, D. (1997) *Underworld*, London: Picador.
Edmonds III, R. G. (2004) *Myths of the Underworld: Plato, Aristophanes, and the 'Orphic' Gold Tablets*, Cambridge: Cambridge University Press.
Heidegger, M. (1993) *Basic Writings*, ed. Krell, D. F., London: Routledge.
Heidegger, M. (2002) *Wegmarken*, Frankfurt am Main: Vittorio Klostermann.
Pike, D. L. (2005) *Subterranean Cities: The World Beneath Paris and London, 1800–1945*, Ithaca: Cornell University Press.
Ponicsanyi, J. (2001) Amazon.com review of House of Leaves. www.amazon.com/House-Leaves-Mark-Z-Danielewski/dp/0375703764.
Streitfeld, A.V. (2008) 'DFW and DeLillo'. http://miravista.typepad.com/cosmopolis/2008/09/delillo-and-dfw.html.
Wallace, D. F. (1996) *Infinite Jest*, London: Abacus.
Wittmershaus, E. (2000) 'Profile: Mark Z. Danielewski'. www.flakmag.com/features/mzd.html.
Wood, M. (1998) 'Post-paranoid' [review of *Underworld*], *London Review of Books*, 5 February, 20(3): 3–5.

3

Houses of leaves, cinema and the new affordances of old media

Paul McCormick, The Ohio State University

Critics of Mark Z. Danielewski's *House of Leaves* (2000) have begun to show how the author thoughtfully and audaciously engages with the American media environment of his time. To date, however, this valuable scholarship has tended to downplay the prominence Danielewski grants cinema in his novel and in his many published interviews, a point that can be illustrated by some of the critical terms for the novel: 'work as assemblage', 'a figure for the digital', a 'networked novel' (Hayles 2003: 278; Hansen 2004: 609; Pressman 2006: 107). *House of Leaves* is all these more fashionable things, but it is also a cinematic novel like Nathanael West's *The Day of the Locust*, John Dos Passos' *The Big Money*, Don DeLillo's *Running Dog* and Thomas Pynchon's *Gravity's Rainbow*. *House of Leaves* uses cinema as its primary interface to interact with its particular media environment through its represented world and with its narrative technique.[1] I show this by first situating it in relation to relevant aspects of the 1990s American media environment, and then showing how the narrative discourse anticipates its later use of cinema as a media interface. Finally, I draw upon rhetorical narrative theory to detail four specific examples of how Danielewski uses cinematic interfaces as formal affordances: by representing a video diary, using the perceptual frame of a surveillance camera, creating rhythmic montage and imitating a documentary film. By focusing on cinema in *House of Leaves*, this essay aims to show how Danielewski disrupts prevalent cultural oppositions between old and new media: first, by representing the formal affordances offered by that old medium, cinema, and second, by demonstrating his skill in remediating those historically contingent affordances.[2]

I. Cinema and *House of Leaves* in the 1990s American media environment

House of Leaves was published in 2000, a year that saw the end of the dot-com bubble in US financial markets. The 1990s had been a period of technological optimism in the US, a technophilia which was driven in large part by widespread financial confidence about internet stocks and other technological start-ups. A measure of this feeling is that several long-standing businesses added 'dot-com' to their names to signify their technological savvy and financial promise. The financial markets were complemented by cultural discourse: *Wired* magazine and books including Nicholas Negroponte's *Being Digital* (1995) and George Gilder's *Telecosm: How Infinite Bandwidth Will Revolutionize Our World* (2000) made grand predictions about how new media would make us happier, smarter and richer in the future. As is still the case today, it was unclear exactly how so-called old entertainment media would adapt to coming changes in the media marketplace, and for many the future of old media did not look particularly promising.

At the same time, however, even casual observers could notice changes in the American media environment through the changing business practices of one old medium – cinema. Over the decade, the relations among entertainment media were transformed by several mergers, including the 1990 merger of Time, Inc. and Warner Communications, the 1993 Disney acquisition of Miramax, the 1993 Viacom acquisition of Paramount Communications, and the largest media merger to date, the 1999 Viacom acquisition of CBS (Lewis 2001: 1–8; Holmlund 2008: 1–26). Film historians emphasise the importance of these mergers for the American movie industry and its business practices: movie studios were now owned by international conglomerates and could depend not just on the renewed vertical integration and economies of scale that came from these media mergers, but cheaper and more frequent multimedia advertising opportunities that included movie trailers, TV advertising, soundtrack deals, product placements, actor interviews, book deals, sequels, newspaper reviews, sponsored internet sites, unofficial websites, online advertising – to name just a few. These multimedia commercial strategies were also modified to promote independent films, many of which enjoyed increased commercial success in the 1990s. Independent films like the unexpectedly profitable and popular *Blair Witch Project* (1999) benefited from a multimedia marketing approach that created increasingly viral advertising using the internet and other strategies and tools. These were of course changes of degree, not kind: media mergers represent a key aspect of twentieth-century American media history (e.g. the Hearst empire and the Warner Brothers' entrance into the TV business) and cinema and other media have long relied on multimedia advertising (e.g. Hollywood fan magazines, gossip newspaper pages and book reviews). Nevertheless, the advertising practices of Hollywood were instrumental in showing American consumers the historically unprecedented scale of the media mergers and the rich possibilities for multimedia advertising in the 1990s.

Readers of *House of Leaves* have good reason to assume that Danielewski was cognisant of these developments, as was his publisher Pantheon (part of Random House). In fact, *House of Leaves* was advertised more like a film than any other formally ambitious novel of its time, and the novel's commercial success must be partly attributed to the way the author and publisher created a low-budget version of movie advertising strategies. Consider the cumulative evidence. The author circulated various hardcopy and online versions of the novel before the first official printing, using his 'first edition' of a few chapters as a preview that helped to create significant commercial buzz. He accepted many interviews and appearances and has succeeded in quickly becoming something of a literary celebrity himself. (This celebrity is furthered by the fact that many of his interviews are in text and often video form online.) His book has a slick official website and the novel's many fan websites offer information about the novel's mysteries. In 2000 Danielewski also published *The Whalestoe Letters*, which copies some of the letters between the *House of Leaves* characters Johnny and his mother Pelafina but also offers new letters, and so doubled advertising efforts for both books. *House of Leaves* was also published simultaneously with the second music album from the author's sister, Poe (Annie Danielewski). One of the more popular songs, 'Hey Pretty', features Danielewski reading a passage from the novel, and he has toured with Poe in a series of Borders Books and Music tours to promote the book and the album, which is also advertised with a link on the back of the second Pantheon edition (for a discussion of the links between *House of Leaves* and Poe's album, see Evans, this volume). The song 'Hey Pretty' was featured on the soundtrack to the MTV original series,

Cinema and the new affordances 55

Spyder Games, and in January 2009 Ford began using the original version of the song in television commercials (http://en.wikipedia.org/wiki/Hey_Pretty). To say that *House of Leaves* became a multimedia event, then, is something of an understatement.

From this perspective, cinema serves as an important precedent and perhaps even a business model for this novel's advertising, but still, the standard critical designations of *House of Leaves* as a multimedia novel, a 'networked novel' (Pressman 2006: 107), or a 'work as assemblage' (Hayles 2003: 278) remain very useful. Such terms describe the dialogical relations among the various media catalogued above, with the novel functioning as one key node in a network of multimedia texts. However, it seems wise to resist the often-related arguments that *House of Leaves* owes a great deal to the internet for its narrative structure and techniques, that it is in some non-trivial way a hyper-textual novel or, as Jessica Pressman claims, that 'it *is* a networked novel that connects up with the contemporary "discourse network" of the Internet' (Pressman 2006: 107; original emphasis). It does connect with the Internet through various paratexts, including a printed link to Poe's *Haunted* album on the book's back cover, but it should be emphasised that it is the total media environment which is this novel's main interest – of which the internet is but one part. And in any case, the novel's primary interface for engaging that media environment is not the internet, but cinema. I develop this argument throughout, but *prima facie* evidence includes the discussion above, the interviews in which Danielewski has repeatedly insisted upon his debt to cinema (the author's father was Tad Danielewski, the avant-garde filmmaker), the novel's main focus on the fictional film, *The Navidson Record*, and the fact that the internet as such is rarely mentioned in the novel's pages.

These arguments are anticipated here because at stake, it seems to me, are two substantially different interpretations of how this novel conceptualises and engages its media environment. In the first interpretation, *House of Leaves* becomes a stock character in the stale story of how an old medium can take advantage of new media to refashion itself – a story that often simplifies and sometimes exaggerates the effect new media have upon a given media environment. In contrast, I suggest that *House of Leaves* uses the new forms of that so-called old medium, cinema, as an interface with its media environment. This interface offers fresh formal affordances for the novel and ultimately functions as a third term to disrupt the simplistic binary between old and new media – suggesting that older media like cinema and the novel are often the most flexible, the most dynamic and, in those important ways, the newest media in their environments.

Below, I explain how *House of Leaves* anticipates its pattern of drawing upon cinema's particular and historically contingent affordances. I borrow the term affordance, originally coined by the psychologist James J. Gibson (1979: 127), to suggest a middle ground or an oscillation between the idea that the media environment determines what techniques and effects an author can use and seek, and the idea that a medium or an entire media environment can make no difference at all for narrative techniques.[3] What we understand as media and media environments are historically and culturally variable and, as they change in time, different media environments encourage or open up certain aesthetic opportunities and ways of thinking for literary artists (and those working in other media). For example, cinema's function in its media environment changed radically from the time Nathanael West published *The Day of the Locust* (1939) to Don DeLillo's *Running Dog* (1978), and these differences offered the respective authors different affordances. In *The Day of the Locust*, West uses Harry Greener's character as a satirical figure for a now-irrelevant vaudeville theatre, while in *Running Dog*, DeLillo parodies the American Western film genre with Vietnamese cowboys and offers authorial commentary on invasive surveillance cameras. When compared to cinematic novels like these, *House of Leaves* can be seen as another, more contemporary example of an American novel that draws upon the historically contingent affordances of cinema for thematic relevance and formal innovation.

II. *House of Leaves* as a cinematic novel

Readers can anticipate Danielewski's ambitions even before they open the book proper, as they read or view or listen to the book's various paratexts that seem to promise a novel that explores and even exploits the affordances of its media environment. In addition, the relations among these texts could also introduce readers to how *House of Leaves* both depends upon and challenges the practice of authorial reading that I follow here – the decision to read a text by hypothesising about the implied author's intention.[4] Because

Cinema and the new affordances 57

readers variously encounter (or not) the book's paratexts before, during and after they read the novel, this fact challenges both the notion of a single, coherent text and the very possibility of different flesh-and-blood readers experiencing a novel similarly by entering the 'authorial audience'. In this way, the paratexts cause individual readers to come to *House of Leaves* with sometimes highly idiosyncratic readerly expectations. From this perspective, the paratexts and the varied reader expectations they engender can appear to initiate the novel's deconstructive play with meaning or its nihilistic interest in absence, its interest in becoming a novel that 'seeks to unwrite its own creation' (Slocombe 2005: 92). However, many of these different reader experiences also lead to a similar awareness (but not an identical awareness) of the significant multimedia strategies employed by Danielewski and his chosen publisher. Remarkably, then, the novel's marketing strategies anticipate: (1) the fact that this book that allows readers choices in how they read it (or view it, or hear it) and in which order; (2) Danielewski's deeply rooted interest and skill in using other media to make his novel more attractive to consumers.

Danielewski's interest and skill are evident in the novel's cover design, itself an interesting product of media interdependence and artistic collaboration. The cover was designed by Eric Fuentecilla, and while Danielewski has claimed in interview to have worked on the book's layout, his exact contribution to the cover design remains unknown. In any regard, if the labyrinth design on the second edition's front cover anticipates the challenging reading experience that is to come, then the binding of the book foregrounds the novel's redefinition of itself *qua* novel. On the binding are seven distinct frames which alternate text and image: text advertising the book's title, author and publisher are intercut with images, still photos of a white house. The final image, as one reads (or views) the binding from top to bottom is 'Pantheon' and the publisher's imprint – which appears as a white building. This is richly significant because this frame manages to suggest some of the main themes of the book: what we will eventually discover as the eerie ubiquity of the haunted white house on Ash Lane, but also the co-existence of text ('Pantheon') and image (the publisher's imprint), to remind us that book publishing and the novel genre's domain has always extended beyond 'mere' text. It is the repetition that makes this case a clear one: not just the seven frames on the binding that evoke cinematic or cartoon frames, not just the intercutting of text and images among those frames, and not just the fact that the final frame combines print and image to doubly symbolise his book publisher, but all of the above. With this binding design, the novel immediately takes as its domain both the image and text together. It is as if the novel is already rebutting those who would conflate 'print media' or 'the novel' with the written word, as if purposely recalling us to the novel genre's long history with images in sketches, cover art, in serial publications, magazines, etc.

The cover and binding prepare authorial readers for the opening of Chapter One, which deserves extended discussion because it signals that cinema will be this novel's primary interface with its media environment. The chapter begins with an epigraph borrowed from the Beatles' 'A Day in the Life' from their famous *Sgt. Pepper's Lonely Hearts Club Band* album, 'I saw a film today, oh boy...' (2000a: 3), a song which is richly suggestive of how the same situation affects an audience differently when it is remediated by film, newspapers or photographs. This epigraph thus chimes with the book's paratexts and cover design, but also the opening paragraph which follows:

> While enthusiasts and detractors will continue to empty entire dictionaries attempting to describe or deride it, 'authenticity' still remains the word most likely to stir a debate. In fact, this leading obsession – to validate or invalidate the reels and tapes – invariably brings up a collateral and more general concern: whether or not, with the advent of digital technology, image has forsaken its once unimpeachable hold on the truth. (2000a: 3)

In the context of Zampanò's narrative situation, this opening paragraph uses cinema to introduce *The Navidson Record*, a fictional blockbuster film that is composed of many film shorts including those of the award-winning photojournalist Navidson, who leads cinematic explorations and documentaries of his own house. His house inexplicably measures longer on its inside than its outside, and its previously non-existent door leads to a labyrinthine hallway that is impossibly long. Zampanò and other commentators, including the young tattoo apprentice named Johnny Truant, will offer their commentary on the film and its contents throughout the novel in a series of footnotes. But in the context of Danielewski's authorial communication, this opening paragraph uses *The Navidson Record* to introduce cinema as Danielewski's interface with his media environment. In this way, the novel's two complementary levels of narrative progression are introduced: first, the frame narration of a story world that includes characters like Johnny Truant, Zampanò and the Navidson family; second, Danielewski's use of those stories for his indirect commentary on his current media environment, primarily through a cinematic interface.

The conclusion of the opening chapter suggests the primary relation between these two narrative levels will be allegorical:

> *The Navidson Record* now stands as part of this country's cultural experience and yet in spite of the fact that hundreds of thousands of people have seen it, the film continues to remain an enigma. Some insist it must be true, others believe it is a trick on par with the Orson Welles' radio romp *The War of the Worlds*. Others could care less, admitting that either way *The Navidson Record* is a pretty good tale. Still many more have never even heard of it.
>
> These days, with the unlikely prospect of any sort of post-release resolution or revelation, Navidson's film seems destined to achieve at most cult status. Good story telling alone will guarantee a healthy sliver of popularity in the years to come but its inherent strangeness will permanently bar it from any mainstream interest. (2000a: 7)

Discussing the topic of 'unnatural narration', narrative theorist Jan Alber has recently noted that when readers try to make sense of narratives featuring unnatural scenarios and events (like the house in this novel), they can employ the strategy of interpreting 'impossible elements as parts of allegories that say something about the world in general rather than particular individuals ("reading allegorically")' (2009: 82). Many passages in the novel – including the passage above – invite us to understand the novel's frequent reference to readers and viewers, to texts and movies, as indirectly saying something about *House of Leaves*. Three basic facts relating to the novel ensure a steady stream of metafictional commentary at each narrative level: the novel's title refers both to the enigmatic house and the book as a material object; Johnny Truant enjoys storytelling and has an intense fascination with Zampanò's text; and Zampanò functions as a kind of film critic of *The Navidson Record*. In the above passage, for example, the metafictional commentary asks us to read the coming narrative of *House of Leaves* just as the imaginary audience received *The Navidson Record*: as 'a pretty good tale' and 'good story telling'. But with this interest, which is only intensified by the story's 'inherent strangeness', also comes a warning that we have received before from Johnny in his equally metafictional introduction: stable meaning in the strange worlds of Johnny and Zampanò will perhaps be as elusive as the house itself, which is as overdetermined as 'Melville's behemoth' (2000a: 3) or, later, Kubrick's black obelisk in *2001: Space Odyssey* (2000a: 60). It is an apt signal of Danielewski's cinematic interface that he chooses to connect his main symbol, the house, to arguably two of the most famously overdetermined symbols of literature and cinema.

If this argument may be provisionally granted, however, the question still remains as to why so much of the novel should relate the commentary of Zampanò and others on *The Navidson Record*. Why use cinema as an interface? Danielewski can take great advantage of the literary affordances of cinema due to an expert knowledge of the medium that may rival that of Don DeLillo or Thomas Pynchon, and there are also good historical reasons for his decision to view 'the advent of digital technology' through a cinematic lens. As new media theorist Lev Manovich (2001: 152) notes, movies like *Terminator 2* (1991) and *Jurassic Park* (1993) convinced Hollywood studios and American consumers that computer animation could now convincingly imitate the photographic image of our perceptual and bodily reality, or Zampanò's 'truth'. In fact, as amateurs gained less expensive access to computer programs to edit still images, video images and animation (e.g. Photoshop), they could subvert cinema's supposed 'unimpeachable hold on truth' by altering their own home videos. As Chris Holmlund puts it, 'The richness of special effects and the ease of shooting and editing that put serious moviemaking within the reach of even unschooled amateurs had been one of the great legacies of the 1990s' (2008: 23). For these reasons, Danielewski's use of cinema as an interface with his media environment is timely and so the novel represents, on one level, an interesting historical artefact of the media environment in 2000.

III. Four affordances of 1990s cinema

The remainder of this essay describes four examples of 1990s cinema that Danielewski uses as formal affordances in *House of Leaves*: a video diary, the perceptual frame of a surveillance camera, the concept of cinematic montage and a documentary film. Most of these affordances were available earlier in cinematic history as well; Danielewski draws eclectically upon cinematic grammars like the director's son he is. As a set of artistic practices now more than a century old, cinema provides contemporary novelists with a wide range of formal registers and historical referents.

However, the first example depends more upon what one might consider contemporary cinema: Navidson's careful editing of his video diary. It is worthwhile to note that this action also allows the character special affordances as well. For throughout his documentary, Navidson uses his film aesthetic to do with his art what he could not do in everyday life: carefully consider and honour the psychological fragilities of his family – particularly those of Tom, his troubled brother, and Karen, the wife he has neglected for his career. When he first chose to explore his own house with video cameras, Navidson forced his brother Tom to participate. But in the course of that exploration, Tom became so frightened that he was eventually left behind with some supplies and a video camera as Navy and the other explorers continued ahead. When Tom dies, he leaves only a video diary in his absence. After his brother's death, Navy edits *The Navidson Record* and Zampanò reveals:

> There is nothing hasty about Tom's story. Navidson has clearly put an enormous amount of work into these few minutes. Despite obvious technological limitations, the cuts are clean and sound beautifully balanced with the rhythm and order of every shot serving to intensify even the most ordinary moment. (2000a: 274)

Detailed and appreciative descriptions of Navy's artistic choices are salient throughout Zampanò's narration, and here the language of cinematic editing provides insight into Navy's subjectivity. Navidson uses his editing to produce an affective response to his brother's lonely video monologue that he was unable to offer when Tom was alive. In the past, Navy rarely gave his younger brother the attention he craved. Driven by his professional ambition as a photojournalist, Navy travelled the world while Tom was out of work and friendless. But the medial opportunities of the video diary allow both of them to change their interpersonal dynamic after Tom's death. Scared and alone, Tom knew that if anyone were to see his monologue after he died, it would be his brother. It is not just Tom's fear, but also the temporal and psychological space provided by his video camera, that allows him to communicate so easily with Navidson through his video diary. It is likely not just the circumstance of Tom's death, but also the aesthetic challenge of editing the video, that allows Navy to do justice to his brother's affective response to the empty hallway after his death.

In short, Danielewski relies on the technological opportunities of new cinema to represent these characters' inter-subjectivity and to show the new human relations possible through this technology. The video diary that Tom composes allows him to communicate with Navidson across a temporal, spatial and psychological distance; in turn, Navidson's careful editing of that video-log reveals his deep and quiet affection for Tom. Perhaps Navidson even believes that he can communicate with his brother by editing his video after his death. On one level, then, we can see evidence of Katherine Hayles' (2002: 112) point that Danielewski's narration remediates various media to show how human subjectivity is created by representation, rather than just shown through representation. Here, Tom and Navidson define their relationship – after Tom's death – with their video art. However, Danielewski accomplishes more than just revealing the interpersonal dynamics that are now possible with the technologies of his media environment. He also shows that literary narration can make us aware of their possibilities, that the novel can theorise about other media and their changing formal potentials by representing those affordances in narrative.

Danielewski also uses his authorial audience's understanding of the virtual reality created by the cinematic frame to describe what Robyn Warhol calls the unnarratable, 'instances of narrators making explicit the boundaries of the narratable' (2005: 221). The two Navidson children, Chad and Hillary, draw disturbing pictures at school to deal with their unnatural experiences in the house, and Zampanò relates that

> In some respects, the distillate of the crayon and colour traced out by the hands of two children captures the awfulness at the heart of that house better than anything caught on film or tape, those shallow lines and imperfect shapes narrating the light seeping away from their lives ... Chad prefers to escape outside ... always well beyond the range of any camera [set up by his father, Navidson], his adventures and anger passing away unobserved. (2000a: 315)

On one hand, one could argue that this passage and others like it simply represent Danielewski's thematic rejection of the orthographic power of new digital media: after all, Chad is 'beyond the range' of the recording camera. But on the other hand, this partial

Cinema and the new affordances

explanation would ignore how Danielewski has used the embedded *The Navidson Record* to show that Chad's misery is beyond the ken of his father's knowledge. The camera becomes a figure for Navy's retrospective conceptualisation of what happened to his family in the house. This figure metaphorises the reach of Navy's perceptual abilities with the physical range of a video camera and functions as a critique of how Navy's career as a photojournalist has left him unaware of his children's fears.

Crucially, it is the hypothetical perceptual space of the camera's gaze that allows Danielewski to show these limits of Navy's knowledge, to narrate what is marked as unnarratable. Rather than merely allegorising the orthographic failure of a particular camera to claim for the technical superiority of the novel in the new media ecology, in this instance Danielewski uses his narration of the empty space off-camera to skilfully reveal Navidson's perceptive failure regarding his own son. In terms of plot, this authorial decision provides new insight into the characters' lives in the storyworld. But it also makes an implicit argument for Danielewski's ability to update narrative technique by thinking carefully about affordances in the new media environment. If the photojournalist Navidson is limited by the range of his camera, we are meant to notice that Danielewski can make art from his narration of a particular camera's frame. Far from deigning to use this particular camera's 'failure' as a figure for an entire medium's failure, the implied author shows how his familiarity with cinema's formal grammar can inflect and sharpen his story.

House of Leaves also successfully modifies its narrative speed by drawing upon the grammars of cinema, concrete poetry and cartoons to experiment typographically. For example, at one point Danielewski quickens the temporal duration by putting one or two words on several pages in a row so that our experience of reading the text parallels the speed at which the explorers race through the hallway; then as characters squeeze through a door we read smaller and smaller boxes of text to parallel that feeling of claustrophobia; then as the characters become disoriented we need to repeatedly flip around our book to read the text; and the spaces between text become affectively charged as they come to represent the empty space in the strange hallway. Such typographic play strengthens our sense of the parallel between the characters' interpretive experiences in their story world and our experience as readers of this text. By manipulating what Jan Baetens and Kathryn Hume call 'the mainstream average rhythm' (2006: 354) of the novel, Danielewski encourages our identification with the explorers through typographic montage. Indeed, it is both instructive and somewhat paradoxical to note how cinematic thinking allows Danielewski to reimagine the page for its imagistic potentials, and thus to return to the very medium and materiality of books, its print, as a resource for formal experiments.

Finally, Danielewski uses documentary cinema and its supposed crisis of authenticity to argue for the novel's relevance in the age of postmodern uncertainty. Over the course of the many explorations, Navidson fails in his effort to capture motion as the hallway grows with Sony Hi8 video cameras and motion detectors (2000a: 28), and later fails in his attempt to understand the hallway by video recording it. In fact, all characters who explore the hallway face an existential emptiness that is not ameliorated by their use of video technology: for example, despite all their exploratory expertise and confidence, Jed is shot to death, Kirby is injured and their intimidating leader Holloway Roberts goes mad and records troubling messages on a video camera before committing suicide. All these explorers try to capture the Unknown on film, but they fail miserably. Their failure as characters to interpret the meaning of the hallway parallels our failure as readers in the novel to obtain 'the truth' about the hallway through their video stories. At first, then, Danielewski would seem simply to echo Zampanò's point about the end of cinema as an arbiter of 'truth'.

But then we reach the climactic scene of both *The Navidson Record* and *House of Leaves*. Navidson's video cameras again fail him at the very moment he needs them – 'nearly six minutes of screen time [in *The Navidson Record*] is black' (2000a: 468). It is only from his remediated audio recording that we learn he reads the book that he brought with him – a book called *House of Leaves* – by burning its pages in the dark as he reads:

> Here then is one end: a final act of reading, a final act of consumption. And as the fire rapidly devours the paper, Navidson's eyes frantically sweep down over the text, keeping just ahead of the necessary immolation, until as he reaches the last few words, flames lick around his hands, ash peels off into the surrounding emptiness, and then as the fire retreats, dimming, its light suddenly spent, the book is gone leaving nothing behind but invisible traces already dismantled in the dark. (2000a: 467)

Cinema and the new affordances 65

On the next page, Zampanò suggests that *The Navidson Record* 'might have absolutely nothing to do with cinema', and he is quite accurate because this passage, which 'serves essentially as the climax to Navidson's documentary' is clearly about Danielewski's *House of Leaves* (2000a: 468). For Danielewski has used the orthographic failure of documentary cinema, its failure to capture the Real as symbolised by the black screen, to suggest why his literary art can thrive in an age of Photoshop inauthenticity and postmodern indeterminacy. The crisis of the unknowable is no crisis for this novel, for while the screen goes black, Navidson's readerly desire remains undiminished. Similarly, those who read about *The Navidson Record*, including Zampanò and Johnny, also experience intense narrative interest as a result of postmodern uncertainty. For novelists with enough skill, *House of Leaves* suggests, one medium's crisis is just another opportunity to ignite reader interest.

In this way, the climactic scene also historicises the orthographic failure of documentary cinema as another cinematic affordance for this novel. Throughout the novel, Danielewski risks a certain level of indeterminacy at the level of plot, and indeed his overdetermined house opens his novel up to multiple interpretations and different readers' interests like Kubrick's black obelisk or Melville's whale. But it is important to see that this local indeterminacy works in the service of a higher authorial purpose. The emptiness that threatens the explorers is also *House of Leaves*, the novel's refusal to function as mere data that can be recorded, easily transmitted, and can be in any way complete or finished. Danielewski has not only shown us that *House of Leaves* cannot end, he has suggested why with his multiple uses of cinema throughout the novel: he has historicised his interest in developing localised indeterminacy as just another tool available in his particular media environment, just another affordance drawn from that other so-called old medium, cinema.

Notes

1 See Manovich (2001: 64) for excellent discussion of media as interface, which I have drawn upon. More generally, this essay is indebted to Manovich's influential conceptualisation of cinema as new media.
2 Special thanks to James Phelan, Brian McHale, Jared Gardner, Brian Hauser, David Herman and the editors of this volume for their helpful criticisms at various stages of this project.

3 For good discussion of the concept's critical history, see Serpell (2008: 226–227). I am indebted to her application of Gibson's concept.
4 Here and throughout I draw upon and am indebted to those critics working in the Chicago School tradition of rhetorical theory, including Wayne Booth, Sheldon Sacks, Ralph Rader, Peter Rabinowitz and James Phelan. See Phelan (2009) on rhetorical theory's interest in similar reading experiences.

Works cited

Alber, J. (2009) 'Impossible storyworlds – and what to do with them', *Storyworlds* 1: 79–96.
Baetens, J. and K. Hume (2006) 'Speed, rhythm, movement: a dialogue on K. Hume's article "Narrative speed"', *Narrative* 12(3): 349–355.
Danielewski, M. Z. (2000a) *House of Leaves*, 2nd edn, New York: Pantheon.
Danielewski, M. Z. (2000b) *The Whalestoe Letters*, New York: Pantheon.
Gibson, J. (1979) *The Visual Perception of Objective Motion and Subjective Movement*, Boston: Houghton Mifflin.
Gilder, G. (2000) *Telecosm: How Infinite Bandwidth Will Revolutionize Our World*, New York: Free Press.
Hansen, M. B. N. (2004) 'The digital typography of Mark Z. Danielewski's *House of Leaves*', *Contemporary Literature* 45(4): 597–636.
Hayles, N. K. (2002) *Writing Machines*, Cambridge, MA: MIT Press.
Hayles, N. K. (2003) 'Translating media: why we should rethink textuality', *The Yale Journal of Criticism* 16(2): 263–290.
Holmlund, C. (ed.) (2008) *American Cinema of the 1990s: Themes and Variations*, New Brunswick: Rutgers University Press.
Lewis, J. (ed.) (2001) *The End of Cinema As We Know It: American Film in the Nineties*, New York: New York University Press.
Manovich, L. (2001) *The Language of New Media*, Cambridge, MA: MIT Press.
Negroponte, N. (1995) *Being Digital*, New York: Vintage.
Phelan, J. (2007) *Experiencing Fiction: Judgments, Progressions, and the Rhetorical Theory of Narrative*, Columbus: Ohio State University Press.
Pressman, J. (2006) '*House of Leaves*: reading the networked novel', *Studies in American Fiction* 34(1): 107–122.
Serpell, N. (2008) 'Mutual exclusion, oscillation, and ethical projection in *The crying of lot 49* and *The turn of the screw*', *Narrative* 16(3): 223–255.
Shackelford, L. (2005) 'Narrative subjects meet their limits: John Barth's "Click" and the Remediation of Hypertext', *Contemporary Literature* 46(2): 227–310.
Slocombe, W. (2005) '"This is not for you": nihilism and the house that Jacque built', *MFS: Modern Fiction Studies* 51(1): 88–109.

Warhol, R. (2005) 'Neonarrative; or, how to render the unnarratable in realist fiction and contemporary film', in Phelan, J. and Rabinowitz, P. (eds) *The Blackwell Companion to Narrative Theory*, Malden: Blackwell, 220–231.

4

This haunted house: intertextuality and interpretation in Mark Danielewski's *House of Leaves* (2000) and Poe's *Haunted* (2000)

Mel Evans, University of Sheffield

> Father: //Communication is more than just words. Communication is architecture. Because of course it is quite obvious that a house... built ... without that desire to communicate, would not look the way your house looks today// (Tad Danielewski, Track 8 '5 ½ Minute Hallway', Poe, *Haunted*)
>
> 'House of Leaves' is one thing. 'Haunted' is another. Together they are something quite different. (Poe, cited in Pressman 2006: fn. 5)

I. Introduction

In an interview given in 2001, Mark Z. Danielewski was asked how the reader should prioritise the multiple narrators within his novel. His response was equivocal: 'Well, there are many ways to enter *House of Leaves*' (McCaffrey and Gregory 2003: 111). Mark B. N. Hansen, in his insightful discussion of digital topography in the novel, has contested this claim, stating that there is only 'one way' to read the novel, a reading which privileges Johnny Truant's narrative as 'first reader' and follows the emphasis his narrative places upon particular events and concepts, often to the 'subordination of [other] potential themes... such as family dysfunction' (2004: 619 fn. 16).

Hansen's assertion hinges on the reader's perception of the novel's narrators, and the 'material-epistemological-ontological hurdles' (2004: 619 fn. 16) the reader faces in reconciling the interaction between Truant, Zampanò and the letters penned by Pelafina, Johnny's mother (the latter also published as a self-contained volume). Even if the reader were to come across the book of letters first, Hansen argues that they serve 'first and foremost to introduce further information about Johnny: in short, they are subordinate to his function as narrator-first reader ... [he] is the primary mediator of the story and the model of interpretation'. Any attempts to maintain a broader thematic understanding fail because of the problematic nature of these narrative 'hurdles' (2004: 619 fn. 16).

However, this essay will counter Hansen's assertion and suggest that there is indeed at least *one* other way to enter *House of Leaves* – a reading which removes the privilege of Truant's position and consequently foregrounds a different set of themes. This reading takes the musical album *Haunted* (2000), written and performed by Poe, Danielewski's sister, as the new entry-point into the house.

II. *House of Leaves* and the open text

The central narrative of *House of Leaves* is a documentary made by Will Navidson recording his experiences at the House on Ashtree Lane. The House is (or contains) a shape-shifting labyrinth which consumes everything that enters it. The resulting film, *The Navidson Record*, is necessarily described to the reader through the narrative voice and pseudo-academic commentary of Zampanò, an elderly blindman. The authenticity of events at Ashtree Lane depicted within *The Navidson Record* is questionable because of the distance from the reader; they are manipulated and edited into a film, which is then represented by text written by a man who, presumably, had the events of the film narrated to him by another (unknown) individual.

These narrative layers are supplemented by the footnotes of Johnny Truant as he prepares Zampanò's text for publication. These constitute a separate but complementary narrative to Zampanò and *The Navidson Record*. In the Appendix there is also a series of transcribed letters penned by Truant's mother Pelafina, during her incarceration in the Whalestoe mental institution. These supplement and contradict the other narratives.

Early in the novel, Truant informs the reader that Zampanò's work is about a non-existent film: 'You can look as I have, but no matter how long you search you will never find *The Navidson Record*' (Danielewski 2000: xix–xx). Similarly the vast majority of Zampanò's copious academic references and sources are fabricated. The central narrative is sustained only by the outer narrative layers; what

Katherine Hayles has termed the process of reconstitution 'through multiple layers of remediation' (2002: 783).

Despite the ontological absence of the central narrative, the influence of the traditional reading process results in the reader attempting to find a coherent rendering of events. The novel repeatedly repels these efforts. For example, there is a scene in Chapter 20 when Navidson – lost in the labyrinth at the centre of the house – reads and burns the novel *House of Leaves*. This of course is impossible within the normal parameters of literary narrative. A similar subversion occurs towards the end of the novel when Truant encounters a band playing a song inspired by the internet edition of *House of Leaves*, a text, from the reader's perspective, he is *still* editing. These violations of the narrative layers and chronology force the reader to contemplate multiple interpretations, and question the authenticity of the whole text. The 'vertiginous inversion of inside and outside', to use Hayles' succinct phrase (2002: 799), leaves the reader scrambling to keep track of the continuously shifting layers.

III. *Haunted* and musical biography

The album *Haunted* (2000), like *House of Leaves*, is atypical of its genre. The 18 seamless tracks – a mix of song and dialogue linked to occlude track changes – form a narrative, telling a story based on biographical events in the artist's life as the album booklet explains:

> This album is dedicated to my father Tad Z. Danielewski (1921–1993). A few years after my father died my brother and I came across a box of cassettes-recordings of my father's voice. One was a letter to my brother ... another was the recording of a speech ... and a few more contained random recordings of forgotten family noise. Hearing his voice again shook me to my foundation. At first I couldn't bear to listen to him, then I couldn't stop. Finally I began sampling him. It was an eerie process. Had I resurrected a ghost? In some ways I had. Ultimately I entered into a dialogue with that ghost. Pieces of that dialogue compose the story contained on this album – Poe. (Poe 2000)

The album explores different facets of Poe's reaction to her father's death, her reflections on their relationship and concludes with her acceptance not only of his passing, but of how he contributed to her life and the adult she has become. To construct this narrative, there are multiple voices on the album: Poe's vocals; the Mother, who Poe tries to contact through a series of phone calls; the Father, constructed from the aforementioned recordings; and Daughter, an actress playing a young Poe. These moments of dialogue occur between songs and occasionally as independent tracks. *Haunted* shares structural and thematic similarities with *House of Leaves*, in that, like the layers of narrative in the novel, the central dialogue is built using edited and manipulated samples of Poe's father.

The album begins with an eerie *a capella* – vocals sung without instrumental accompaniment – entitled 'Exploration B'. Framed as a phone call to Mother, it establishes the narrative (throughout this essay // marks spoken vocals).

> I thought you should know,
> Daddy died today at 12.03, he sends his love.
> He wanted you to know, he isn't holding a grudge
> and if you are you should let it go.
>
> //Pick up, pick up please. . .Mom? Hello?//.

Throughout the album, the samples give insight into Poe's relationship with her father. For instance:

> //Father: And at the end of it all lies of course the final phenomenon of deterioration: Entropy. Which is a predictable disintegration where the creative life ceases: everything has to fall apart. Daughter: Why are you always so serious?!//

Elsewhere, the samples are edited to comment on the present, a ghostly evocation of the father's voice:

> Father: It is November 6th, and we are in Madrid Spain. It is a very special day, and to celebrate it Annie [Poe's real name] will sing a song ('Spanish Doll').

The album narrative is meaningful in its own right. However, as the title for Track 1 indicates, there are intertextual links to *House of Leaves* ready to be explored.[1]

IV. Representing the (intertextual) reading process

Before discussing the effects of intertextuality, it is necessary to examine how *House of Leaves* comments upon and encourages the experience of its reader. The novel uses several tropes to represent and comment on the reading process, the most prominent being the labyrinth (or maze) at the centre of the House. The maze provides the propulsion for the Navidson narrative, yet is also symbolic of the reader's interpretation – as Chapter 9 conveys through its manipulative textual layout. Zampanò also emphasises the link with the reading process:

> The anfractuosity of some labyrinths may actually prohibit a permanent solution ... no one, not even a god or an Other, comprehends the entire maze ... Navidson's house seems a perfect example. Due to wall-shifts and extraordinary size, any way out remains singular and applicable only to those on that path at that particular time. **All solutions are necessarily personal.** (Danielewski 2000: 115; my emphasis)

Hayles (2002) has suggested that the reader must become immersed within the novel – the labyrinth – and so surrender to their incomplete knowledge of events. The maze is thus a subjective experience representing a reader's personal exploration through the novel, bound by their competence and knowledge. This perspective is supportive of Danielewski's claim that there are multiple ways to read *House of Leaves*.

Zampanò, in his descriptive critique of *The Navidson Record*, also foregrounds the significance of echoes within the documentary. They play a significant part in Navidson's exploration of the maze within the House, the sound revealing the spatial parameters. Symbolically, the echo is also an imperfect representation of the original. In a lengthy deviation from his main subject, Zampanò discusses the curiosity of echoes in myth and science: 'repetitions that are far from digital, much closer to analog[ue] ... [colouring] the words with faint traces of sorrow ... or accusation ... never present in the original' (2000: 41). Their role within the maze thus symbolises the reader's interpretation based upon the author's words, which can never achieve a true replication of the author's intended meaning.

Both of these metaphors were used by Umberto Eco to describe the 'open' text. This text type lacks a central cohesive meaning, but instead has multiple readings 're-echoed by the others'. The open text has a 'maze-like' structure: 'You cannot use the text as you want, but only as the text wants you to use it' (Eco 1979: 9). The utilisation and development of these metaphors by Danielewski may be coincidental, but neatly articulates the challenge *House of Leaves* poses for the traditional reading experience.

However, whilst *House of Leaves* may only let the reader use the text as the text dictates, that is not to say that Hansen's claim is valid regarding the single entry-point (via Truant) into the novel. Eco theorised that a text controls the reader only according to what the reader brings to the text, termed the reader's 'competence' (Eco 1979: 21–22). One particular type of competence is intertextual – intertextuality being the way in which a given text refers back to previous texts (1979: 21). A reader's intertextual competence, therefore, refers to his or her ability to recognise the references between texts, such as between *Haunted* and *House of Leaves*, and to build an interpretation based upon this particular information.

V. Intertextual hauntings in the *House of Leaves*

This essay adopts the stance of novel first – that is, the reader encounters the novel *House of Leaves* before listening to the album. The analysis considers how the reader will reconcile and reconstruct their previous understanding of the novel as a consequence of the new intertextual information.

The links between *House of Leaves* and *Haunted* have been previously recognised by both the general reader and the critic. Jessica Pressman provides an astute assessment of what she terms the 'hypertext' between the novel, album and also the website *houseofleaves.com*: 'these clues are rewards that confirm the reader's strategy of venturing outside the novel for keys to its narrative' (Pressman 2006: no pagination). Her reading identifies an interpretative emphasis upon the role of Pelafina, as narrator and potentially as the fictional 'author' of the novel (Pressman 2006: no pagination); coherent with one of the approaches mentioned by Danielewski in the interview (McCaffrey and Gregory 2003: 111). However, Pressman does not consider the potential effect of the album's self-contained narrative on the interpretation of *House of Leaves*. Nor – as she acknowledges – does she have the space to explore specific examples of intertextuality (Pressman 2006: fn. 19).

VI. Re-emphasising the author

The recognition of the link between novel and album does not impact solely upon the fictional narrative. Indeed, its most immediate and significant effect is upon the reader's appreciation of the author. In a musical album, the artist (singer, perhaps also musician and songwriter) retains an explicit presence in the authorship, ownership and performance of their work. Conversely, this artistic identity is far less pronounced for the modern-day author. The reader cannot hear the author's voice, due both to the distance created by narrative voices and to the limitations of the textual medium. However, the influence of *Haunted* reidentifies Danielewski as the creative author behind *House of Leaves*.

References to Danielewski-as-author within the novel itself are minimal – even the traditional attribution on the novel's front cover is reduced in significance because it appears alongside a reference to Zampanò. Truant, at one point, does wonder if the text 'has just been made up and what's worse, not made up by me or even for that matter Zampanò. Though by whom I have no idea' (2000: 326). But this is one of few explicit references to the implied author – and, as will be seen, can be understood within the narrative-frame of the novel as a reference to Pelafina. The novel's narrative structure thus places the reader's focus on the central narrative, upon which each subsequent voice has been layered.

The intertextual reading from *Haunted* back to *House of Leaves* shifts this focus away from *The Navidson Record*. Because the album functions outside the narrative layers of the novel, both as an independent material product and as an independent biographical narrative, the reader acquires a new perspective on the novel as a created whole, narratives and voices created by one individual. From this external position, armed with the new information, the reader can then re-enter the text from a truly outside-in perspective and reconcile and rebuild their interpretations accordingly.

VII. Novel to album – priming the reader

Whilst the analysis will focus on the references in *Haunted*, it is important to illustrate how key points within *House of Leaves* prime the reader and prepare them for the audio experience outside the text. As Pressman has shown, there are several references to Poe within the novel. Her edition (not the UK edition used in this essay) contains an instruction on the back cover to 'listen to the house ... 'HAUNTED' the new CD from Poe on Atlantic Records, www.p-o-e.com'. She also identifies the citation at the beginning of Chapter 20 attributed to Edgar Allan Poe, as Poe lyrics (Pressman 2006: no pagination).

There is another instance, typifying the word- and text-play found within *House of Leaves*. In the transcript of Karen's interviews

'What Some Have Thought', immersed within the pseudo-comments of renowned individuals such as Stanley Kubrick there is a single contribution from 'A Poe t. 21 years old. No tattoos. No piercings' (Danielewski 2000: 360). The textual arrangement makes 'Poe' a clear reference for the competent reader; effectively, Poe is making a cameo in her brother's novel. The reference further emphasises the interwoven nature of novel and album and also foregrounds Danielewski's role as author, as only he possesses the necessary knowledge to make such a reference, a winking tribute to his sibling.

The priming is also thematic. The significance of cinematic devices – particularly the use of space and text in Chapter 9 – has been well documented by critics, including the role of sound and music (e.g. Hayles 2002). It seems these latter also serve to prepare the reader for the soundtrack to the novel found in *Haunted*. Early in *The Navidson Record*, Zampanò praises Navidson's editing: '[he] has permitted the action and subtlety of the composition to represent the profound sentiments at work without the molestations of some ill-conceived voice-over or manipulative soundtrack . . . disingenuous musical cues' (2000: 11). Yet, as the story progresses the value of sound is emphasised. For example when Navidson is lost within the labyrinth he sings to himself, and the inability of print to convey this dimension is acknowledged. Lyrics are transcribed, and the musical notation is provided, but of course neither can be heard (2000: 476–479). Sound also becomes integral to the plot. When Karen waits for Navidson to return from the labyrinth a terrifying void appears in the children's bedroom. Rather than fleeing, Karen pauses – and the critical opinions supplied by Zampanò suggest that she did so 'because of something she hears . . . the sound is obviously imagined'. Karen then steps into the void and rescues Navidson (2000: 522–523). These examples have been perceived as a comment upon the failure of the print text in the digital age (Hansen 2004). But they can also be perceived as a hint of how these failures can be overcome – if the traditional limitations of the fictional novel are expanded into an intertextual cross-genre experience such as that offered by the intertext in *Haunted*.

VIII. Album to novel – material intertext

The first intertextual references encountered by the reader coming from novel to album are in fact material. On the back of the album case beneath the track listing, the reader is instructed to 'Read the House – "House of Leaves" by Mark Z. Danielewski' and also to 'listen to the House...[sic] **www.p-o-e.com**' (Poe 2000). The connection between the two texts is immediately established with the House being the focal link. The directions also echo the instructions on the back of the US edition of the novel noted by Pressman (2006).

Upon opening the album case the reader encounters the CD itself, the top surface printed with multiple photographs. One of these is Poe's logo, but the rest are Polaroids of the exterior of a white house. The same photographs are found in Appendix A of the novel, 'Exhibit # 081512' (2000: 572). The House no longer exists solely within the narrative frame and physical space of the print book, but is placed within the real world of the reader and literally fused to the audio CD. Because the images are of a house's exterior, the inference is that to enter the house one must listen to the CD – a very literal realisation of Danielewski's comments.

The accompanying album booklet consists of a series of manipulated images. The first three in the booklet depict a black background with faint perspective lines: a long dark hallway. In the first two images, monochrome photograph portraits are positioned in the doorway, the overlaid text implying that they are Poe's parents. This material union between one of the key tropes of the *House of Leaves* (hallways) and the biographical narrative of the album is one of the most explicit signs that the two have been created and should be read together. The final page of the album booklet lists specific page numbers for each song on the album. For example, under Track 1 the reader is directed to the passage describing Holloway's death (2000: 337), a Truant footnote discussing Zampanò's creative 'anguish' (2000: 337) and to a letter by Pelafina, in which she discusses her missing memories of her son's visits (2000: 616–617). These provide some guidance for the reader's interpretation.

IX. Intertextual lyrics – method and effect

The intertext between *Haunted* and *House of Leaves* is varied both in explicitness and effect. One of the more identifiable methods, as discussed above, is the use of track titles. This continues beyond the title and into the song itself. For example, 'House of Leaves' is a short, atmospheric track composed of dialogue and sound effects:

This haunted house   77

> Father: //We hear of a lovely daughter, shot down in her mistaken flight, unaware yet of how her life will be affected by this experience.
> Daughter: Why is it a House of Leaves?
> Unknown Voice: Into the House.
> Daughter: I can hear myself, I'm somewhere in there. What's happening?
> Mother: Nobody's home.
> Daughter: Daddy?
> Father: I thought he was dead.
> Daughter: Where are you?
> Father (emphatically): Dead
> Father's Ghost: Try now to take the next step// (Poe 2000)

The dialogue on this track is distorted by extensive reverb – by echo – aurally recreating the text-based experience of the House. What previously must have been imagined by the reader, due to the limitations of print media, can now be known and experienced. This chilling effect is enhanced by the contribution of the biographical narrative. The competent reader is able to identify and foreground particular themes, such as human mortality and grief, and consider the relationship of these to the House, both as symbol and as novel. Additionally, the track's personal narrative emphasises Poe's role as author and creator and correspondingly Danielewski's own role as author of *House of Leaves*.

Another track to make an explicit titular reference is 'Dear Johnny'. This song uses intertext differently to 'House of Leaves', in that rather than an in-song fusion between album and novel content, Poe addresses one of the narrators Johnny Truant:

> Johnny dear, don't be afraid.
> I will keep your secrets safe.
> Bring me to the blind man who
> Lost you in his house of blue. ('Dear Johnny', Poe 2000).

Here the intertextuality reinforces the outside-in reading; Poe's position – in order to possess the relevant knowledge to address Johnny and Zampanò – must be outside the text. This is confirmed by the reference to the 'house of blue', which refers to the typesetting of 'house' in the colour edition (greyscale in the monochrome edition). Poe engages and interacts with the characters not as individuals within a world but as specific voices within a print-text, emphasising her perspective – and the competent reader's – from the higher outside level. This pulls the narratives and voices in the novel together, linked like the songs on a music album by their omniscient authors.

X. Intertextual foregrounding

A subsequent effect of the outside-in reading promoted by the *Haunted* intertext is to foreground particular objects or events marginalised in the novel on first reading. Telephone calls, for example, are a key narrative device in the structure and plot of *Haunted*. Poe makes three phone calls to her mother – for the first (Track 1, cited above) and second she has to leave a message on the machine. The third, however, is answered and Poe's response 'Mom?' is full of surprise and relief (Poe 2000). The role of the telephone within the novel is subsequently highlighted, all 23 indexed references. Perhaps the most salient link is the phone call made after Jed's death between Karen and Jed's fiancée, the adjective *terrified* a possible reference to Track 6 'Terrified Heart':

> Karen tells her the truth [about Jed's death]. A panicked shout cracks over the speaker phone and then decays into **terrified** cries. Abruptly the phone line goes dead. Karen waits for the woman to call back but the phone does not ring again. (2000: 319; my emphasis)

Thematically, the telephone emphasises the difficulties of communication, the possibility of 'decay', and the impact this may have upon relationships, contradicting Hansen's belief that the theme of family dysfunction is necessarily quashed by the primacy of Truant's narrative (2004: 619 fn. 14). Yet, as a consequence of the biographical narrative in *Haunted*, a connection is also made between Poe and Danielewski and their experience of grief. It is not that there is any particular mapping between the characters and authors themselves, but instead the resonance arises through the message of the phone call itself.

Elsewhere, intertextual references foreground specific scenes in the novel. For example, the title-track 'Haunted' describes Poe's initial reaction to her father's death, but also paraphrases dialogue from *House of Leaves*:

> I'm haunted by the lives that wove the web, inside my haunted head.
> **Hallways. Always.**
> I'll always love you.
> I'll always need you.

I'll always want you.
And I will always miss you. (Poe 2000; my emphasis)

The first reference paraphrases the scene in *The Navidson Record* when Daisy asks her father to play the game 'Always'. The album booklet directs the reader to this passage. Zampanò's commentary observes how: '"always" slightly mispronounces "hallways". It also echoes it' (2000: 73). The reader is invited to make the interpretative step between the echo of 'always' and 'hallways' and Daisy and Navidson to Poe and her father. Just as the young Poe on the album protests that 'You never listen to me' (Poe 2000), so Navidson ignores Daisy's words and simply tickles her (2000: 73). The security of the fictional narratives, bound within the *House of Leaves*, is now being broken by the invasive intertext and biography of *Haunted*.

XI. Reshaping the interpretation

The intertext encourages the reader to reconstruct their previous interpretation of events within the novel. Track 8 '5 ½ Minute Hallway' is a particularly strong and convincing example affecting not just a particular scene, but the narrative composition as a whole.

The track links to a section in the Truant narrative, in which Johnny watches a band perform a song of the same title:

> Anyway I kicked back and began listening to the songs, enjoying the strange melodies and wild, nearly whimsical words . . . We were still talking . . . when **out of the blue** some very weird lyrics spiked through our conversation . . .: '**I live at the end of a Five and a Half Minute Hallway**'. I couldn't believe my ears. (Danielewski 2000: 512–513; my emphasis)

The lyric Truant transcribes is the opening lyric of Poe's '5 ½ Minute Hallway'.

As Truant 'becomes aware that the narrative he edits extends beyond its pages, so too does the reader learn the same about the book' (Pressman 2006: no pagination). Of course, recognition of the direct citation and the coded synecdoche of Johnny's phrase 'out of the blue' (outside the House) requires the necessary competence. However, this scene and intertextual link is perhaps the most explicit of them all, a clue planted by Danielewski and his sister to invite the uninitiated reader to explore the intertextual maze.

Within *House of Leaves* the impossible hallway is lexically prominent; the index gives 28 distinct references occurring across the three narratives. The hallway is the location of Truant's 5 ½-minute childhood trauma, when Pelafina attempted to kill him and was then incarcerated in the institution (Danielewski 2000: 517). Pressman proposes that the foregrounded 'hallways' construct a link across the narrative layers, a passageway between the fictional voices of the novel. She cites the following lyric as the key to resolving the jigsaw of the narrative layers: 'But there's more to this story than I have exposed. There are words made of letters, unwritten, and yes I forgive you, for leading me on.' (Poe 2000). Pressman interprets the above lyrics as if spoken by Pelafina herself – the writer of the Whalestoe Letters – and thus evidence that Pelafina can be read as the author of both the Truant and Zampanò narratives (2006: no pagination). This interpretation is highly coherent and viable.

However, the interpretation can be extended. The hallway is a linking device throughout the narratives, an architectural metaphor for communication, but this communication is not restricted to voices within the novel. It also extends outside it. So, whilst Pelafina may be the author within the novel, the intertext also foregrounds Danielewski and Poe as the overall creators who selected 'hallway' for this purpose. In this reading, 'hallway' is merely one of many signals indicating the relationship between the authors and between their texts.

Pressman also overlooks the lyrics' meaning within their original context. On the album 'words made of letters, unwritten' refer to the taped letter and recordings made by Poe's father; tapes she explicitly states that 'my brother and I found' (Poe 2000). The prior admission, therefore, that 'there's more to this story' is an acknowledgement of the intertextuality – that the 5 ½ Minute Hallway extends far beyond song lyrics not just into the fictional narrative of *House of Leaves* but into the biography of the authors and their own personal experiences.

Additionally, Pressman's resolution to the narrative complexity is rejected by both album and novel. The album notes direct the reader to the '5 and a Half Minute Hallway' segment of *The Navidson Record* where the hallway is described as 'meaningless' (Danielewski 2000: 60). It is compared to the artefact in Kubrick's *2001: A Space Odyssey* – a mysterious object in a film which has been the subject of innumerable interpretations (see Fry 2003: 332–333). The novel thus mocks the reader who believes they have found a stable reading, even when looking beyond the narrative layers.

The 'hallway' example, as a concept and entity, represents the sheer interpretative complexity facing the competent reader. It is emblematic of the innovativeness of *House of Leaves*, a text breaking outside its print boundaries and into the digital media of the twenty-first century.

XII. Rebuilding the narrative

The final example of intertextuality to be discussed in this essay is also the most innovative. Track 16 'Amazed' is the culmination of the album's narrative, describing Poe's new-found appreciation and respect for her father as she addresses his ghost:

> I'm amazed
> When push comes to shove what I'd give to you
> Everything
> I'm amazed
> The hallways I wouldn't mind crawling through
> And I'd do it for days and days
> I'm amazed, I'm amazed
> The places you're taking me to (Poe 2000)

In the novel and earlier on the album the hallway is an unknown, threatening space; it links the narrators by being the symbol and source of their fear. Here, however, the singer perceives them as a necessary route to the new experiences being offered. The second chorus takes this a step further, replacing the line with 'The walls that I wouldn't mind crashing through' (Poe 2000). The lyrics represent the power of the intertextuality to change interpretations and build something new, found in the wordplay of the song's title and repeated refrain: 'amazed = a maze'. The labyrinth has been redefined.

The concept of redefinition is established throughout Track 16, and reaches its peak in the closing verses:

> Johnny your suitcase was finally received
> She's packed up her things and she's ready to leave
> It's amazing
> All of the ink that was bled from your hands
> Has painted a picture that she understands
> It's amazed

Poe addresses Johnny Truant as she did in the song 'Dear Johnny', but here adds narrative information, a process legitimised by the intertextual system constructed throughout the album and novel. The stanzas refer to an incident described in the Appendix letters. Pelafina asks her son for a large suitcase so she can leave the institution, but her request is not fulfilled. She writes: 'Dear John, With no luggage to speak of . . . I've had nowhere to put my things and so I've lost all of it' (Danielewski 2000: 642). This is Pelafina's last letter. The next informs Johnny of her death.

The lyrics of 'Amazed' however provide a different conclusion to the story, offering the reader a happy ending. The narrative is not a representation or echo of the novel's, but an original contribution. Any notion held by the reader that *House of Leaves* is a conventional narrative bound within the physicalities of the print-text have been fully dispelled.

For 'Amazed' the album booklet directs the reader to the final letter in the Appendix, the aforementioned document informing Johnny of Pelafina's death. A key feature of this letter is the misspelling in the final paragraph of Pelafina's surname Lievre: 'our sympathies over the death of Ms. Livre [sic]' (2000: 643). Another example of wordplay ('livre' is French for 'book'), this is a metatextual comment on the demise of the traditional print-text. However, in interpreting this misspelling, the reader must oscillate between the two potential referents of 'li[e]vre': 'Pelafina' and 'novel', and this implies a link between the two endorsing Pressman's (2006) reading of Pelafina-as-author. Yet the relationship with the narrative additions within 'Amazed' suggests that whilst Pelafina may be the author, she is also still a character within the print-text; she is subject to the interpretative process of the reader, as they engage with the misspelling and in turn subject to the author, Danielewski, who placed the error in the text. Pelafina's transient identity – as both author and character – questions the nature of authorship and creativity as an individual, independent event. The collaborative intertextual narrative between *House of Leaves* and *Haunted* reinforces this insecurity, as seen in the final stanzas of 'Amazed':

> And here by the ocean the sky's full of leaves
> And what they can tell you depends on what you believe
> It's a maze
> The ash is a tree and the voices were three

And all that is gone is here sweeping through me
It's amazing (Poe 2000)

The lyrics convey a sense of resolution, a coming to terms with bereavement and the face of mortality. But they also reflect upon the interpretative reading process of the *House of Leaves* experience – 'full of leaves' – and its reliance upon the reader's competence and ability. The three 'voices', referred to in conjunction with the ash tree, implies the three narrators: Pelafina, Johnny and Zampanò; whilst also matching the well-established biographical narrative of Poe, her father and feasibly Mark Z. Danielewski. This consolidates the link between fiction and biography. Thus the line 'all that is gone is here sweeping through me' forces the reader to oscillate between several significant and legitimate readings built by album, novel and the intertext between them. Within the album context, it can be seen as Poe's acceptance that her father lives on as an 'echo' in his daughter. It also echoes Johnny Truant's words to the reader: 'Just as you have swept through me. / Just as I now sweep through you' (2000: 518). As a commentary upon the reading process it positions the reader as the final, subjective determinant of a text's meaning. In the space between the two, in the intertext between fictional novel and biographical narrative, the fictional work becomes a manifestation of 'all that is gone' – the past experiences and relationships of Danielewski, author and sibling, brought to fruition within the fictional narratives and voices of *House of Leaves*.

XIII. Conclusion

The analysis has discussed a reading of *House of Leaves* that – contrary to Hansen's belief (2004) – does not prioritise Truant's narrative and instead enables a new appreciation of the themes within the novel. Whilst it is true that 'no one ever sees that labyrinth in entirety' (Danielewski 2000: 114), the intertextuality between *House of Leaves* and *Haunted* extends the text and emphasises the role of the author. The links between character and author are never wholly explicit or confirmed, and the reader can be left to wonder to what degree Pelafina, or Johnny, or Zampanò occupy the author's real world.

The effect of the intertext to foreground previously marginalised or unnoticed themes, events or objects within the novel cannot be underestimated; and indeed, it is testament to the abilities of both Danielewski and Poe that the force of the intertext permeates all levels. This essay will conclude with a final example. In Chapter 9 where the textual layout replicates the experience of exploring the labyrinth in the House, there is a paragraph which describes Jed and Wax's decision to return without their missing team-mate Holloway, with a footnoted critical reference: 'Hank Leblarnard's *Grief's Explorations* (Atlanta: More Blue Publications, 1994)' (2000: 125). This is a fictional resource created by Danielewski (http://artsandpopularculture.com/List_of_fictional_books), and garners new significance in light of the intertextual reading. The name of the publication company, the comparative 'more blue' ('blue' an established synecdoche for the novel), points to the House outside the novel. For the competent reader, the book's title *Grief's Explorations* could also be that of the overall project between M. Z. Danielewski and Poe. For the competent reader, these clues are scattered throughout both novel and album and the satisfaction arises from their identification and positioning within the interpretative puzzle.

The unification between the biographical narrative of the album and the complex layers of *House of Leaves* may appear indulgent – perhaps a dumbing-down of Danielewski's magnificent textual experiment. Yet the subjectivity of this reading, the necessary intertextual competence, embodies the essence of the House and the reading process – 'All solutions are entirely personal' (Danielewski 2000: 115). This, to paraphrase Danielewski, is another way to enter the House.

Note

1 The full track listing of *Haunted*:
   Exploration B
   Haunted
   Control
   Terrible Thought
   Walk the Walk
   Terrified Heart
   Wild
   5 & ½ Minute Hallway
   Not a Virgin
   Hey Pretty
   Dear Johnny

Could've Gone Mad
Lemon Meringue
Spanish Doll
House of Leaves
Amazed
If You Were Here
Hey Pretty (Drive-By 2001 Mix)

Works cited

Danielewski, M. Z. (2000) *House of Leaves*, London: Doubleday. Black and white edition.

Eco, U. (1979) *The Role of the Reader: Explorations in the Semiotics of Texts*, Bloomington: Indiana University Press.

Fry, C. L. (2003) 'From technology to transcendence: humanity's evolutionary journey in *2001: Space Odyssey*', *Extrapolation* 44(3): 331–343.

Hansen, M. B. N. (2004) 'The digital topography of Mark Z. Danielewski's *House of Leaves*', *Contemporary Literature* 45(4): 597–636.

Hayles, N. K. (2002) 'Saving the subject: remediation in *House of Leaves*', *American Literature* 74(4): 779–806.

McCaffrey, L. and Gregory, S. (2003) 'Haunted house: an interview with Mark Z. Danielewski', *Critique: Studies in Contemporary Fiction* 44(2): 99–135.

Poe (2000) *Haunted*, Atlantic Records.

Pressman, J. (2006) '*House of Leaves*: reading the networked novel', *Studies in American Fiction* 34(1): 107–122.

5

Trickster authors and tricky readers on the MZD forums

Bronwen Thomas, Bournemouth University

I. Virtual Danielewski and his fans

Mark Z. Danielewski is an author whose work routinely engages with and remediates new modes and forms of representation, and who appears extremely adept at manipulating the resources of various new technologies to promote his work (e.g. see Evans, McCormick; both this volume). Yet to date little attention has been paid to his online presence or to the web-based activities of his fans. Danielewski once had a MySpace profile (the removal of which caused some disquiet to fans) and still has an account on Facebook (as of August 2009), though access to the latter is by invitation only. These social networking sites also feature accounts created by fans adopting the profiles of fictional characters from the novels: Will Navidson and Zampanò both appear on MySpace. Editions of Danielewski's works carry website addresses, and publishers Transworld have even set up a dedicated site for the author. Meanwhile, sites such as Exploration Z provide links to information about Danielewski and Poe, his musician sister, and a link takes the user through to www.onlyrevolutions.com, a multimedia resource which explicitly elicits involvement through inviting users to upload photographs. In addition to all of this, www.youtube.com carries numerous video clips of Danielewski at book signings, readings and in interview, as well as fan videos mainly consisting of trailers for movie versions of *House of Leaves*.

It would seem, therefore, that like so many contemporary artists and writers, Danielewski's influence, and his ability to connect with his audience(s), are enhanced by these various online resources. Yet Danielewski's relationship with his readers, mediated by these various resources, is much more complex and ambivalent than first appearances might suggest. This chapter draws on my analysis of this relationship via discussion forums devoted to Danielewski and his work, as well as some follow-up interviews I conducted with prominent forum members. When asked if they considered themselves to be fans of Danielewski's work, or members of a distinct community, participants' responses ranged from the noncommittal ('Maybe', fatwoul, 31 July 2009) to the enthusiastic ('definitely', Shadow Girl 23 July 2009). However, true to the style and culture of the MZD forums, users tended to be critical and questioning of the terminology itself, and wary of being labelled. In particular, some users wanted to draw a clear distinction between admiration for the work, and fascination with the author. For example, John B, a regular and much respected contributor to the MZD forums, remarked that '"Fan" is a strong word' (9 July 2009) and expressed his reservations about Danielewski's propensity for self-promotion ('I think he thinks he's better than he actually is, and that's a bit grating'). Meanwhile Norkhat (21 July 2009) seemed surprised to find the term 'fan' being used at all in the context of literature, but concluded on reflection that his behaviour 'pretty much makes me a hardcore fan'.

Fan cultures can arise in response to specific fictional works or to celebrate the life and output of an individual writer. The most popular fandoms online tend to focus on narrative texts that create a distinctive fictional world, for example Tolkein's *Lord of the Rings* trilogy or the *Harry Potter* novels. Often fans set about recovering aspects of the texts, or the author's life, hitherto marginalised, and invent and imagine their own extensions of the fictional world, or relationships with the characters, by means of writing fanfiction. Fans are often fiercely protective of the legacy of the authors whose works they admire: on the self-styled Republic of Pemberley, the forum administrators stoutly defend their 'matriarchal governance' of all things Austen (www.pemberley.com/faq.html#bios). But while some fans are motivated to help try to consolidate or establish the reputation of writers whom they believe to be neglected or misunderstood, others prefer to keep their communities of interest close-knit and cultish.

The fascination with Danielewski exhibited online follows similar patterns, as alongside interest in the texts, and in textual matters, it is undoubtedly the case that fans are intrigued by the author and his life. Questions of authorship dominate many of the discussions that take place, and the fact that so many different editions (and translations) of the novels exist, also poses questions to do with the whole idea of the stability of the text. The novels themselves, with their dizzying and highly eclectic range of references and complex narrative structures, seem to necessitate endless rereading, and lend themselves to the kind of collective activity and ongoing unravelling that discussion forums facilitate. Indeed, it might be said that, like the house in Danielewski's novel, his books resist containment or fixed boundaries. Fans are prepared to devote endless energy to the task of interpretation because they clearly believe that these works are important and their potential meanings inexhaustible. While there is always the tantalising prospect that the author is enjoying an elaborate joke at his readers' expense, and that they are being teased into chasing up blind alleys, the thrill of entering the maze seems irresistible. Indeed, there has perhaps never been a body of work so suited to the creation and pursuit of endless labyrinthine 'threads', and while discussions still coalesce around individual interpretations and readings of the texts, they are also shaped and influenced by the spirit of participation and need for constant updating that characterises network culture (Bolter 2001).

Studies of fan cultures have hitherto tended to celebrate their 'democratic' (Pugh 2005) potential and participatory ethos (Jenkins 1992), whereby hierarchical relations between author and reader are disrupted, and the boundaries between creation and reception are fundamentally blurred. I have argued elsewhere (Thomas 2007) that this somewhat utopian vision can obscure the extent to which access and power is unevenly distributed, and glosses over the very real tensions that may exist within and between fandoms. In the case of the Danielewski forums, there is often barely concealed contempt between members, and, as I have already indicated, some dispute about the extent to which users even see themselves as 'fans', or recognise themselves as a part of a community. Nevertheless, while recognising these limitations, the chapter will draw on fan studies in order to better understand the operation of the MZD forums and the behaviour of its users, and so as to draw comparisons with other fan cultures. At the same time, I will also focus on evaluating the contribution that these specific forums make in terms of offering insights into Danielewski's work and the extent to which this interpretative work locates itself in opposition to mainstream criticism and the academy.

II. The MZD forums

The MZD forums represent the most well-established and well-populated of the discussion forums dedicated to Danielewski's work and as such will be the main focus of this chapter. Activity on the site amply bears out Hayles' claim that 'we will not be able to leave [*House of Leaves*] alone because it will not leave us alone' (2002: 129), as huge numbers of posts are generated by members who appear more than happy to pore over textual minutiae and endlessly debate their meanings. Hayles, a self-confessed lurker, includes some discussion of the *House of Leaves* website (which forms part of the MZD forums) in her chapter on Danielewski in *Writing Machines* (2002). There she claims that most of the participants are between 15 and 30 years old, basing this supposition on her observation of 'their rhetoric and interests' (2002: 125). Such a view accords with Danielewski's own assessment that his work 'has become part of that angst-driven youth element' (Benzon 2007) in which internet culture plays such a prominent role. Though the anonymity of the net makes generalisation problematic, as with any online forum much information can be gleaned from navigating the site itself, for example about the number of members, their personal profiles (often including links to their own websites) and their activity on the site, including links to all of the threads and posts they have so far contributed. The information provided on the MZD forums seems to bear out Hayles' hunch, as most users profess or reveal themselves to be young male college grads, mainly though not exclusively from the US and the UK.

Each member of the MZD forums has the opportunity to upload images and to personalise their profiles with epigraphs and tags. The latter are usually utilised to help establish the credentials of the user, as most select quotations from literature or philosophy or involve a direct allusion or play on words relating to Danielewski's work (e.g. 'ftaires!'). Personalisation of this kind can offer tantalising clues as to the identities of the users (especially their ages, nationalities or gender), but there is too much evidence of mischief on the site to make identification anything like straightforward. For example, sutrix (as of August 2009) gives his occupation as 'Knob Adjuster', while Stencil includes amongst his interest 'Breathing through nostrils'. In addition to their public profiles, users are able to private message each other and can set up a facility to ignore posts by particular individuals if they so choose, leading to the emergence of certain cliques and factions.

The MZD forums have been active since shortly after the publication of *House of Leaves*, and while forums have subsequently been set up for *Only Revolutions* and other works by Danielewski, the House of Leaves forum remains the most populous. While some members such as John B move freely between the forums, there is also an element of healthy competition between them as comparisons are drawn not just in terms of the respective merits of the two texts, but also in terms of the quality of members' comments. While some mention will be made here of the Only Revolutions forum, most of my analysis focuses on House of Leaves. I will also be focusing only on the English-language discussions, though it should be noted that the website also hosts discussions for French, Dutch, Greek, Serbian and German participants.

MZD forums currently boast 24,222 members (as of 3 August 2009), of whom 1,314 are described as 'active'. For comparison, a fansite for *Dune*, the cult fiction by Frank Herbert, boasts 1,215 registered users (http://forum.dunenovels.com/phpBB2/, accessed 10 August 2009). Thus while the vast majority of members of MZD are 'lurkers', regular contributors exhibit remarkable loyalty to the site, often posting up to three or four times a day. One of the interesting features of online discussion forums is that the members may become just as much of a focus as the topics and subjects that supposedly bring the community together, and the MZD forums are no exception in this regard. Certain members such as fatwoul have achieved a kind of cult status for their online displays, and two forum members even contributed their own video for youtube (www.youtube.com/watch?v=TnO4NF56ByY), stepping out of the shadows and thereby blurring the boundaries as the audience become the performers. In addition, face-to-face meetings are regularly suggested, often coalescing around book signings or appearances by Danielewski, again extending the reach of the forums beyond the website into the 'real' world and everyday lives of users.

There is ongoing speculation on the site as to whether 'Mark' is a member of the forums operating under a pseudonym, and various references to the House of Leaves 'ghost' also suggest that users are wary of the fact that their contributions may be being monitored or at least observed by him. The site administrators certainly have inside knowledge of the author's movements, and the idea that 'Mark' is

Trickster authors and tricky readers 91

interested in and even influenced by the discussions taking place on the forums seems to have been validated by the fact that early proofs of *Only Revolutions* were made available to a select group of regular posters for their perusal and comments. Danielewski's views on the forum may be viewed on youtube (www.youtube.com/watch?v=zH A_7HCZF2o&feature=related), where he is asked about whether or not he follows the discussions and what he thinks of them. After a typically provocative opening ('those fools, I have them in my trap!'), Danielewski goes on to express enthusiasm for the interest and involvement of his fans, and conveys his hopes that his work invites participation and dialogue.

III. Style and tone

New users to both the House of Leaves and Only Revolutions forums are directed towards lists of 'useful threads' and assured that 'your opinion, as long as it is new, counts just as much as the opinion of a veteran poster' (Stencil, 12 May 2003). The key here is that new users are warned that asking the same old questions? will be met with impatience, and members also clearly have very little time for people who have not yet read the books. The tone adopted in many of the posts and threads (e.g. 'Codes for Dummies') adds to the impression that this is not a place where fools will be suffered gladly. Persistent flouting of the site's conventions can attract hostility from the more established members, resulting in some intimidating behaviour. Whilst still fairly new to the site, Norkhat described the experience of posting as 'like being a new pupil in class' (1 January 2009) and when interviewed, he expresses some disquiet about what he calls the 'Ozymandian' nature of the constant injunction 'it's been debated elsewhere' (21 July 2009). Nevertheless, once initiated into the forum, Norkhat becomes one of its stoutest advocates, referring to it as a 'democratic, unorthodox, apocryphal, cybernetical APPENDIX'.

The kind of routine misspelling and poor grammar characteristic of so many other online forums is virtually unheard of on MZD forums, perhaps because members do not shy away from pointing out errors and slips in each other's posts. The failure to observe typographical conventions and misreadings of the texts similarly attracts opprobrium. Yet posts also typically make widespread use of capitals and exclamations to help enliven the debates and to convey paralinguistic information. What we have, then, is a curious blend of highbrow pedantry with a style and tone more familiar from online chat rooms or social networking sites. Thus the copious use of emoticons appears rather incongruously alongside references to Ovid or Derrida, and quotations in Latin or Greek are followed by outbursts of obscenities and expletives. Site administrators do of course have the option of barring members who cross certain boundaries of taste, but even where this occurs (as in the case of the infamous Bonemaster 3000, accused of stalking other users), previous posts by debarred users are still accessible. Perhaps one of the things that distinguishes the language of the forums most is the amount of direction that goes on, with members routinely intervening to remind fellow users of the accepted conventions, to demand that they elaborate or clarify what they have said, or simply to instruct them of their shortcomings and errors. For this community, then, there seems to be an understanding that they come together to share knowledge and to learn, and this helps shape their interactions and the ways in which they relate to one another.

IV. Collectivity and the pooling of knowledge

In many respects, the discussions on the MZD forums bear a striking resemblance to those observed by Henry Jenkins (2006a) on fansites devoted to the cult TV show *Twin Peaks*. Jenkins found that the reading practices and interpretative strategies of these fans centred on resolving narrative enigmas and appeals to extratextual discourses. On the MZD forums, many users testify that they first came to the website looking for answers, and the number of extratextual references made is quite staggering, as shall be explored more fully later. Jenkins further found that the fans he studied had a complex relationship to the 'author' (David Lynch) and perceived themselves as sophisticated viewers outside the mainstream. As has already been suggested, users of the MZD forums enjoy an ambivalent relationship with 'Mark' and pride themselves on the breadth and depth of their knowledge, often comparing themselves favourably with less erudite readers of Danielewski's work. While the *Twin Peaks* fans looked for continuity errors in the show, users of the MZD forums look for errors and typos in the text, but are unsure as to the extent to which these are intentional or accidental. Like the fans studied by Jenkins, members on the MZD forums seek confirmation for their

Trickster authors and tricky readers 93

own hypotheses from others while also staking a claim for superior knowledge. Thus as with the *Twin Peaks* fans, the invocation of collective problem solving does not necessarily ensure harmony or agreement between users, with competing and often contradictory formulations of events and their meanings being offered.

Jenkins contextualised the behaviour of the *Twin Peaks* fans as being typical of 'the informational economy of the net' (2006a: 125) where 'knowledge equals prestige, reputation, power'. In a related essay on collective intelligence (2006b), Jenkins describes how fans are often motivated by epistemaphilia, but learn to pool their knowledge and to value knowledge as something that can be exchanged between them. It is here that Jenkins sees the radical potential of the fans' behaviour, as he argues that the 'dynamic, collective, and reciprocal nature of these exchanges undermines traditional forms of expertise' (2006b: 140), as fans discover that the value of information they possess in effect increases through social interaction.

Pooling knowledge and contributing to an evolving 'Republic of Letters' (Norkhat 21 July 2009) is certainly a core feature of the exchanges taking place on the MZD forums, as is the participants' desire for validation for their interpretations and hypotheses from those whose opinions they respect. But as Jenkins seems to allow, such behaviour can carry its own risks where 'what might previously have been private meditations [becomes] . . . the basis for social interaction' (2006a: 124). Thus while the ability to recognise obscure or arcane references brings plaudits from fellow contributors on the MZD site, displaying one's hand and thereby implying gaps in others' knowledge can elicit reactions of a less favourable kind. One of the interesting but problematic aspects of these kinds of sites is that it becomes very difficult at times to distinguish between personal attacks and criticisms of opinions or beliefs that are being put forward, and, as has already been shown, the MZD forums are certainly not immune from infighting and the formation of certain cliques.

V. Factions and Fractures within the 'community'

The kind of humour and adversarial banter that characterises many of the exchanges on the MZD forums has arguably led to the emergence of a distinctly male culture. In his study, Jenkins contrasted the behaviour of male fans of *Twin Peaks* with that of female fans of *Star*

Trek, claiming that the latter are much more interested in paradigmatic relationships, not as clues to help resolve plot questions (as is the case for the *Twin Peaks* fans), but as the basis for gossip which draws on personal experiences. On the MZD forums, it has been observed (John B 9 July 2009) that female users tend to gravitate to the 'Other Stuff' section in which discussions range from sharing personal problems, to flirting and trivia bearing little or no relevance to the work of Danielewski. Such segregation of topics (and of users) helps contribute to the impression that users on the 'main' discussion threads see themselves as sophisticates engaged in the serious intellectual business of trying to resolve the enigmas and complexities of Danielewski's work, and while all threads from time to time wander off topic, and the language of many of the posts descends into insults and obscenities, boundaries and hierarchies have clearly become well established within the site.

Members' grumbles and complaints about the operation of the site or the conduct of other users occasionally becomes a topic of conversation in itself. In addition, members may reflect on how the site is changing, or make explicit reference to those who have left or stopped posting. One example is the thread 'i miss' started by girl 2 (8 May 2003) where she lists a variety of members who have fallen by the wayside, and looks back with nostalgia to 'no gab or drivel, just straight up intelligent conversation'. Harking back to a 'golden age' is not uncommon (e.g. ThomasJ, 9 May 2003) and is usually imagined as a time when the intellectual content of posts is high, and when harmony between members is the norm. In contrast, the present is often described in terms which suggest division or splintering, as when lazysmurff remarks on the development of a 'pseudo hierarchy of newbie and oldtimer' (10 May 2003) on the House of Leaves forum.

In response to a question I asked about hierarchies on the site, John B (9 July 2009) suggests that it is only natural that some members gain more respect than others, as posts vary in quality, with some proving to be much more 'valuable'. Though the criteria for quality and value remain undefined, it is evident that more established members see it as their right and their duty to sort the wheat from the chaff as it were. Fatwoul (31 July 2009) happily admits to having taken on the role of enforcer in the past, chasing away 'trouble makers', though he feels that this role has evolved into his becoming a more mischievous and 'prolific poster of useless comments'.

Perhaps most memorably and poetically, Norkhat describes the site as undergoing a process of 'sedimentation' (21 July 2009), and compares the community variously to a stone circle and to a collection of 'dinosaurs and gnats', suggesting almost a process of natural selection in the way in which groupings emerge. The participants I interviewed seemed to feel that such a process was one that they were familiar with from other sites and forums, and seemed to assume that it would not take long for new members to become familiar with the prevailing tone and conventions of the site. Of course, their views may not be representative of those who have left the site, or never contributed in the first place, but for these users at least the quirks and tensions that surface from time to time are fundamental to what gives the site its sense of identity.

VI. The trickster author

Jenkins' study of *Twin Peaks* fans revealed that fans held in great reverence the 'author' figure as a kind of master programmer able to tap into a wide network of previously circulating cultural texts which they then set about to track down and identify. A similar preoccupation with tracking down intertexts and pinpointing extra-textual references also characterises much of the discussion on the MZD forums. However, this gives way to a growing reflexivity on the part of users of the forums that, on the one hand, full enlightenment might be an ultimately unachievable goal and, on the other hand, that it is precisely the ongoing nature of such activity that makes Danielewski's work, and discussion of it, so appealing and rewarding in the first place.

Again, very reminiscent of the MZD forums is Jenkins' observation that fans of *Twin Peaks* perceived David Lynch as a trickster figure, able constantly to anticipate and undermine the expectations of his audience, and possessing almost supernatural powers in terms of his ability to monitor and respond to the expectations and desires of his fans. Jenkins found that Lynch's perceived unpredictability was an important part of his appeal to fans, justifying their most outrageous speculations, and thwarting the efforts of professional critics or reviewers to 'make sense' of his work. On the MZD forums, 'Mark' enjoys a similar kind of mystique, so that although there is speculation about his intentions, and even his private life, users also seem to recognise that keeping the author at a distance may help to prolong the pleasure which they get from his work.

As is fairly commonplace in online forums, many members of the MZD forums appear anxious to preserve their anonymity, and give very little away about themselves. In turn, this helps to stoke the rumours about the author's participation on the site, culminating in an occasional attempt to 'out' Danielewski. For example, many members became convinced that fallingquarters was in fact Danielewski perhaps because the posts contributed by this member seemed so provocatively enigmatic, adding to the mysteries and puzzles suggested by *House of Leaves* rather than attempting to resolve them. Many threads on the MZD forums are devoted to reports of users meeting 'Mark' at readings, discussing interviews and reviews of his work, and generally speculating about his whereabouts and his activities. However, in my correspondence with individual members of the forums, participants were careful to distance themselves from any fan-like behaviour. For example, sutrix describes Danielewski's role as being akin to that of 'a proficient director or musician' (10 July 2009), and mocks those who 'follow his every move... [and] treat him like a Rock Star'. Shadow Girl similarly contrasts her own interest in the author with that of 'hysterical high school girls' (23 July 2009) but she does recognise that the 'mystique' surrounding this figure is an important draw for forum users. While forum users had different opinions regarding the extent of Danielewski's participation in the discussions, and about the extent to which the work should be considered separately from the author, there is a certain watchfulness that comes from the uncertainty about his presence on the site which occasionally borders on suspicion and even distrust. Similarly, just as users engage in intellectual jousting with one another, there is also a sense in which, as Norkhat (21 July 2009) puts it, 'people breaking codes feel like they wrestle with a master-mind', much as the *Twin Peaks* fans perceive the 'trickster' Lynch. The implication is that while there is huge respect and admiration for Danielewski, users want to try and engage with and even match him by displaying their own prowess and knowledge.

VII. Self-reflexivity

Like the convoluted narrative and puzzles of Lynch's *Twin Peaks*, Danielewski's writing teases and tantalises readers into following up intertextual references, chasing down clues, and interpreting symbols. In my correspondence with users of the site, most revealed that they found the MZD forums either after or while reading *House of Leaves*, a natural process for them, it seems, as they perceive the internet as the best place to go to find out things. One participant (sutrix) revealed that he had discovered the site before he read the book, but for all of the respondents, the initial impulse to 'go looking for answers' (Shadow Girl, 23 July 2009) is described as only the starting point. Reflection on why users come to the site, and why they stay, is fairly commonplace. For example, welladjusted initiated a thread called 'Why do you use this website?' (11 April 2008), provoking some interesting insights (including Norkhat's reference to the site as 'a Republic of Letters' (3 January 2009)), the odd flippant comment ('I come here to share my gay love with Ellimist' (sutrix 3 January 2009)), as well as some overt hostility ('Stop trying to waste our time, troll' (Ellimist 3 January 2009)). Indeed, one of the distinctive features of the MZD forums is the level of reflexivity of the posts and the amount of metacommentary that takes place as regards both the relative merits of contributions, and the behaviour of users and their interactions with others. Of course in any discussion forum, participants respond to and evaluate what others have said, but here participants are quick to criticise (and occasionally to praise), and as was said earlier, few allowances are made for those new to the site or unfamiliar with its practices.

It appears, however, that users are protective of the level of debate within the forums rather than being closed to new insights. Participants are impatient to discover more, and are particularly receptive to users who contribute references or identify possible codes not previously recognised. For example, John B celebrates the way in which the forum draws out the 'encyclopedic quality' of Danielewski's writing, and welcomes the fact that his own range of references (acknowledged as itself being encyclopaedic by fellow users) is supplemented by those more 'science-oriented people' (9 July 2009), whose views he might never have encountered other than via this site. The language of the forums is thus peppered with references to laws of physics, alongside references to film, Norse mythology, literary theory and narratology.

VIII. Relationship to academia

As was said earlier, while contributions to the MZD forums can be playful, and the language colourful, failures to observe shared conventions are met with contempt, and loose claims and suppositions are treated with disdain unless they are supported by textual evidence of some kind. In this respect, much like the fans of the TV show *Lost* studied by Debra Journet (2008), forum users behave rather like literary critics, favouring close reading and engaging in interpretative work. This was an aspect of the website picked up on by N. Katherine Hayles, who noted that 'readers pursued the book with an intensity rivalling the most devoted literary critics' (2002: 125). Indeed, the attention to detail and commitment demonstrated by users are often quite astounding, as with the elaborate timeline of events in *House of Leaves* painstakingly put together by girl 2 (28 June 2002). It might even be said, therefore, that this 'community' is very much located within a framework of learning and instruction, most evident perhaps in the deference occasionally afforded to the site's 'elders' such as John B.

Like much of the discussion that takes place on these forums, academic criticism of Danielewski's work has tended to focus on textual issues and typographical pyrotechnics, or on tracking down and tracing the various ways in which the books allude to or remediate other texts. Yet on the MZD forums the question of whether *House of Leaves* is a parody of academic discourse is often explicitly raised, as in the thread ('Academia', 15 May 2003) initiated by bigholfan. While many, if not most, of the contributors to the site are college students or faculty, and are clearly schooled in the conventions and intellectual practices of the academy, they tend to position themselves against orthodoxies and the mainstream. For example, John B, a college tutor in the US, allows that the forums 'tend to attract geeky and nerdy people from all over', but finds that the site offers him the freedom to say things 'that I'd never have dreamed I'd write about in any book' (9 July 2009). In John B's 'useful threads' section on the Only Revolutions forum (18 September 2006), 'reviewing the reviewers' perhaps provides the best evidence of the protectiveness forum users feel towards the books and their author, but also suggests that they perceive their own interpretations and activities to be in many respects vastly superior to that of professional reviewers and critics. Thus MicheleVR5 admits to enjoying reading

Raminagribis 'snarking on the bad reviews' (3 September 2006) even while allowing that she herself found many of the reviews interesting.

IX. 'Useful threads' and active reading

The 'useful threads' sections provide a good snapshot of the kinds of topics being discussed on the forums. On the House of Leaves site, recurring topics include colours, images, different editions of the novel, influences, textual issues, the significance of names and the presence of codes in the text. Useful threads for Only Revolutions include discussions of how people are reading the book, the significance of the history gutter, recurring themes and contexts. As was said before, repetition is actively discouraged on the site, which can create the impression that topics and threads are gradually wound down or even abandoned. Moreover, one of the most prolific and colourful of posters, fatwoul, perceives a wider drift away 'from book-related site to online community, with no specific focus' (31 July 2009). But such concerns belie the participants' (including fatwoul's) willingness to take up and play with ideas and suggestions circulating on the site, and the setting up of a group (3 June 2009) to collectively reread *House of Leaves* section by section indicates that the discussions are not likely to run out of steam any time soon.

As was suggested earlier, individual contributions often impress in terms of sheer effort, indicating hours of research into a particular name or word, or a painstaking attempt to crack a code or devise some elaborate theory of how the meanings of the texts can be pieced together. For example, Tim-and-Carl's (2 September 2008) 'Interesting Summation of Clues' is apparently the result of two weeks of 'hardcore study', and while all may not concur that the results are that 'interesting', the enthusiasm and attention to detail may at least be readily applauded. Thus while the theories put forward and codes and meanings suggested by users may sometimes appear rather bizarre, taking the forums as a collectivity, one cannot but be impressed by the range of specialisms and references on offer.

X. Conclusion

In many respects it is precisely the fact that the variety and breadth of interpretations offered cannot be neatly swept up into one overarching theory that is the most important contribution of the forums. Norkhat (21 July 2009) makes the point that not only do the forums support vast quantities of opinions and readings of the novels, but that the specific and unpredictable ways in which users of the site connect these fragments together compound the possibilities so that they become infinitesimal. A user can choose to navigate between posts relating to different time periods, different threads, different texts. He or she can follow the threads and posts made by individuals, mark threads as read, and generally jump in and out of the forums and the discussions as he or she chooses. Many users make reference to the fact that they have taken breaks from the forums, sometimes returning because they want to reimmerse themselves in the community, sometimes because they are returning to reading the novels, or to discover new ways of reading them.

Again, while it is dangerous to generalise, for most users there seems to be a basic trajectory away from seeking answers towards embracing and celebrating the open-endedness of the discussions. For example, in one of his earlier posts, John B attempts to steer the discussions of the novel away from clue hunting and an obsession with codes and symbols, towards 'describing the experience of just reading the bloody thing' (23 April 2002). To the casual observer, therefore, what might seem like inconsequential or disjointed chatter may link up to previous threads and discussions, to private disputes between individuals, as these are never closed but may be reopened at any point, by anyone who so chooses. As Rryssa puts it, 'Reading the book was half the fun ... This is the other half' (20 October 2008). Whether or not the discussions that take place on the site will filter out to influence Danielewski's standing and reputation as a writer remains to be seen. Similarly, while he evidently takes an interest in the site and in some of its individual members, thus far he has stopped short of the kind of overt endorsement of fan-generated content displayed by other authors, for example J. K. Rowling.

Some contributions and some of the contributors to the forums offer highly sophisticated analyses and densely formulated arguments which could be seen to rival more formal academic criticism. For example, John B's 'unbound book theory' (17 August 2009) is frequently referred to and is clearly much respected by the forum users, and his reflections on his own experience of reading the novels, and on the contributions and interpretations offered by others, play an important function in setting the standard for the discussions. In particular, John B's claim that *House of Leaves* serves an important function in 'teaching the reader about the act of reading' (14 January 2009) might almost be extended to the forums themselves, as contributors offer vivid and engaging accounts of their engagement and frustrations with the texts, and reflect on their own experiences and those of others.

Thus the forums are interesting and insightful not just for offering different interpretations of the novels, or identifying and glossing the vast range of references and allusions they contain, but in mapping the journeys of readers of Danielewski's work, and in illustrating the ways in which these journeys are endlessly unpredictable and enriching. While the squabbling and infighting that takes place can be tedious and irritating, they may also perhaps be best understood as part of this journey, where factions are formed and disbanded, and where readers' experiences of the 'bloody things' created by Danielewski may at times be as frustrating as they are rewarding.

Notes

Throughout this chapter, italics are used for editions of the novels, while the names of the associated discussion forums appear in roman.

Interviews with forum members fatwoul, Norkhat, sutrix, John B and Shadow Girl were conducted via email, July 2009. All have given permission for me to quote from this correspondence and to refer to them by their forum names.

Website addresses:
www.houseofleaves.com/forum/
www.republicofpemberley.com
http://forum.dunenovels.com/phpBB2/

Works cited

Benzon, K. (2000) 'Revolution 2: an interview with Mark Z. Danielewski', *Electronic Book Review*. http://www.electronicbookreview.com/thread/wuc/regulated.

Bolter, J. D. (2001) *Writing Space: Computers, Hypertext and the Remediation of Print*, 2nd edn, London: Lawrence Erlbaum Associates.

Hayles, K. (2002) *Writing Machines*, Cambridge, MA: MIT Press.

Jenkins, H. (1992) *Textual Poachers: Television Fans and Participatory Culture*, London: Routledge.

Jenkins, H. (2006a) '"Do you enjoy making the rest of us feel stupid?" alt. tv.twinpeaks, the trickster author, and viewer mastery', in *Fans, Bloggers and Gamers: Exploring Participatory Culture*, New York: New York University Press, pp. 115–133.

Jenkins, H. (2006b) 'Interactive audiences? The "collective intelligence" of media fans', in *Fans, Bloggers and Gamers: Exploring Participatory Culture*, New York: New York University Press, pp. 134–151.

Journet, D. (2008) 'Literate acts in convergence culture: *Lost* as transmedia narrative', paper presented at Project Narrative, Ohio State University.

Pugh, S. (2005) *The Democratic Genre: Fan Fiction in a Literary Context*, Bridgend: Seren Books.

Thomas, B. (2007) 'Canons and fanons: literary fiction online', Dichtung-digital 37(1). http://www.dichtung-digital.org/2007/thomas.htm.

II

The Fifty Year Sword

6

Reading the graphic surface of Mark Z. Danielewski's *The Fifty Year Sword*

Glyn White, University of Salford

I. Introduction

Mark Z. Danielewski's *The Fifty Year Sword* (2005), described on the author's website as 'an illustrated short story', is much slighter than the author's novels but is entirely in keeping with them in the way that it thoroughly problematises its narration. As with Danielewski's larger works the narrators are distinguished by striking typographic devices and page design, in this case by, as the dust jacket puts it, the author 'mischievously playing with layout [and] colour'. *The Fifty Year Sword* is unavailable from usual retail outlets though it can be obtained through a Dutch website (www.debezigebij.nl). Where it is found in libraries, it is unlikely to be shelved normally with other works by the same author because of its unusual dimensions. Its black hardback or cloth binding is approximately 325 x 165mm (or 12 ½ × 6 ½ inches): an exceptionally tall and narrow form.

The dust jacket reminds us that this book is, to some extent, a collaboration with 'Dutch artist and entrepreneur' Peter van Sambeek, but if we check the reverse of the title page we note that: 'Jacket design and book lay-out: Mark Z. Danielewski/ Studio Jan de Boer' (4, all references to the 2006 second edition). I take this to mean that the latter were employed to carry out the intentions of the former.

Set mainly at the Halloween party of 112-year-old Mose Dettledown in East Texas, the narrative concerns recently divorced Thai dressmaker Chintana, and her encounter with the American woman Belinda Kite, who has wronged her by sleeping with her husband, Pravat. *The Fifty Year Sword* is possibly a ghost story but, if so, is certainly not a straightforward one. The most clearly uncanny element comes in the shadowy form of the Story Teller – not the one hired by the host – who carries his Fifty Year Sword in a black box and whose nature, identity and motives remain mysterious. The Story Teller embeds his tale in Chintana's but both of these characters are narrated to us simultaneously by five separate narrators, each of whose access to the 'facts' of the narrative is ambiguous.

In this essay I will not discuss links to the rest of the Danielewski canon (other than to suggest that its lyrical style, compounded words, interest in flora and fauna and its coloured printing prefigure these elements in *Only Revolutions*). Instead, I will focus on how this neglected text employs page design and how its graphic devices inform the experience of reading *The Fifty Year Sword*. Fulfilling this aim will involve some discussion of genre, theme and reader engagement.

II. MD explains a possible ghost story with five coloured narrators

There is an author's note (signed 'MD' not 'MZD') on page 6. Centred on the page and in a smaller type than the main text it goes some way to disguising itself as further technical information. The note begins with 'Maybe' and, as a single sentence, has tortuously extended syntax but does offer a number of clues and considerations that may help us interpret the text.

The note first discusses genre: 'the history of any ghost story is a ghost story unto itself, which is to say another story completely, assuming any of what follows can rightly even be considered a ghost story' (6). In making this teasing generic identification the note implies that ghost stories are haunted by their history. But which history? As Peter Buse and Andrew Stott note in their 'Introduction' to *Ghosts: Deconstruction, Psychoanalysis, History* (1999: 1–20), the idea of the ghost is inherently an anachronistic one, conceptually and historically, despite the fact it survives to haunt even the twenty-first century: 'anachronism might well be the defining feature of ghosts, now and in the past, because haunting, by its very structure, implies a deformation of linear temporality: there may be no proper time for ghosts' (1). The history referred to in MD's note may be that of the story's inspiration and composition, but could also be interpreted to mean the story within the story, since ghost stories feature hidden histories in the form of the reasons for the (albeit supernatural) presence of the ghost. A third possible history might be that of the tale since its first telling. MD's note on page 6 thus makes suggestive links to the ghost story genre while it refuses conclusive identification within it.

The central part of MD's note concerns the sources of the narrative and the manner of its presentation, stating that the text is based on 'independently conducted interviews' of five subjects and that the author 'has done nothing more than lend together these gathered and rerelated bits' (6). This offers us a factual truth-claim, a disavowal of authorial responsibility and the gathering of accounts worthy of an empirical ghost hunter (see Buse and Stott 1999: 3). Ultimately, however, the note closes with an ambivalent statement of the results of its method: 'so as to present here a pretty peculiar and perhaps altogether alternate history of one October evening in East Texas'. The material is 'rerelated' (i.e. third hand) and produces either something doubtful ('pretty peculiar') or simply false ('altogether alternate').

Once again these concerns and the ambivalence drawn out are consistent with the ghost story genre in which the manoeuvre of placing responsibility for the tale on sources is a regular trope. For example, Joseph Sheridan Le Fanu's authorial narrator of 'The White Cat of Drumgunniol' learns of a family curse from a survivor of that line and states: 'I mean to repeat it, as nearly as I can, in his own words' (1994: 58). Similarly his 'Madame Crowl's Ghost' is presented in the idiom of an old servant recalling her teens but Le Fanu does not use quotation marks in either of these tales. The narrator of Le Fanu's 'An Account of Some Strange Disturbances in Aungier Street' argues that to write his experience, rather than speak it, is disadvantageous because: 'Pen, ink and paper are cold vehicles for the marvellous, and a "reader" a decidedly more critical animal than a "listener"' (1994: 68). Such disingenuous phonocentric desire to recapture the feeling of being told a tale is often present in M. R. James' ghost tales, too, as in 'A Neighbour's Landmark' which does not place the teller's tale in quotation marks, only his dialogue with his auditor (1992: 281). In fact many of James' tales were produced for seasonal tellings with print as a secondary outlet. *The Fifty Year Sword*, with its embedded Story Teller speaking to five orphans, recreates this storytelling ambience internally, but the ghost tale is not the only influence here. The magical realism of the Story Teller's narrative recalls the picaresque African folk tale in the manner of Amos Tutuola's *The Palm Wine Drinkard* (1952). Yet *The Fifty Year Sword* differs from all these examples of recounted tales in its insistence on quotation marks throughout. It retains the marks not just of one source but of the author figure's stitching together of five source narrators line by line, and sometimes word by word.

The note on page 6 performs the function of a preface but it is one particularly concerned to explain the installation of the quotation marks that both enclose and pepper what follows. Jacques Derrida in his 'Outwork, Prefacing' to *Dissemination* argues that the presence of a preface indicates the already written nature of the content and asks: 'what historical and strategic function should henceforth be assigned to the quotation marks, whether visible or invisible, which transform this into a "book"?' (1981: 4). While other ghost stories suppress the graphic signs of quotation, *The Fifty Year Sword* never lets us forget them. Yet the tale is not satisfied by simply revealing its quoted nature, it wishes, without employing speech attribution, footnotes or dramatic form, to indicate exactly which narrator has supplied which word (and in some cases which silence). This is to be accomplished, as page 6 tells us, by the use of different colour inks for the quotation marks.

The employment of coloured inks in the novel (or at the very least varied tones of print), exploiting contemporary print technology, has become a virtual trademark of Danielewski. The use of coloured inks in addition to black remains, however, a costly mode of printing not only because of the extra materials but also because of the extra synchronisation required. Despite the desirability of accurate quotation, the reproduction of the colours used in Danielewski's texts is beyond the budget of an academic publication such as this.

The quotation marks in *The Fifty Year Sword* are presented in five colours: 1) deep yellow, 2) orange, 3) red-brown, 4) mid-brown and 5) dark brown. The colour printing is not limited to these colours, and in fact it uses almost the whole colour spectrum at one point or another, but each of these colours appears on almost every spread. The colours of the five quotation marks are related closely enough so that the darker ones often require comparison between one another to be definitely attributed.

What do we gain from this careful plotting of each narratorial contribution? MD's note insists that the system is employed to essentially anonymise the narrators: 'rather than delve into the devices and biases and oddly canted idiom of the five persons ... or represent them throughout with characterising phrases, temporal references or even more quotation marks' (6). Indeed, the lines

Reading the graphic surface

are mainly so brief as to give the reader little purchase on any individuality the colour-attributed narrators might have. It might be possible to say that narrator 3 (red-brown quotation marks) gets more than his or her fair share of the compound words employed (see, for example, page 46) but this is certainly not a characteristic exclusively attributable to this individual narrator. Similarly, if we isolate or ignore the contributions of any one narrator a new narrative does not emerge nor is the original enhanced in any meaningful sense.

If the individual narrators are unrevealing, we do find that the number five appears significant: there are five latches on the Story Teller's sword case, five scented candles in the room he selects (cloves, nutmeg, ginger, cinnamon, molasses) and five mysteriously opening windows to blow them out. Most significantly, there are the five orphans that the Story Teller tells his tale to. Aged between four and nine, and trailed by the harassed Social Worker, they are given unusual names (Tarff, Ezade, Iniedia, Sithiss and Micit) perhaps most distinct for their lack of particular class, gender or ethnic markings.

I suggest that the reader in search of significance for these orphan auditors maps them on to the five narrators using the author's note which suggests that the narrators have a shared past and that one 'from the prison of a later life hates them all' (6). We may take a further liberty by equating this last with the authorial narrator (another identity), but their number and the comparable anonymity of narrators and oddly named orphans prompts us to look at this connection. What other characters could have been interviewed? The proper-named characters are Chintana, her ex-husband Pravat, Mose Dettledown and Belinda Kite, and only Chintana and Belinda appear to hear any of the Story Teller's narrative. A second tier of characters are named by their profession (the Social Worker, the Gas Station Owner, the Park Ranger, the Car Dealer, the Taxidermist, the City Alderman, the Caterer) and an otherwise unnamed woman who calls Belinda Kite '"'a hateful whore'"' (34). Try as we might to find a better fit, we are left with the orphans as our best candidates, knowing that this is far from conclusive. Conditioned by most of the fiction we read to seek significance in narratorial identity, the reader may sustain, in hope rather than in expectation, an unsupported hypothesis for some time. The difficulty of arriving at any kind of satisfying identification of the five narrators ultimately throws us back on an awareness of the technical functions of narration:

But who is it that is addressing you? Since it is not an 'author,' a 'narrator,' or a *'deus ex machina,'* it is an 'I' that is both part of the spectacle and part of the audience; an 'I' that, a bit like 'you,' attends (undergoes) its own incessant, violent reinscription within the arithmetical machinery; an 'I' that, functioning as a pure passageway for operations of substitution, is not some singular and irreplaceable existence, some subject or 'life,' but only, moving between life and death, reality and fiction, etc., a mere function or phantom. (Derrida 1981: 325)

Our narrators are a gaggle of ghosts. Each purely functional narrator generates a thread which ties in to the others, weaving a pattern and a text (*textere* = to weave). This is a metaphor appropriate to Chintana's occupation and, since the narrative warns us at its opening: ""No matter how you cut it . . ."" (8), we ought, perhaps, to have been prepared to find that unstitching the strands of narration will avail us nothing more than an awareness that it is their weaving *together* which makes them substantial. It is the text's numerous quotation marks which stitch these strands together, not the presence of a single editor or author, and holding together – mentally, physically, narratively – is what *The Fifty Year Sword* is about. Closer examination of the quotation marking of the narrators, focusing on some instances where the system varies, will bear out their importance for the narrative.

III. Complications with quotation marks

There are five complications to the use of quotation marks during the narrative that are worth noting. The first is that when the narrators quote overheard speech a set of single quotation marks nests inside their double ones. This initially occurs when the Social Worker tells Chintana that the Halloween party will end at midnight with ""'someone's birthday'"" (22). This is just an increase in quotation marks of the same colour, but over the page a second complication occurs. The line that reveals it will be the birthday of ""that bitchwitch Belinda Kite"" uses two colours; mid-brown double and yellow single marks. Taken literally, this narrator-quoting-narrator is confusing (how would it be possible if the interviews are independent as claimed?) but it becomes the norm during the Story Teller's narrative and, as a third complication, the closing single quotation marks no longer match the colours of their opening ones.

The fourth complication occurs later on in the Story Teller's narrative when he quotes the impossible grey swordmaker, The Man with No Arms, and his italicised dialogue receives its own set of double quotation marks (66). Almost immediately (his second speech) the fifth complication occurs when the colour of the closing double marks does not match that of the opening ones. The result is that there can be as many as four different coloured sets of marks in a line, outweighing the words in length (e.g. on page 74).

    The dramatically enlarged yellow quotation marks that the narrative opens with are also worthy of note. Such larger marks indicate new sections of the story. Page 8 is the only larger mark for narrator 1, but there are two for narrator 2 (36, 52), two for narrator 3 (34, 86), one for narrator 4 (66) and two for narrator 5 (76, 94). There are also two other larger quotation marks, both closing quotation marks, in different colours. The first, in grey, appears on page 52, introducing a single, exceptionally long line of text before another attributably coloured, larger quotation mark returns us to the quoted text. The note on page 6 tells us that: 'Where no quotations appear only the worst should be assumed: an interruption by someone other than one of the before mentioned persons, the reader or even the author . . .' Apart from condemning itself (page 6 is outside quotation marks), this cues us to expect much from the 'unquoted' line but what we read is two long nonsense words, the first beginning with a capital and six lower case Zs. The narrative has this interruption introduced by the storyteller "singing": ""a series of clucks, trills, sputters and odd clicks caught in / "whistles and the back of his throat." We may thus read the nonsense line as the storyteller's indecipherable song (though its numerous Zs might suggest the missing initial in the attribution of the note on page 6). When the narrative resumes, the storyteller explains that in the ""Forest of / "'Falling / "'Notes sounds could not hold / "'together"" and that ""'this was only the song I sought to sing, not what ultimately spilled / "'out of my lips. That sound was completely different."" (52). What happens outside the quotation marks is not what was intended, it does not even make sense. The text's quotation marks are a necessity if meaning is to be conveyed, if sound and spoken language is to be mastered.

    The second larger closing quotation mark, in pink, ends the book on page 100, that is when the narrative no longer holds together. The closing mark is significant because it reminds us of how the narration of the supposed five narrators stays open. The convention for rendering ongoing speech is for the opening quotation mark to be repeated and for the closing one to occur only when the speech ends. The narrators' lines thus stay open, despite the others cutting in, and never close (or at least are never closed by marks of the same colour). Each thread and each opened quotation mark remains open with the narrative depending on the reappearance of the next thread to continue. How the fabric is eventually cut to size is something we shall return to in the conclusion. Before that, we must engage with a final element of the page design of *The Fifty Year Sword* and what is actually its dominant aspect.

IV. Blank space

We have already noted the tall format of the book, but the use of the pages within this format is highly particular. Excepting the title pages and the 12 illustrations, the recto (right-hand) page is always blank. This explains, for any reader without a copy of *The Fifty Year Sword*, why I have only been quoting from even-numbered pages. The one mark on the recto page (again excepting pages with illustrations) is the folio (page number) which appears halfway down the right-hand margin sectioned off by a single (opening) square bracket. Furthermore, the text area on the unnumbered verso (left-hand) pages is unusually narrow. Though some lines of the text reach 80mm (3 inches) in length the left-justified column only appears to range over slightly more than half the page. Looking at the 50 spreads, just over a quarter and considerably less than a third of the potentially available text area is used.

    The overall impression created by this white space, flicking through the book, is one of prestige, since it is only important, expensive books which can afford to include large measures of blank space at the openings of chapters (always, for example, opening a section on the recto page). This impression is increased by the 12 Van Sambeek illustrations, eight of which occupy recto pages and four of which are given full spreads to themselves. Yet when we start to read the text, the effect is somewhat different. Though there is clearly room to say much more, the short lines, often imparting only a single word, show the text stretched thin. It might be argued that the layout of the text looks like poetry (if not for those quotation marks) and invites us to read it as such. Yet the self-confession of the text as a story, or history (6), does not really support this. The reader is challenged to react to and reflect upon the presentation of a narrative accompanied by so much empty space.

Nick Frankel (2000), writing about James McNeill Whistler's *sui generis* book *The Gentle Art of Making Enemies* (1890), notes how asymmetrically placed paragraphs, often of quoted critical sources, float vulnerably on pages where they are sniped at by Whistler's cutting (printed) marginal commentary. A sense of vulnerability hangs over the narrative of *The Fifty Year Sword*, too. Where does this impression come from?

Derrida's *Dissemination* (1981) engages with several French texts which utilise white space in unconventional ways and, while discussing Mallarmé's radically laid-out poem Un coup de dés, Derrida makes the following point about white space in general: 'the "blank" marks everything white [*blanc*] ... *plus* the blankness that allows for the mark in the first place, guaranteeing its space of reception and production' (1981: 253). The French connection of white (*blanc*) and 'blank' allows Derrida to show the integral role of paper and its colour in printed text, a role performed whether or not the text in question arranges print in new or in traditional ways. The significance of this observation is in the way that it lets us see the extraordinary complexity of the exchange (reading) that print on paper allows; the creation of something out of nothing as, by the addition of a few words, the meaning of a page is dramatically altered. Dealing with Phillippe Sollers' experimental novel *Numbers*, Derrida argues that: 'The whiteness of the virgin paper, the blankness of the transparent column, reveals more than the neutrality of some medium; it uncovers the space of play or the play of space in which transformations are set off and sequences strung out' (1981: 345). By making a point of the white space, by rejecting the conventional, pragmatic way of filling it with as much text as is easily readable, *Numbers* (and by extension *The Fifty Year Sword*) shows us that 'what is said or written ... is already the performing of a cut within a graphic substance that retains and distorts traces of all sorts: forms, sketches, colors, half-silent ideograms and spoken words, etc.' (1981: 339). Though no one has to cut open (separate) book pages any longer, the expanses of white space mean that idea of the cut threatens the narrative of *The Fifty Year Sword*.

In Reif Larsen's *The Selected Works of T. S. Spivet* (2009), a novel with wide margins in which illustrations and observations related to the central narrative are regularly offered, the precocious

12-year-old narrator reads the contents of a handwritten notebook, which are rendered as if printed in the nineteenth century. A long gap between sections is noted by a dotted line and linked to an aside where T. S. notes: 'Here there was a break in the text, and the white space made me suddenly remember that it was my mother who had been writing all of this, that it had not simply happened' (2009: 237). The gap has reminded him of the author and her fiction. This is a fictional description of the reader's consideration of attribution, which we have already discussed at length. Why should white space make us, like T. S. Spivet, think of this? The most spacious pages in most novels are the title pages and the beginnings and endings of sections and chapters. Such expanses of space are only the refocusing of the paragraph break writ large but they are so often associated with attributing authorship that this may even be a learned response. When there is an excess of space that is without a conventional explanation, as in *The Fifty Year Sword*, the effect is disruptive.

According to Brian McHale: 'Against [the] background convention of a page of solid print . . . the introduction of blank space has the effect of foregrounding the presence and materiality of the book, and disrupting the reality of the fictional world' (1997: 181). This is a good explanation of what Larsen has Spivet experience and even suggests why Derrida's language of the cut and the mark is so violent; without content the graphic mark only sullies the page. McHale also describes the relationship between print and content as a cut: 'A major ontological "cut" divides the book as real, material object from the text as intentional object' (1997: 180). He goes on to argue that in William H. Gass' *Willie Masters' Lonesome Wife* (1968) 'the reality of the fictional character is constantly jeopardized and undermined by the book's insistence on its own reality: its distractingly coloured pages and distorted typography' (1997: 180). This reading might easily be extended to *The Fifty Year Sword* which, with virtually every line reminding us of its quoted nature and white space prompting questions about attribution, seems intent on maintaining what McHale calls 'ontological hesitation' (184) or 'flicker' (187). There are risks for texts that do this as McHale tells us: 'never losing sight of the ontological "cut" between the projected world and the material book . . . can be annoying . . . but even annoyance can become a device of foregrounding' (1997: 192). The possibility of irritation in texts that utilise the graphic surface in unconventional ways reminds us of a familiar (rather outmoded) accusation: that such texts mark themselves as not novels (or stories) in the traditional sense at all.

V. Immersion in the postmodern

Though critical fingers can easily be pointed at what is different about postmodern literature when it uses unconventional page design, as Danielewski consistently does, what is supposedly missing in such literature is rarely theorised. Marie-Laure Ryan's *Narrative as Virtual Reality: Immersion and Interactivity in Literature and Electronic Media* (2001) supplies this gap. The key term is 'immersion' which Ryan defines as the creation of emotional intimacy with fictional characters and the collapse of awareness of the real/fictional distinction. Immersion in a narrative requires comfort and familiarity since: 'We can no more observe the stages of our immersion than we can watch ourselves falling asleep. It is only retrospectively, like a person awakening from a dream, that the reader realizes that the virtual has come to be experienced as primary reality' (Ryan 2001: 170–171). Ryan does not specifically address texts that foreground page design but argues more broadly for recognition of the value of immersion in contemporary/postmodern literary fiction. Danielewski's novels and *The Fifty Year Sword* would be placed among those works which replace immersion with textual play in what Ryan describes as 'text as game'. This, she argues, is a literary response to poststructuralist theory that shows us language itself is a game without purchase on reality (2001: 187).

Extending the argument, Ryan attempts to oppose text as game and immersive texts as conflicting approaches:

> The text as game metaphor is esoteric and elitist; readers need literary competence to appreciate the text . . . Text as world is a much more populist conception. All the reader needs to gain access to the fictional world is a basic knowledge of language, life experience and reasonable cultural competence. If there are rules to be learned in order to navigate the textual world, these rules can be learned on the fly. (Ryan 2001: 195)

The division of fiction posited here is too hard and fast. I have argued elsewhere (White 2005: 13–22, 38, 57–58) that interpreting complex literary fictions requires a model of a determined and adaptable reader. If we are to address the reader's competences then we need to consider several overlapping levels, all of them learned:

1. Reading competence.
2. Competence reading fiction.
3a. Competence with a particular genre of fiction (including the genre of literary fiction).
3b. Competence that may be required by a certain author.
4. Text-specific competence.

It is only at level 4 that the text as game may become an obstacle. Some games might be more conducive to a given reader than others, just as for other readers picaresque narratives, sagas with great numbers of characters or elaborate fantasy settings may not be easily absorbed. The point is that to navigate any individual text we have to learn the rules that allow us to enter into the world *or* the game. Unless the text comes with an instruction manual these rules must always 'be learned on the fly'. Ryan makes an excellent observation that 'it takes much more time to read the first fifty than the last fifty pages of a traditional narrative, because during those first fifty pages the reader must construct character, setting and motivations, while in the last fifty pages she can harvest the fruit of this labor' (167). This is, I would argue, equally true of the non-traditional text as game (and, rather neatly, applies to the hundred pages of *The Fifty Year Sword*).

Ryan explicitly identifies two influential critics who have written about the game/world split in literary texts: McHale (see Ryan 2001: 198), who is happy to positively categorise texts that expose their nature as 'world-making machines' as postmodern fictions (McHale 1997: 196), and Roland Barthes, whose earlier model of readerly and writerly texts (1975: 4) gives a sense of 'text as world' and 'text as game'. Ryan (2001: 195–196) argues for a reversal of current critical preference for non-immersive texts. The extreme pole of 'text as game' is invoked as a theoretical whipping boy (2001: 350) as if it were the ultimate aim of postmodern writing which is perceived to be dominating literary studies. In fact, Ryan is overstating her case for effect and, in practice, is willing to acknowledge that the meeting of text as game and text as world may be subtle, and appeal to readers who enjoy 'the intellectual delight of playing a game of in and out between a world-internal and a world-external, medium-conscious stance' (2001: 353). Ryan suggests 'The best compromise of all is simply to regard the concepts of game and world as complementary points of view on the same object, much in the way modern physics uses the metaphors of wave and particle as alternative conceptualizations of light' (2001: 199). Yet while Ryan recognises that text as game is not 'radically incompatible with immersion' (352), and the two approaches should not be mutually exclusive in the same text, she maintains that

> because an observer cannot simultaneously occupy two different points in space, the complementarity of the two metaphors ... means that we cannot experience both dimensions at the same time. We must therefore immerse and deimmerse ourselves periodically in order to fulfil, and fully appreciate, our dual role as members of the textual world and players of the textual game. (2001: 199)

The implication that readers need to be consciously immersing and deimmersing sits awkwardly. Ryan effectively demonstrates that Italo Calvino's *If on a Winter's Night a Traveller* (1979) is 'a tale of frustrated immersion' (2001: 168), but that novel's most striking effect is that even when we have understood that the novel's titled chapters lead us nowhere we are still capable of becoming immersed in them. Calvino's exemplary postmodern text demonstrates that our role as readers is both dual and radically disjunctive; but also shows that joining a textual world, even an immersive one, is always joining in a game. In highlighting frustrated immersion in postmodern writing, much as McHale (1997) focuses on ontological shifts, Ryan is emphasising postmodern literature's rejection of traditional narrative at the expense of recognising what it retains (and indeed what it cannot do without).

Larsen's T. S. Spivet seems to have the right idea about reading. Through questioning the nature of the narrative he is reading he finds that: 'Though the unstable verifiability of the narrative made me nervous it also kept me turning the page. I was hooked on believing and not believing. Maybe I was becoming an adult' (2009: 237). My intention here is to point out that the simultaneous awareness of text as game *and* world is a positive and mature response to reading. To reduce texts, critically, to one or the other will invariably do them a disservice.

VI. Conclusion

How does this play out in relation to this essay's title? Even *The Fifty Year Sword* with what appears to be a schematic game orientation offers the possibility of a kind of immersion as we get used to, and therefore less mindful of, its idiosyncracies. *The Fifty Year Sword*'s graphic devices certainly are not geared towards reader immersion as they are in, for example, B. S. Johnson's novels featuring internal monologue (see Barton 2008), Alasdair Gray's *1982, Janine* (1984), or even Larsen's first-person novel about an obsessive mapmaker. *The Fifty Year Sword*'s devices are focused on engaging the reader with the content at a *thematic* level. This certainly makes it more recognisably a text as game rather than a text as world, but in practice the game played is a referential one, using a relatively traditional critical approach to unify design and narrative.

The narration and design of *The Fifty Year Sword* give it a particular texture: the texture of fabric(ation). Meanwhile, throughout, the content thematises the idea of the cut. It is there in what happens, from Chintana's accident to Belinda's injury, in what is said, such as Chintana's joke that the caterer offering the orphans cake ""'could lose a hand'"" (28), in Chintana's thoughts, such as ""Crossing up with a ghost, thought Chintana, was about the only thing that would keep her from cutting her appearance short" (14), and in the narration of her feelings: "she felt bleak,/ "as if a thousand vengeances upon vengeances were dicing her suddenly / "into hail." (34). The uncanny Story Teller ignores ""'ropes, knives, poisons, explosives and guns" (44) for swords that will allow him to cut and to kill. The Fifty Year Sword itself is an invisible/imaginary blade that menaces the orphans (82) before being seized by Belinda Kite who dismisses story and Story Teller (84) and

> "to further substantiate her claim,
> "proceeded to swing, and
> "to no effect
> "stab, gash, cross,
> "flay, chop, slash,
> "cube, pare, lop,
> "perforate, puncture, slit,
> "pierce, sunder, and jab the
> "handle
> "at herself, all over. (84)

This theme of cutting builds up to the climax of the narrative which is delivered to the reader in a new section (large quotation mark on 94) as an essentially cinematic cut to the orphans' point of view: "''From their window [they] were the first to see the snow / "splash / "red." The illustration on pages 96–97 gives us another angle on this scene, using the same blue as the other images but introducing red for seven drops of blood as Chintana embraces the injured Belinda Kite (the hand to be injured is first seen in the illustration on 16–17).

What has happened in the narrative? Have Belinda's self-inflicted cuts with the insubstantial Fifty Year Sword become real at the stroke of midnight, the hour of her birth 50 years ago? Or is there a less uncanny, but no less disturbing, explanation? Has Chintana, conditioned by her own accidental wound, the Story Teller's tale and her need for revenge, then provoked by Belinda's taunt "''Baby, your hubby was a lousy fuck'" (94), lashed out violently? Different choices put different inflections upon the last lines: "she also continued to wonder / "just how long one tiny stitch of, / "well you know, // "could really hold."'" Is the missing word 'restraint' referring to Chintana's ability to rein in her anger? Is it 'flesh' (perhaps cued by the pink closing quotation mark) as we await the total dissolution of Belinda Kite? Or, if we choose to interpret by remaining outside the text as world, is the missing word 'narrative'?

The Fifty Year Sword weaves its five threads of narration into a pattern designed to deliver a climax as cryptic as the origins of the Story Teller's hate. This is a text that uses graphic means to highlight its narrative's fragility, its intertextuality and its end. The last line, which is given a virtually blank spread to itself, hangs – like the sword of Damocles – by a thread. Yet identifying the thematic payoff of design and narrative does not exhaust the text: 'Writing does not simply weave several threads into a single term in such a way that one might end up unravelling all the "contents" just by pulling a few strings' (Derrida 1981: 350). We are left grasping for meaning at the end of this writerly ghost tale, a postmodern take on a genre that thrives on ambivalence and narrative sleight of hand. We may or may not be disturbed by the ghostly, impossible presences within *The Fifty Year Sword* or hooked by the arcane and unique methods they have been conjured by, but if we cannot see them, or refuse to believe in them, then it is our loss.

Note

I would like to thank Simon Barton for assistance with this essay.

Works cited

Barthes, R. (1975) *S/Z*, trans. R. Miller, London: Jonathan Cape.
Barton, S. (2008) 'Measuring silence: textual gaps in the works of B. S. Johnson', in *Proceedings of the Salford Postgraduate Annual Research Conference*, Salford: University of Salford.
Buse, P. and Stott, A. (1999) *Ghosts: Deconstruction, Psychoanalysis, History*, Basingstoke: Macmillan.
Danielewski, M. Z. (2006) *The Fifty Year Sword*, Amsterdam: De Bezige Bij.
Derrida, J. (1981) *Dissemination*, trans. B. Johnson, Chicago: University of Chicago Press.
Frankel, N. (2000) 'The meaning of margin: white space and disagreement in Whistler's *The Gentle Art of Making Enemies*', in Bray, J., Handley, M. and Henry, A. C. (eds) *Ma(r)king the Text: The Presentation of Meaning on the Literary Page*, Aldershot: Ashgate, pp. 87–104.
James, M. R. (1992) *Collected Ghost Stories*, Ware: Wordsworth Classics.
Larsen, R. (2009) *The Selected Works of T. S. Spivet*, London: Harvill Secker.
Le Fanu, J. S. (1994) *Madame Crowl's Ghost and Other Stories*, Ware: Wordsworth Classics.
McHale, B. (1997) *Postmodernist Fiction*, London: Routledge.
Ryan, M-L. (2001) *Narrative as Virtual Reality: Immersion and Interactivity in Literature and Electronic Media*, Baltimore: The Johns Hopkins University Press.
White, G. (2005) *Reading the Graphic Surface: The Presence of the Book in Prose Fiction*, Manchester: Manchester University Press.

III

Only Revolutions

7

Only evolutions: Joyce's and Danielewski's works in progress

Dirk Van Hulle, University of Antwerp

Whereas Mark Z. Danielewski's *House of Leaves* already showed several correspondences with James Joyce's *Finnegans Wake*, *Only Revolutions* seems even more explicitly related to Joyce's last work. Even the title can be read as a succinct summary of *Finnegans Wake*'s circular structure. With regard to structural aspects, however, circularity is only one of several, more complex structures in both these 'works in progress'. At the same time, on a meta-level, the matter of circularity revolves around the notion of what the situationists called *récupération*, etymologically derived from the Latin *re-capere*, to take again. Based on the examination of structural differences and correspondences, the research hypothesis of the present essay is that *Only Revolutions* is less successful as a *récupération* of *Finnegans Wake*, than as a cunning *détournement* of the situationists' 'revolutionary orientation'.

I. *récupération* versus *détournement*

The term *récupération* was coined by the Situationist International, a French experimental avant-garde group. In 1957, at a convention in Cosio d'Arroscia in Italy, delegates from several avant-garde groups, such as the Lettrist International, the International Movement for an Imaginist Bauhaus and the London Psychogeographical Committee, joined forces in what they decided to call the Situationist International. In their magazine, *Internationale Situationniste*, they developed a critique of art and society, based on Dadaism, Surrealism and modernist architecture, which Edward Ball characterizes as follows: 'From the Dadaist vanguard of the teens and twenties they took an urge to destroy art; from the surrealists, an aim to reconstitute it at the level of everyday life. From modernism in architecture they developed a utopian urbanism, in part derived from the Bauhaus, but superseding it in an effort to widen its formalist and populist tendencies into a general political study of urban space. Out of these three positions, the S.I. developed a kind of phenomenology of urban life' (Ball 1987: 24). By construing situations, the group tried to examine the effects of urban geography on the minds of individual human beings. On the basis of their psychogeographical findings, the situationists suggested a revolution resulting in a better society which would fulfil people's 'real' needs, as opposed to the needs imposed on them by consumer society.

One of the situationists' 'tools' was the so-called *détournement*, or the reuse of pre-existing artistic materials with a double aim: to destroy existing art by ignoring its present value and to reuse it as a tool for their own purposes. *Détournement* is defined as 'le réemploi dans une nouvelle unité d'éléments artistiques préexistants' ('the reuse of preexisting artistic elements in a new ensemble') according to two laws: 'The two fundamental laws of *détournement* are the loss of importance of each detourned autonomous element – which may go so far as to completely lose its original sense – and at the same time the organization of another meaningful ensemble that confers on each element its new scope and effect' (Knabb 2006; originally published as 'Le détournement comme négation et comme prélude' in the third issue of *Internationale Situationniste* (Paris, December 1959)). In 1956, Guy Debord and Gil J. Wolman wrote a 'users' guide' in which they stressed the revolutionary nature and aim of this technique:

> The literary and artistic heritage of humanity should be used for partisan propaganda purposes. It is, of course, necessary to go beyond any idea of mere scandal. Since opposition to the bourgeois notion of art and artistic genius has become pretty much old hat, [Marcel Duchamp's] drawing of a mustache on the Mona Lisa is no more interesting than the original version of that painting. We must now push this process to the point of negating the negation. Bertolt Brecht, revealing in a recent interview in France-Observateur that he makes cuts in the classics of the theater in order to make the performances more educative, is much closer than Duchamp to the *revolutionary orientation* we are calling for. (Knabb 2006; originally published as 'Mode d'emploi du détournement' in the Belgian surrealist journal *Les Lèvres Nues* 8 (May 1956)).

Guy Debord illustrated this use of *détournement* in *La Société du Spectacle*: 'Les idées s'améliorent. Le sens des mots y participe.

Le plagiat est nécessaire. Le progrès l'implique. Il serre de près la phrase d'un auteur, se sert de ses expressions, efface une idée fausse, la remplace par l'idée juste.' ('Ideas improve. The meaning of words participates in the improvement. Plagiarism is necessary. Progress implies it. It embraces an author's phrase, makes use of his expressions, erases a false idea, and replaces it with the right idea.') (Debord 1967: 207). This statement not only formulates the idea behind *détournement*, but 'performs' it, since the statement itself is a *détournement* in the form of a literal re-employment of a passage from the Comte de Lautréamont's *Poésies II*: 'Le plagiat est nécessaire. Le progrès l'implique. Il serre de près la phrase d'un auteur, se sert de ses expressions, efface une idée fausse, la remplace par l'idée juste.' ('Plagiarism is necessary. Progress implies it. It embraces an author's phrase, makes use of his expressions, erases a false idea, and replaces it with the right idea.') (Lautréamont 1870: 6). If Debord's version of this statement is a *détournement*, it presupposes a different conception of 'progress' since the derailment or turnabout of existing materials in a new work implies a different message and a so-called 'revolutionary orientation'.

This 'revolutionary' manner of reusing the art of the past in order to serve present purposes, however, is not to be confused with that other situationist notion, referred to as *récupération*. The notion of 'récupération' is sometimes translated as 'cooption', because the most common meanings of the English verb 'to recuperate' are to return or restore to health and to recover from financial loss. An alternative translation is 'appropriation', in the sense of an appropriation of originally subversive ideas by the mainstream. In preparation for the 1957 convention, Debord wrote a 'Report on the Construction of Situations' in which he analysed the 'bourgeoisie in its period of decline' and noted that one of its paradoxical characteristics is that it usually resists artistic creations when they first appear, but subsequently exploits them. For instance, the Dadaists and Surrealists were rejected at the moment they made their artistic creations, but they were 'rediscovered' by the 'bourgeois' establishment as soon as it had found a way to 'exploit' them, for instance by buying avant-garde works and selling them at a huge profit or by exhibiting them in museums of fine arts. The worst form of exploitation, however, was *récupération*, because it turned Dadaist anti-art into harmless neo-Dadaism. Avant-garde was thus diverted into decorative, marketable 'spectacles' by means of these reactionary 'mécanismes spectaculaires autonomes' ('autonomous spectacular mechanisms'), as it was formulated in the essay 'Domination de la Nature, Idéologies et Classes', in the eighth issue of *Internationale Situationniste* (Paris, January 1963). The essay opens with the sentence: 'The human appropriation of nature is the real adventure we have embarked on.' According to the situationists, 'the very core of the revolutionary project' is the possibility of replacing work with a new type of free activity – a possibility that was opened up 'by the domination of nature' (Knabb 2006).

To explain this mechanism of *récupération*, the situationists compared it to Darwin's theory of evolution and the Spencerian principle of the 'survival of the fittest'. In 'Domination de la Nature, Idéologies et Classes', published in the eighth issue of *Internationale Situationniste* (January 1963) the process of appropriation was described as follows: 'Ainsi, sur la bohême, la bourgeoisie a fait son darwinisme, applaudissant les valeurs sélectionnées qui entrent dans son paradis quantitative.' ('Invoking a sort of aesthetic Darwinism, the bourgeoisie applauds the bohemian values that have proved fit enough to survive and enter into its quantitative paradise.'). The problem with this situationist analogy with Darwin's theory of evolution, however, is the opinion that the history of ideas implies 'progress' (as suggested in Debord's *détournement* of Lautréamont's passage on progress quoted above). On the one hand the mechanism of *récupération*, based on (the rather reductive situationist interpretation of) Darwin's theory, is rejected; on the other hand the idea that 'ideas ameliorate' is said to be implied by 'progress' (*le progrès*). The resulting tension indicates the problematical and apparently quite arbitrary nature of the situationists' distinction between *détournement* and *récupération*, which depended on the (respectively situationist or non-situationist) intention of the re-employment. This tension raises the question how Darwin's theory of evolution relates on the one hand to what the situationists regarded as laudable 'progress' and on the other hand to what they loathed as bourgeois *récupération* in terms of the survival of the fittest.

To investigate this question with a view to assessing the 'revolutionary' nature of *Only Revolutions*, a useful point of reference is James Joyce, whose 'work in progress' playfully refers to the 'sowiveall of the prettiest' (Joyce 1975: 145). By way of a working definition, the notion of *détournement* will be used in the present essay in the sense of the reuse or derailment of existing ideas to create a new work with a deviating message, in contrast with the notion of *récupération* as the mainstream reappropriation of originally subversive ideas.

II. Circular

One of these originally subversive ideas was Joyce's way of problematising both the traditional teleology of linear narratives and the notion of 'progress' in general, notably by means of *Finnegans Wake*'s circular structure. 'Remounting aliftle towards the ouragan of spaces' (Joyce 1975: 504) Joyce introduces Darwin's *On the Origin of Species* in connection with the 'tree of life', intentionally confused with the biblical tree of knowledge. In reply to the question '[j]ust how grand in cardinal rounders is this preeminent giant' (i.e. the tree), the answer goes as follows:

> Your Ominence, Your Imminence and delicted fraternitrees! There's tuodore queensmaids and Idahore shopgirls and their woody babies growing upon her ... and culprines of Erasmus Smith's burstall boys with their underhand leadpencils climbing to her crotch for the origin of spices and charlotte darlings ... and cock robins muchmore hatching most out of his missado eggdrazzles. (Joyce 1975: 504)

These 'eggdrazzles' allude to the same Yggdrasil from Norwegian mythology, mentioned on the last page of *House of Leaves*: '• / Ygg/ d/r/a/s/i/l / What miracle is this? This giant tree. / It stands ten thousand feet high / But doesn't reach the ground. Still it stands. / Its roots must hold the sky. / **O**' (Danielewski 2000: 709). Joyce's fusion of the Yggdrasil, the biblical tree of knowledge and the Darwinian tree of life suggests an interchange between one idea (creation) and another (evolution) – '*For Ark see Zoo*' (Joyce 1975: 104) – without however implying the replacement suggested by the situationists: Joyce does *not* 'efface une idée fausse, la remplace par l'idée juste' ('erases a false idea, and replaces it with the right idea'); he rather makes them coincide. To some extent one could argue that he applies a form of 'détournement', recycling words from hundreds of source texts; this *détournement* also implies a turn or twist. For instance, Darwin's words are twisted into the 'ouragan of spaces' (Joyce 1975: 504) or the 'origin of spices and charlotte darlings' (Joyce 1975: 504). Joyce starts with a 'species', which gradually evolves into two slightly different ones: 'spaces' and 'spices'. Joyce is not looking for an Adamic language; instead, he makes language perform its own evolution and thus creates 'logodiversity' or literary 'biodiversity'. In that sense, Samuel Beckett certainly had a point when he referred to 'Mr Joyce' as a 'biologist in words' (Beckett 1984: 31).

In the section on the Ondt and the Gracehoper, for instance, he fills the fable with names of insects in different languages. In a way, he partly performs the Adamic task of giving names to all creatures. The passage in Genesis 2:19, recounting how 'Adam gave names to all cattle', is retold in Wakese: 'he had put his own nickelname on every toad, duck, and herring before the climber clomb aloft, doing the midhill of their park, flattering his bitter hoolft with her conconundrums' (Joyce 1975: 506). This is where Joyce is at his best: the matter of language. But there is a difference from Adam's task. Joyce does not simply give new names to things; he rather turns the process around. He starts off with names and turns them back into what they stand for.

A similar mechanism is applied in the chapter on Anna Livia Plurabelle, full of river names. Here, the names of rivers are used, not to 'contain' the water they designate, but to become the particles out of which a river is made, that is, to make the words 'perform' what they stand for. In the last part of *Finnegans Wake*, this technique is used again, when Anna Livia Plurabelle flows into the sea. One of the source texts on which this passage is based is Fritz Mauthner's *Beiträge zu einer Kritik der Sprache*. In the introduction to this work, Mauthner refers to Heraclitus, claiming that the old Greek aphorism that 'one cannot bathe twice in the same river' also applies to language, since its words and forms have changed continuously (Mauthner 1923: I.7). Joyce jotted down in one of his *Finngans Wake* notebooks (VI.B.46, page 15): 'not bathe twice in / same R'. And a bit further in the same notebook (page 50): 'Δ name for Poddle / name of bed.'[1] In the published text of *Finnegans Wake*, this became 'a poddlebridges in a passabed' (Joyce 1975: 600), part of the description of Anna Livia as a 'Polycarp pool, the pool of Innalavia, . . . wherein once we lave 'tis alve and vale, . . . a poddlebridges in a passabed, the river of lives' (Joyce 1975: 600).

The Heraclitean idea that everything flows and Joyce's favourite metaphor of the river are contained in the *Wake*'s opening lines: 'riverrun, past Eve and Adam's, from swerve of shore to bend of bay, brings us by a commodius vicus of recirculation back to

Howth Castle and Environs' (Joyce 1975: 3). Page H4² of Mark Z. Danielewski's *Only Revolutions* opens with the words 'Bend by bend I lead every curve / blossomingly' (H4). On the same page (upside down), Sam's text (S357) mentions 'swerves of Peace'. Whether or not these bends and swerves are direct allusions to *Finnegans Wake* and its 'commodius vicus', the latter's circular structure, based on Giambattista Vico's cyclical view of history, sheds an interesting light on Danielewski's treatment of time in *Only Revolutions*.

Both the time indications and 'THE CREEP' are printed in purple ink, suggesting the possibility that the creep is time, which Sam and Hailey try to outrun. But no matter how creepy the chase may become, in the end there is always the pause button – or what looks like a pause button – in front of / at the end of each version of the story and marking the 'beginning' and the 'end' of the novel, while at the same time emphasising its endlessness.

Time in *Only Revolutions* is divided into two periods (22 November 1863 – 22 November 1963 and 22 November 1963 – 19 January 2063). The word 'period', etymologically derived from the Greek *periodos* (cycle), from *peri* (around) and *odos* (way), can also mean 'full stop' and in that sense *Finnegans Wake* famously ends without a period. The line 'A way a lone a last a loved a long the' is not followed by a full stop. After having finished his novel with a periodless 'the', Joyce interestingly started adding periods after the word 'the' elsewhere in the text. For instance, 'who oped it closeth thereof the. Dor' (Joyce 1975: 20) or 'what hopped it dunneth there duft the. Duras.' (Joyce 1975: 334). The period between 'the' and 'Dor' was added by Joyce in 1936, during his revision of the *transition* 1 pages for the printer. Though this procedure of adding periods after definite articles may seem strange, there is method in it, for each time a door is being closed. Thus the closing of a door is always simultaneously presented as a potential opening. The door needs to be closed in order to be able to be opened again. Even after the publication of the first edition, by means of the list of errata, Joyce added a period after this definite article: 'the. Lukkedoerendunandurraskewdylooshoofermoyporter toryzooysphalnabortansporthaokansakroidverjkapakkapuk' (Joyce 1975: 257.27-28). This 100-letter combination of the phrase 'Shut the door' in several languages is one of the so-called thunderwords, marking the Fall and at the same time the beginning of everything. One other definite article followed by a period emphasises that link between the Fall and the closing / opening of the door: 'Of manifest 'tis obedience and the. Flute!' (Joyce 1975: 343) – Joyce's *détournement* of 'Of Man's First Disobedience, and the Fruit / Of that Forbidden Tree, whose mortal taste / Brought Death into the World', the opening lines of Milton's *Paradise Lost*.

In *Only Revolutions*, a similar insertion of 'periods' marks the top margins, referring to the cinematic technique of movie projection. The upper right corner of one in 20 (two times five pairs) pages features a dot, which resembles the changeover cues marking the end of a reel in movie projection. The first dot of each pair marks the end of the reel, signalling to the technician operating the projector to prepare the next reel. The second dot indicates the time of the moment of the changeover between two reels (Goulekas 2001: 72). In *Only Revolutions*, this cinematic detail is functionally applied to structure the narrative. For instance, page(s) 67 feature a first cue in the upper right corner. The text on these pages does not indicate any obvious narrative turn, but the reader is warned that a change is imminent, and indeed four pages further on (S71: 'I slow. Pull over.' / H71: 'He slows. Pull over.') the text prepares the next 'reel'. The actual changeover takes place on page 73, where the new location is made explicit (S73: 'New Orleans! My town!' / H73: 'LZ New Orleans!'). In this way, the book can be divided into five chapters: Chapter 1 (1–72): The Mountain, on the road; Chapter 2 (73–144): New Orleans; Chapter 3 (145–216): St Louis; Chapter 4 (217–288): leaving St Louis; Chapter 5 (289–360): Marriage and the Mountain.

Page 355, with a dot in the upper right corner announcing the changeover cue, alludes to *Finnegans Wake*'s 'bend of bay' again, announcing the imminent 'pause' button (359), the final changeover cue: 'What bending she allways resolves. / What evolving she allways ends.' (S355); 'What resolving he allways bends. / What ending he allways evolves.' (H355).

Implicitly, the changeover cues turn the readers into projector operators. The typography invites the reader to play an active role in the story, as in Danielewski's previous works – for instance when in *House of Leaves* the act of reading and turning the pages becomes functional in the narrative: the reader performs the function of doorslammer and the pace of turning the (almost blank) pages increases, to match the increasing pace at which the doors are closing. The reader is invited to imitate the content in an almost childlike way when 'all those doors // behind // the man // are slamming shut,

// one // after // another // after // another.' (Danielewski 2000: 216–225). In this way, Danielewski gives a whole new meaning to the notion of a page turner. Moreover, by reading or 'projecting' more into the story than what the text says, the reader turns the house into a *House of Leaves*, a text that is bigger than what is printed on its pages. What may seem like a gratuitous game at first sight, can be read as the process of creating meaning in terms of what Linda Hutcheon called 'process mimesis'. Unlike 'product mimesis' this form of 'process mimesis' implies a higher degree of engagement from the readers, because they are given the chance to participate in the creative process as a witness of the way in which the book analyses itself (Hutcheon 1984: 9). Before even realising it properly, the reader unwittingly speeds up the narrative pace and becomes the one who shuts the. Door – to paraphrase *Finnegans Wake*. In a similar way, the readers of *Only Revolutions* are involuntarily made into projector operators, fully aware of the act of projecting (while reading), actively involved in dividing the book into five chapters (according to the traditional structure of a tragedy) and making the changeover to a new reel, cycle or *periodos*, right on cue.

III. Hexagonal

Joyce's last work was called 'Work in Progress' by Ford Madox Ford, but the circular structure of his book undermines the notion of progress. In a similar way, the title of Danielewski's book seems to imply that evolution does not imply progress, only revolutions. As the author of the theory of evolution, Charles Darwin was preoccupied throughout his career with the question whether evolution implies progress. Robert J. Richards suggests that 'Darwin embedded his developing theory of natural selection in a decidedly progressivist and teleological framework, a framework quite obvious when one examines the initial construction of his theory.' (Richards 2009: 54). According to Dov Ospovat 'the explanation of progress was a persistent problem for Darwin from 1838 on' (1981: 214),[3] but Ospovat also draws attention to moments in Darwin's notebooks when he suggests that degradation is always possible.[4] In his notebook E, for instance, he expresses his intention to try and formulate a law of progressive tendency, but he immediately reminds himself that evolution does not necessarily imply progress and draws attention to the 'non-necessity of the so-called progressive tendency law' (notebook E, page 70; Darwin 1987: 415). Moreover, especially in the transmutation notebooks, Darwin shows himself extremely aware of the relativity of the notion of 'progress'. What human beings call progress may be perceived in a totally different way by other species. For instance, in the first so-called transmutation notebook (notebook B: 74), he notes: 'It is absurd to talk of one animal being higher than another. We consider those, where the cerebral structure, intellectual faculties, most developed, as highest. – A bee doubtless would whe[re] the instincts were' (Darwin 1987: 189).

Darwin chooses the bee as an example to indict any form of anthropocentrism. His admiration of the bees' qualities and accomplishments also shows at several instances in *On the Origin of Species*, for instance when he mentions that 'a large store of honey is indispensible to support a large stock of bees during the winter' (1859: 93). In Danielewski's *Only Revolutions*, bees also play a more important role than any of the numerous other species mentioned throughout the book (apart from 'US'), and Sam and Hailey consume only honey (S/H42). After finding the 12 jars of honey (42) the supply gradually dwindles. Whenever the honey is mentioned again, the supply has diminished by a jar: 8½ by page 123, 7½ by page 152, 6½ by page 180, 5½ on page 181, 4½ on page 209, 3½ on page 238. Hailey finds out she is allergic to bee pollen and is given the advice to avoid bees, but '*Honey's fine*' (H117); what is more, honey is necessary: '*Honey you need*' (S117). When the honey is consumed, both Sam and Hailey recognise its power: 'It's the HONEY. All along. By it I succeed. Without it I retreat. Begin to freeze.' (H353); 'It's the HONEY. All along. By it I thrive. Without it I recede. Start to die.' (S353).

In *On the Origin of Species* Charles Darwin particularly admires the way hive-bees 'make their cells of the proper shape to hold the greatest possible amount of honey' (1859: 248), and he assesses the difficulty of this special skill by comparing it to human activities: 'a skilful workman, with fitting tools and measures, would find it very difficult to make cells of wax of the true form, though this is perfectly effected by a crowd of bees working in a dark hive' (224). Darwin describes the hive-bees' cells as 'an hexagonal prism, with the basal edges of its six sides bevelled so as to join on to a pyramid, formed of three rhombs' (225). Whereas the bees keep their honey in hexagonal cells, each of the protagonists in *Only Revolutions* has six jars of honey. The form, containing this content, is materialised in 360 pages, each of which consists of $6 \times 6 = 36$ lines of text.

With the exception of 'US' the bee seems to be the only creature that is still alive toward the 'closing' pages of the book, for all other fauna and flora have been extinguished typographically. The symbolic presence of the bee (as the only creature whose name is homophonous with the most existential verb in the English language) seems to mark the notion of rebirth, especially when the natural environment's 'renaissance' is announced by means of 'explosions of **Roughlegged Hawks, Mallards** and **Crows**' (H357) and 'explosions of **Aster, Yarrow, Buttercups** and **Clover**' (S357), introducing flora after the extinction of fauna in the ark or zoo that is Sam's part of the novel. Not unlike Joyce's technique of creating literary biodiversity by means of inserting hundreds of insect names in a creation 'writing its own wrunes [runes/ruins] for ever' (Joyce 1975: 19), Danielewski both introduces and sends off various species – '**Wild Boars** grow up around our trestle' (S133), 'and **Wild Boars** die too' (S228). Thus, 'thousands of **Honey Bees**' (S40) are also introduced, after which Sam and Hailey find one dozen jars of honey (S/H42); later on a beehive is gassed with pesticide / Zyklon mist (S/H175); and eventually 'a **Bee** . . . ends *its* life' (S321) by stinging Sam (to death?): 'But O what a sting! Now? Me? Over with?' (S322). The next page starts with the word 'Wake?' (S323). The corresponding page in Hailey's part (after her fall, H321) opens with 'Hit? / But softly', recalling Anna Livia Plurabelle's moving end on the *Wake*'s last page: 'Finn again! Take. Bussoftlhee, mememormee!' – echoing in its turn Dido's moving 'Remember me' in Purcell's *Dido and Aeneas*.[5]

Throughout the story Hailey's allergy to pollen is linked with her aversion to another form of organic seed. Since Sam promises to '*allways only come outside*' (S/H48), Hailey's aversion to semen is matched by his conscious decision not to reproduce. Nonetheless, they wish to marry or '*to get circled*' (S256), and in order to do so they have to assert themselves against the insinuations that they may be '*unfit*' – as the District Clerk suggests (H256). During the second encounter with the Creep, they proclaim themselves 'fit beyond fitness' (S/H276). Finally, Sam and Hailey manage to get married (S/H297) and when they have reached the mountain (S/H312) and the climax ('*I'm coming*' (S313) / '*I'm becoming*' (H313)), Sam does not '*pull out*' (H314), which implies at least the willingness to reproduce. They thus make a choice that is potentially advantageous to the continuation of the species. Evolution by natural selection also includes sexual selection, which is directed by choice. And choosing is – literally – central in *Only Revolutions*:

> —*Everlasting Whims & Everlasting Loss.*
> *Against Horrors passing with Love's passing.*
> *Between Them you must choose.* //
> —*Choice then is allways Them?*
> —*Love & Horror's impermanence forever against*
> *Loss & the Caprice of endurance.* (S/H180–181)

IV. Chiastic

This middle passage of the book (repeated on the same pages, but upside down) is the core of the book's chiastic structure. The 'Everlasting Whims & Everlasting Loss' can be read as an allusion to Thomas Carlyle's *Sartor Resartus*, in which Chapters 7 and 9 ('The Everlasting No' and 'The Everlasting Yea') are separated by the 'Centre of Indifference'. In many ways, *Only Revolutions* can be read as a criticism of indifference, not so much the indifference of Uncle Sam/the US towards the world around it but, in more general terms, the indifference of 'US' human beings towards the environment and the species surrounding us. Danielewski's stress on biodiversity (even typographically, using bold type for the different kinds of fauna and flora) implies an increased awareness of mankind's modest place within evolution as a whole – an awareness reminiscent of Darwin's indictment of mankind's arrogance and all forms of anthropocentrism. Darwin explicitly emphasised the circular movement of evolution when he exemplified his notion of continuous variation. A change in one species (say, 'US') will influence other species, but in the end it will also influence itself:

> if certain insectivorous birds (whose numbers are probably regulated by hawks or beasts of prey) were to increase in Paraguay, the flies would decrease – then cattle and horses would become feral, and this would certainly greatly alter (as indeed I have observed in parts of South America) the vegetation: this again would largely affect the insects; and this, as we just have seen in Staffordshire, the insectivorous birds, and so onwards *in ever-increasing circles of complexity.* (Darwin 1859: 73; my emphasis)

In *Only Revolutions*, everything seems to be evolving in ever-increasing circles of complexity around 'US' – the restaurant ('The

St. Louis Pub' (S194), 'The St. Louis Bistro' (S199), 'The St. Louis Juke Joint' (S211), 'St. Louis Beanery refreshed' (S148), 'St. Louis Eatery renewed' (H148)), the people ('Viapiponacci' (S159), 'Viapoponacci' (S159), 'Viazazonacci' (H195), 'Viazozopolois' (H146)), the cars ('VW Rabbit' (H139), 'the Dodge Omni' [H142], 'the Chevrolet EC' (S138)). But Sam and Hailey always claim they remain unchanged: 'we're allways sixteen' (H/S194). The feeling of being sweet 16 is reflected in the overconfidence and self-centredness of US: 'For there are no countries. / Except me. And there is only / one boundary. Me.' (S3). In the perspective of literary history, this sentence sounds like an echo of a line from John Donne's poem 'The Sunne Rising': 'She is all states, and all princes, I' (Donne 1985: 61). The mirroring effect of the chiasmus expresses the illusion of self-sufficiency, especially since the line is followed by 'Nothing else is.' At the same time the chiasmus turns everything around. After suggesting that the whole world – represented by his love's breasts, 'both the India's of spice and Myne' – lie in his bed, the narrator makes a suggestion to the sun: since 'the world's contracted thus' and 'since thy duties bee / To warme the world, that's done in warming *us*. / Shine here to *us*, and thou art every where; / This bed thy center is, these walls, thy spheare' (Donne 1985: 61; my emphasis). Donne does not capitalize 'US' typographically, but content-wise the jesting and playful self-importance of the couple in love is similar to 'US' in *Only Revolutions*. The narrator's bed is the centre of indifference in which the whole world is contracted, not unlike Danielewski's attempt to make the world's past and future meet in the present of his book, and not unlike Joyce's effort to put 'Allspace in a Notshall' (Joyce 1975: 455).

Joyce's works are full of chiastic structures, from *Dubliners* to the discussion in *Finnegans Wake* of the big X (Christ) in the middle of the so-called *Tunc* page of the Book of Kells. Moreover, according to Thomas Cousineau, Joyce even applied chiastic patterns to the structure of his works, for instance to *A Portrait of the Artist as a Young Man* (with its five chapters, of which the third serves as a pivot). Joyce often used a chiasmus to signal an epiphany. In the last paragraph of *The Dead*, Gabriel Conroy's epiphanic moment is marked by means of a double chiasmus: 'It [the snow] was falling on every part of the dark central plain, on the treeless hills, *falling softly* upon the Bog of Allen and, farther westward, *softly falling* into the dark mutinous Shannon waves . . . His soul swooned slowly as he heard the snow *falling faintly* through the universe and *faintly falling*, like the descent of their last end, upon all the living and the dead' (Joyce 1994: 59; my emphasis). In *Only Revolutions* the 'falling snow' (S/H325) is counterpointed by Sam's 'falling frequently' (S325), albeit without chiasmus, while Hailey is 'spilling often' (H325), evoking a more watery image. In *A Portrait of the Artist as a Young Man*, when Stephen Dedalus has his artistic vision while he sees the 'birdgirl' standing in midstream, gazing out to sea (Joyce 2000: 185), Joyce emphasises this epiphanic moment by means of a (double) chiasmus: 'Her bosom was as a bird's *soft and slight, slight and soft* as the breast of some darkplumaged dove. But *her long fair hair* was *girlish*: and *girlish . . . her face*' (186; my emphasis).

The question is whether Mark Z. Danielewski employs the chiastic structures for the same purposes. The chiastic structure has the effect of marking a centre of indifference in the middle of the whirlpool of revolutions. Joyce seems to have employed this marker as a kind of stylistic equivalent of the penciled *x* with which one marks an interesting passage in a book, thus drawing attention to epiphanic moments, comparable to Marcel Proust's *mémoires involontaires* or Virginia Woolf's 'moments of being'. But *Only Revolutions* does not seem to imply the same modernist suggestion that a special meaning could be attached to such moments of 'beeing'. Danielewski does however employ the chiastic structure to freeze-frame the moment of the choice, an ecological choice around which the survival of the biodiverse world revolves – 'it's never too late to keep a World' (S/H315). Unlike the modernist belief in some kind of aesthetic transcendence in privileged moments of being, Danielewski's chiastic structure seems to relate more closely to John Donne's use of the chiasmus in the early modern period. At the moment when Copernicus' thesis that the earth revolved around the sun was confirmed by Tycho Brahe and Johannes Kepler, Donne poetically gave this Copernican revolution yet another ironic twist. Similarly, Danielewski makes 'US' so important that the irony of this self-centredness puts mankind in its proper place among his fellow-species.

V. 'Allspace in a Notshall' (Joyce 1975: 455)

In terms of the situationists' vocabulary, the question remains whether this ironic twist can be regarded as a form of *détournement*. From a situationist point of view, *Only Revolutions* – with its label 'national bestseller' prominently on the cover of the paperback edition – is not the *Finnegans Wake* of the twenty-first century, but a case of neo-experimental *récupération*. From a more positive perspective, *Only Revolutions* could be regarded as a functional re-employment of *Finnegans Wake*'s circular bends and swerves; or of John Donne's chiasmus in 'The Sunne Rising'. Whatever works can be re-employed. To some extent, this attitude corresponds with that of the bee in Jonathan Swift's *Battle of the Books*. Not unlike the 'erring' Johnny Truant in *House of Leaves* (Van Hulle 2002), Sam and Hailey answer to the spider's description of the bee in Swift's fable: 'what art thou but a vagabond without house or home, without stock or inheritance? . . . Your livelihood is an universal plunder upon nature' (Swift 1990: 111). The spider also accuses the 'free-booter over fields and gardens' of being indiscriminate and robbing 'a nettle as readily as a violet' (1990: 111). If, to some extent, this reproach also applies to Danielewski as a writer, the bee's response seems equally appropriate: 'I visit indeed all the flowers and blossoms of the field and the garden; but whatever I collect from thence enriches myself without the least injury to their beauty, their smell, or their taste.' (Swift 1990: 112).

In terms of poetics – in the etymological sense of the Greek verb 'poiein', to make – the old battle between the ancients and the moderns, notably the bee's 'enrichment', adds an extra dimension to the prominent motif of the bee in *Only Revolutions*. But at the same time, this enrichment or re-employment is as common as what Stephen King simply calls his 'toolbox' (King 2000: 114). Whatever used to be considered 'experimental' at some point in time can be functionally employed or appropriated as a new tool, even in a best-seller. Only those techniques that are 'fit' or seem to work for him will be re-employed. Evidently, from a situationist point of view this is a blunt recognition of 'bourgeois' *récupération*, but on the other hand such a commodification of literary experiments has also had its modest effects on the mainstream. What matters, though, is that the result has to work, and in the case of *Only Revolutions*, the re-employment of experimental techniques is not always effective. The intellectual sophistication and artificial numerology often end up in mannerism that sometimes lacks narrative persuasiveness.

But even if, to some degree, the experiment has to be considered a failure, it is an important failure. Danielewski's attempt to keep revolutionising literature answers to Samuel Beckett's notion of always failing better: 'All of old. Nothing else ever. Ever tried. Ever failed. No matter. Try again. Fail again. Fail better' (Beckett 2009: 81). While the book may fail as a *récupération* of *Finnegans Wake*, *Only Revolutions* successfully turns the situationist approval of the human domination of nature round. According to the situationists 'the very core of the revolutionary project' came down to 'replacing work with a new kind of free activity' by means of 'the domination of nature'. If *détournement* is understood as a direct re-employment of an existing idea or work to create a new work with a deviating message (in contrast to the mainstream *récupération* or appropriation of an originally subversive idea), the title *Only Revolutions* can just as well be interpreted as a *détournement* or derailment of the situationists' 'revolutionary orientation' towards this domination of nature. In that sense, Danielewski's book is an important Darwinian statement in that it questions the human species' self-importance and suggests that in a broader perspective all anthropocentric 'revolutions' are only evolutions.

Notes

1 This entry is based on another passage in Mauthner's *Critique*; the only difference is that Mauthner uses the example of the Danube, which Joyce replaces by the river Poddle. Mauthner's point is that the name 'Donau' is just the name of a riverbed, not the river itself; similarly, the name Peter Müller only stands for a set of organs and vessels through which a continuously changing mass of blood is flowing.
2 The page references to *Only Revolutions* will be preceded by an S or H, to indicate Sam's (green) or Hailey's (golden) side of the story.
3 See also Ospovat 1981: 213: 'Once Darwin had concluded that natural selection works on chance variations, he could no longer treat man or any other species as a preplanned, an inevitable, goal of the process of transmutation. But he continued to think that progress in general was inevitable, and he appears to have believed that the production of some intellectual being was inevitable.'
4 For instance in notebook D, page 49: '27th. August. There must be some law that whatever organizations an animal has, it tends to multiply & IMPROVE on it. – Articulate animals must articulate. <i> in vertebrates tendency to improve in intellect, – if generation is condensation of changes. then animals must tend to improve. – yet fish same as, or lower than in old days' (Darwin 1987: 347).
5 'When I am laid in earth, may my wrongs create / No trouble in thy breast, / Remember me, but ah! forget my fate.' *Dido and Aeneas*, Act III, libretto by Nahum Tate.

Works cited

Ball, E. (1987) 'The great sideshow of the Situationist International', *Yale French Studies* 73: 21–37.
Beckett, S. (1984) 'Dante...Bruno. Vico..Joyce', in *Disjecta*, New York: Grove Press.
Beckett, S. (2009) *Company, Ill Seen Ill Said, Worstward Ho, Stirrings Still*, ed. Van Hulle, D., London: Faber and Faber.
Cousineau, T. J. (2007) 'Demented vs. Creative Emulation in *Murphy*', in *Samuel Beckett Today/Aujourd'hui* 18, '"All Sturm and no Drang": Beckett and Romanticism, Beckett at Reading 2006', ed. Van Hulle, D. and Nixon, M., Amsterdam: Rodopi, pp. 355–365.
Danielewski, M. Z. (2000) *House of Leaves*, New York: Pantheon Books.
Danielewski, M. Z. (2006) *Only Revolutions*, New York: Pantheon Books.
Darwin, C. (1859) *On the Origin of Species by Means of Natural Selection, or the Preservation of Favoured Races in the Struggle for Life*, London: John Murray.
Darwin, C. (1987) *Charles Darwin's Notebooks 1836–1844*, ed. Barrett, P. H., Gautrey, P. J., Herbert, S., Kohn, D. and Smith, S., Ithaca: Cornell University Press.
Debord, G. (1967) *La Société du spectacle*, Paris: Buchet-Chastel.
Donne, J. (1985). 'The sunne rising', in *The Metaphysical Poets*, London: Penguin Classics, pp. 60–61.
Goulekas, K. E. (2001) *Visual Effects in a Digital World: A Comprehensive Glossary of over 7000 Visual Effect Terms*, San Francisco, CA: Morgan Kauffman.
Hutcheon, L. (1984) *Narcissistic Narrative: The Metafictional Paradox*, New York and London: Methuen.
Joyce, J. (1975) *Finnegans Wake*, London: Faber.
Joyce, J. (1994) *The Dead*, ed. Schwarz, D. R., New York: Bedford-St. Martin's.
Joyce, J. (2000) *A Portrait of the Artist as a Young Man*, London: Penguin.
King, S. (2000) *On Writing: A Memoir of the Craft*, New York: Scribner.
Knabb, K. (ed.) (2006) *Situationist International Anthology*, rev. edn, n.p.: Bureau of Public Secrets. Online versions: 'Report on the construction of situations' www.bopsecrets.org/SI/report.htm; 'Ideologies, classes, and the domination of nature' www.bopsecrets.org/SI/8.nature.htm; 'Détournement as negation and prelude' www.bopsecrets.org/SI/3.detourn.htm; and 'A user's guide to détournement' www.bopsecrets.org/SI/detourn.htm#6.
Lautréamont, Comte de [Isidore Ducasse] (1870) *Poésies II*, Paris: Librairie Gabrie, Balitout, Questroy et Cie.
Mauthner, F. (1923) *Beiträge zu einer Kritik der Sprache*, 3 vols, Leipzig: Felix Meiner.

Ospovat, D. (1981) *The Development of Darwin's Theory: Natural History, Natural Theology, and Natural Selection, 1838–1859*, Cambridge: Cambridge University Press.

Richards, R. J. (2009) 'Darwin's theory of natural selection and its moral purpose', in Ruse, M. and Richards, R. J. (eds) *The Cambridge Companion to the 'Origin of Species'*, Cambridge: Cambridge University Press, pp. 47–66.

Swift, J. (1990) *The Battle of the Books*, in *A Tale of a Tub, and Other Works*, Oxford: Oxford University Press.

Van Hulle, D. (2002) '"erronymous" intentions from Joyce to Danielewski', in *Variants: The Journal of the European Society for Textual Scholarship* 1: 123–141.

8

Only Revolutions, or, The most typical poem in world literature

Brian McHale, The Ohio State University

The claim that my title makes is manifestly absurd – isn't it? Whatever else it might be, Mark Z. Danielewski's *Only Revolutions* (2006) is surely *not* the most typical poem in world literature – far from it. Neither the title page nor the book-jacket copy identifies it as a poem at all, and some of the promotional material actually calls it a novel. Moreover, given Danielewski's track-record as a novelist, author of the celebrated first novel *House of Leaves* (2000), one would surely be justified in expecting that the new book would also be a novel.

Novel or not, *Only Revolutions* is certainly a *narrative* text. It recounts the adventures of Sam and Hailey, a pair of teenagers who become lovers and set out on a road-trip, part joyride, part (inadvertent) crime-spree, across the United States, from the heights of the Appalachians, where they meet, southward to New Orleans, then northward to St. Louis. After a longish hiatus there, where they try to settle down and make a living, they return to the road, continuing northward from St. Louis into the upper Midwest, and then westward into the Rockies, where they are finally separated by death – though which of them dies differs between the two versions of the story. For the story is told twice, once in Sam's voice and from his point of view, the other in Hailey's, and the two versions are often at odds. In other words, *Only Revolutions* is a classic exercise in narrative perspectivism, in the spirit of modernist novels such as *The Sound and the Fury* or *Manhattan Transfer* (though, unlike cases of modernist perspectivism, here the divergent versions of events cannot always be reconciled). It is also, as I trust my plot summary makes clear, a variant on the classic American genre of the road novel or road movie, in the tradition of *On the Road*, *Easy Rider*, *Thelma and Louise* or (maybe most pertinently of all) Terence Malick's *Badlands*.

Much more even than its narrative content, the *form* of *Only Revolutions* surely undermines any claim that it might have to typicality. The book is designed to be read in both directions: beginning at the title page, one reads the top parts of every page; then, rotating the book 180 degrees and flipping it over, one *re*begins at a *new* title page, again reading only the top portions of every page. At the foot of every page, one glimpses the *other* text, printed upside down. Hailey's narrative runs in one direction, Sam's in the other; each narrative mirrors the other, but from opposite ends of the book, and with literally opposite orientations. The two narratives converge in the middle, so that on pages 180–181 the same events are narrated in unison by Hailey and Sam, though in passages of opposite orientation, one upside down relative to the other; then they diverge again. There are other formal complications (some of which will be discussed below),[1] involving parallel columns of print, changing type-size, colour-coding, and even the book's end-papers, but none so radical in their effect as the obligation (not option) to physically *manipulate* the book, to rotate and reorient it in real-world space (not virtually) in order to read it at all. To call *this* bizarre object the most typical poem in world literature makes as much sense as calling Danielewksi's *House of Leaves*, with its many anomalies of typography, layout and structure, the most typical novel in world literature.

That last remark should give us pause. The claim that I make in my title, as I suppose many readers will have recognised, is a variant on one that the Russian Formalist Viktor Shklovsky notoriously made about Sterne's *Tristram Shandy*, when he called it the most typical novel in world literature (1990: 170). This is characteristic Shklovskyan provocation, of course, because *Tristram Shandy*, far from being a typical novel, may be one of the most *anomalous* novels in world literature. It is anomalous in many of the same ways that *House of Leaves* is anomalous; indeed, we might be tempted to describe Danielewski's novel as a hypermediated updating of Sterne's, but for the fact that *Tristram Shandy* was *already* hypermediated relative to the (print) media environment of Sterne's own era. In any case, *House of Leaves* is certainly a novel in the tradition of *Tristram Shandy*, and Shklovsky might have regarded them both as typical novels, in the same rather special sense of 'typical'. In Shklovsky's view, *Tristram Shandy* is typical because it 'lays bare' the poetics of the novel, and so, in a way, shows us how *every* novel is made, and above all because it subordinates *mimesis* to its own aesthetic laws, which, according to Shklovsky, is the case with *all* novels, including putatively 'realistic' ones.

I want to make a parallel argument about the typicality of *Only Revolutions*. First of all, its narrative content, far from undermining its typicality, actually aligns it with the mainstream of poetry world-wide, if we take the long view. As I have argued elsewhere (McHale 2009), it is an accident of relatively recent history that the lyric has come to be seen as prototypical for *all* poetry. Before the nineteenth-century 'lyric transformation' that affected the full range of verse genres (Fowler 1987: 250–261), many if not *most* poems were narrative poems. Moreover, narrative poetry has continued to be written in the twentieth century and since, despite Modernism's efforts to 'purify' poetry of its narrative content (McHale 2000). In this respect, *Only Revolutions* finds its rightful place in the epochs-long history of poetic narrative that runs from oral literature and the epic traditions that sprang from it, through medieval verse romances, Renaissance sonnet cycles, folk ballads and their Romantic literary imitations, novels and autobiographies in verse, and so on, right down to the eras of Stephen Vincent Benét, James Merrill, Ed Dorn, Anne Carson, Les Murray and other moderns and postmoderns.

The formal and physical anomalousness of *Only Revolutions* presents more of a challenge. In what sense can a book-length poem be regarded as *typical* if it must be physically rotated and flipped to be read properly? Narrative poems abound in world literature, but I think it is safe to say that no previous poem has ever been structured in this way. If *Only Revolutions* is typical in the way that Shklovsky claimed *Tristram Shandy* was typical – that is, if it lays bare the poetics of poetry in something like the way that *Tristram Shandy* (according to Shklovsky) laid bare the poetics of the novel – then it remains to be demonstrated what exactly *Only Revolutions* shows us about poetry. Or, to put it the other way around, what would our definition of poetry look like if we assumed, for the sake of argument, that *Only Revolutions* really *was* the most typical poem in world literature?

This is the question that I aim to pursue in the remainder of this essay. I want to consider two definitions of poetry – one recent and relatively obscure, the other canonical and celebrated – that seem to me sufficiently capacious and radical to accommodate Danielewski's poem, or rather, capacious and radical in ways that make it possible to locate *Only Revolutions* near the centre of poetic practice instead of on its fringes.

I. Segmentivity

To accommodate a text like Danielewski's, we need a *radical* definition of poetry. It obviously cannot be one that relies on traditional formal criteria of rhyme or metre, since *Only Revolutions* is essentially a free-verse text in which, though rhymes and scannable lines occur throughout, they do so sporadically and ad hoc, not systematically. Nor will the criterion of metaphorical or figurative language serve, not because *Only Revolutions* lacks figurative language – in fact, it abounds with figures[2] – but because, as the cognitive linguists have shown, metaphor is constitutive of language and thought generally, and not a criterion of poetry in particular.

We need, in other words, a definition basic enough – radical enough – to accommodate free verse and even 'prosaic' poetry alongside traditionally metrical, lyrical and figurative poetry. Just such a definition is the one proposed by the poet Rachael Blau DuPlessis (see also Shoptaw 1995; McHale 2009). Poetry, according to DuPlessis, is defined by the criterion of *segmentivity*. Poetry is *segmented* writing, 'the kind of writing that is articulated in sequenced, gapped lines and whose meanings are created by occurring in bounded units ... operating in relation to ... pause or silence' (1996: 51). Segmentivity, 'the ability to articulate and make meaning by selecting, deploying, and combining segments', is 'the underlying characteristic of poetry as a genre' (51).

The segments she has in mind as constitutive of poetry come in a variety of kinds and sizes. They range from words, or even just letters, which may 'hang alone in an open space', through lines, up to 'larger page-shapes' such as stanzas or other configurations of language and spacing. The ends of segments may be signalled by special devices, or not:

> Line terminations may be rounded off by rhyme, or by specific punctuation marks, but they are basically defined by *white space*. Recurrent patterns of parallel sounds (rhyme) are not necessary to mark line ends, though rhyme is popularly taken to indicate poetry (or its lack), a fact which should actually draw our attention to the crucial importance of articulated segments in the definition of poems. (1996: 51)

Segments of one kind or scale may be played off against segments of another kind or different in scale; for instance, 'Sentence or statement may be draped, or shaped, across a number of lines' (51). Traditional metrics, of course, accommodates this practice under the rubric of *enjambment*, but DuPlessis in effect generalises and radicalises *enjambment* to include *all* interactions among segments at *all* levels: 'The specific force of any individual poem occurs in the intricate interplay among the "scales" (of size or kind of unit) or comes in "chords" of these multiple possibilities for creating segments' (51).

All such interactions are, in DuPlessis' view, meaningful, or rather meaning-*inducing*. Poetry, for her, crucially involves 'the creation of meaningful sequence by the negotiation of gap (line break, stanza break, page space)' (51). 'In short,' she concludes, 'all the meanings poetry makes are constructed by segmented units of a variety of sizes' (51).

Clearly, *space* and *spacing* are key to DuPlessis' definition. Poetry, for DuPlessis, is distinguished from other kinds of writing by its *spacing* of language, its placing of language *in space*. Prose writing, by contrast, and narrative prose in particular, tends to neutralise the spacing of language, rendering it invisible.[3] When poetry and narrative coincide, as in narrative poems, two different ordering principles interact (cooperate and compete) – *narrativity* and *segmentivity* (McHale 2009).

A narrative text, *Only Revolutions* is also conspicuously a *segmented* text, one in which language has been subjected to spacing, placed in space.[4] Any passage chosen at random would bear this out, but let us consider a particularly 'action-packed' one, from the narrative point of view – a moment of emergency. As a consequence of their overindulgence in the pleasures of New Orleans, Hailey becomes violently ill, and Sam, worried, takes her to a hospital emergency room, where she foolishly ingests a 'CURIOUS PILL' offered her by a 'RASTAFARIAN MEDIC' (100 gold). The capsule's contents send her into anaphylactic shock. Since this is Hailey's side of the book, she narrates:

        Panic. PHYSICIANS furious for time.
—*It's shock!*   —*It's cardiac!*
        Sam above me. Peaked and gaunt.
        Slap. Someone pounds my chest.
—*It's a reaction!*   —*Anaphylactic!*
        But the Wheel seizes.

>   —*Epinephrine!*
>   Losing it. Nearer. Now.
>   And all I can do is hold him.
>   —*Needle!*
>   Ow. Outandout relief. Rush.
>   A turning, returning, release. Pleasing.
>   I want Sam to kiss me awake but
>   ALL PRACTITIONERS unclasp my hand
>   and whisk me away to recover.
> Allone.
>   With allready The Healing, stinking
>   of gangrene, and Visiting Ailing
>   guarding their spleens, anxiously
>   motioning me to join Them. (104 gold)

Even a cursory glance confirms the foregrounding of space in this passage. First of all, it is justified on the right, like all the verso pages in *Only Revolutions*, and not on the left, as one conventionally expects in poetry, so that we are immediately confronted with a ragged left margin, white space infiltrating the text from the 'wrong' side. But white space infiltrates from the straight-edge right margin as well, and even bubbles up in the middle of lines. These are certainly what DuPlessis might call 'gapped lines', and in concert with other visual features, including changing typefaces (*italics*, SMALL CAPS), anomalous capitalisation and spelling, and letter-*O*s colour-coded gold, they create a distinctive 'page-shape'.

Segments of different scales are played off against each other in this passage. Individual words ('*Anaphylactic!*' '*Epinephrine!*' '*Needle!*' 'Allone') and short sentences ('*It's shock!*' etc.) 'hang alone in an open space.' Counterpointed against these stand-alone units are somewhat longer lines, four to eight words long, decisively 'rounded off' by punctuation in the first 12 lines of the passage, but sometimes allowed to terminate without punctuation in its last eight lines. In other words, syntax and lineation tend to coincide in the first part of the passage, while sentences are 'draped, or shaped, across a number of lines' in its latter part. Finally, words, lines and sentences are counterpointed against the overall configuration of text on this page (or, more exactly, this quadrant of a page). Together, words, lines, sentences and page-shape produce a rich, resonant 'chord'.

If poetry, according to DuPlessis, entails 'the creation of meaningful sequence by the negotiation of gap', then what meanings arise from our negotiation of this passage's manifold gaps? Obviously, one set of meanings is *iconic*: spacing partly serves here to orchestrate – or choreograph, or stage – the narrated events. The voices of the hospital staff, signalled by italics, are distributed to the left and right, and then in the middle (head? foot?), of a space that we might infer is that occupied by Hailey, supine on a gurney. At the height of the emergency, abrupt line-terminations signal tension, constriction (of Hailey's respiratory passages?) and speed. As the crisis passes, after the needle-jab, the end-stopping relaxes, and sentences begin to flow again from line to line; the poem 'breathes freely' again.

Beyond its iconic mirroring of narrative events, however, spacing here also *troubles* meaning-making, challenging the reader to integrate disparate segments, and disparate *kinds* and *scales* of segmentation, into a semantic whole. This challenge emerges clearly as we move *outward* from this passage to the rest of the page. For the bloc of lines we have been examining is only one component of a more complexly configured page-space. It is framed below and to the right by straight-edged strips of blank paper. We might call them 'gutters', a term borrowed from the poetics of comics, where it designates the ribbons of white space that divide one panel from another – the place, according to Scott McCloud's classic account (1993), where the comics reader is recruited to make meaning by negotiating the gaps between images (see also Berlatsky 2009).

Across the gutters from the emergency-room passage are other blocs of text, but how (if at all) we are to integrate their meanings with those produced by our passage remains an open question. Opposite our passage, on the same upper part of the page, across a vertical gutter on the right, appears a separate, parallel column of text. Printed in smaller typeface, and justified on the left (whereas our passage is justified on the right), this text lists (somewhat obliquely and cryptically) real-world news events and news-makers from the period between 10 September 1972 (the heading at the top of this column) and 29 October 1972 (the heading at the top of the column on the next page):

Sept 10 1972
Frank Shorter's marathon.
Uganda, US
& $3 million loan.
Tonsure.

E Howard Hunt,
G Gordon Liddy & 5.

Cairo's Joint capital.
Mitsubishi & Harvard.

Vietnam, US & 0.
Manila Martial Law.

And so on, for another 29 lines of print, interrupted here and there by blank lines. Some of these events and actors are readily recognisable (the 1972 Olympics, the Watergate break-in, etc.), others are more obscure, but in either case, the question is, how are they related to the fictional events narrated parallel to them, on the other side of the vertical gutter? Are we meant to treat these public events as in some sense *contextual*, 'framing' (literally and figuratively) the fictional events displayed to their left? Only one thing is certain: there is no way to read *straight across* from the lines on the left (the emergency-room scene) to the lines on the right (public history), because, though they are roughly parallel, they literally do not *line up*; the different typefaces and different number of lines (20 on the left, 39 on the right, excluding skipped lines) preclude that. Integration of meaning, negotiation of gap, if it is to take place at all, can only occur here on the scale of *bloc to bloc*, not line to line.

Nor is this the only gutter to be negotiated. Below the horizontal gutter at the bottom of our bloc is another, more compressed bloc, only 16 lines long, printed in a smaller typeface, and oriented upside down relative to the emergency-room passage. From the point of view of our passage, this one is literally illegible. To render it legible, the reader must physically rotate the book 180 degrees, in the process rendering *our* passage illegible relative to the newly legible one. Thus it is impossible to read both passages together at once, and to integrate them at all requires a dimensional shift from the 2-D space of the page to the 3-D space of the book. This implies segmentation on a whole different scale, unanticipated by DuPlessis – beyond the space of the page to the space of the *whole book*.[5]

Poetry is the kind of writing that produces meaning through spacing, DuPlessis tell us. This is certainly borne out by *Only Revolutions*, a text segmented on multiple scales, in units ranging in size from the isolated word up to the whole book, superimposed to sound rich, complex chords. But there is no guarantee that the meaning that spacing produces will be *determinate* meaning, and *Only Revolutions* bears that out, too. Spacing here produces determinate meaning, if at all, only at the scale of the line and bloc of lines; negotiating across the gutters, let alone across the space of the whole book, yields meanings that remain open, fluid and improvised, richly indeterminate.

II. Parallelism

DuPlessis' definition of poetry is expressly designed to accommodate untraditional and avant-garde practices of the modern and postmodern era – in other words, just the sort of poetry that DuPlessis herself writes. Her definition is a 'big tent' under which many diverse kinds of writing can shelter, including the kind we find in *Only Revolutions*. To get a different perspective on the putative typicality of *Only Revolutions*, it might be worthwhile to consider a different 'big-tent' definition of poetry, one at least as radical as DuPlessis', but more attuned to poetry's traditional resources. Though differently focused, the two definitions are compatible, it seems to me (but that is an argument for some other occasion).

I have in mind Roman Jakobson's celebrated definition, not of poetry exactly, but of the *poetic function*. Recall that Jakobson identifies the poetic function as one of the six functions that co-occur in many, if not most verbal communications. In most speech events, the poetic function is subordinated to other functions – to the *referential* function of communicating information about the world, to the *emotive* function of expressing the addresser's interior state, to the *conative* function of influencing the addressee, to the *phatic* function of ascertaining that the communication channel is open, and/or to the *metalinguistic* function of reflecting on the code being used. But in some speech events, the poetic function is dominant, and these are the instances we call *poetry* (or *literature* more generally). The poetic function is characterised, Jakobson says, by an orientation towards the *message as such*, in contrast with the referential function's orientation towards the context of the message, the emotive function's orientation towards the message's addresser, the conative function's orientation towards its addressee, the phatic function's orientation towards the communication channel and the metalinguistic function's orientation towards the code.

Orientation towards the message is achieved by exploiting the most basic structuring principles of language itself. Language, as Saussure taught over a century ago, is structured on two axes: a paradigmatic *axis of selection* and a syntagmatic *axis of combination*. The paradigmatic axis can be pictured as a set of silos, from each of which items may be selected that are, not identical, but functionally equivalent. Thus, we could imagine one such silo in which all the synonyms and near-synonyms of the noun *house* are stacked: *home, residence, dwelling, abode, domicile, quarters*, etc., all the items that a search of the Thesaurus yields. To produce an utterance, one selects an item from the paradigmatic silo and fits it into the appropriate slot in the syntagmatic sequence, alongside other items filling other slots: *Your house is on fire, your children are gone*; *Your domicile is ablaze, your offspring are dead*; *Your abode is being consumed, your youngsters are lost*; etc. The slots are *different* from one another in the grammatical functions they perform, while the respective slot-fillers for each position in the sequence are functionally interchangeable, belonging to the same grammatical category.

All this is very basic indeed – which is what gives Jakobson's definition such scope and power. 'The poetic function,' he writes (1987: 71), '*projects the principle of equivalence from the axis of selection into the axis of combination.*' Where the paradigmatic axis of selection is normally the axis of (quasi-) identity, and the syntagmatic axis of combination the axis of (grammatical) difference, the poetic function imposes identity upon the successive items in the sequence, thereby, according to Jakobson, directing the focus away from the informational, expressive, interpellative, etc. functions of the speech event and onto the *message as such*.

Jakobson's famous example, miniature in scale, is that quintessential political slogan of the 1950's, *I like Ike* (70). The three words constituting this sequence belong to different grammatical categories – subject, verb, object – but phonemic near-identity has been imposed on them: that /ay/ sound, repeated three times, twice as part of the same /ayk/ unit. The last two words *rhyme*, we might say; all three are *assonant*; or we could say that the three words *parallel* each other at the level of sound, though not at the level of grammatical category or meaning. Of course, *I like Ike* is *not* an utterance in which the poetic function dominates. As a slogan, it serves a predominantly *conative* function, *interpellating* its addressee, inviting him or her to identify with the *I* who likes Ike. In short, *I like Ike*, while not a poem, nevertheless displays the poetic function, albeit in a subordinate role.

Similarly structured lines, where phonemic identity overrides grammatical or semantic difference – or, just as often, reinforces grammatical or semantic similarity – abound throughout *Only Revolutions*: 'A turning, returning, release. Pleasing.' (104 gold; see above). Phonemic parallelism here – rhyme, assonance and stress – reinforces the semantic relationship between *turning* and *returning* (they share an etymology, after all), and create specious, ad hoc relationships between *returning* and *release* and between *release* and *pleasing*. This is a micro-scale example of the poetic function in action, unconstrained by any other superordinate function (such as political sloganeering).

Parallelism among successive items in a sequence – what Jakobson calls the projection of equivalence into the axis of combination – operates at different levels in different kinds of poetry. It is the constitutive principle of *metre* – the succession of equivalent patterns of stress and unstress (or length or brevity of syllables) – as it is of *rhyme*. The most spectacular manifestations of parallelism, however, involve *syntactic-semantic parallelism* within or between lines, an organising principle in many traditions of poetry, ancient and modern alike:

1 Canst thou draw out leviathan with an hook? or his tongue with a cord which thou lettest down?
2 Canst thou put an hook into his nose? or bore his jaw through with a thorn?
3 Will he make many supplications unto thee? will he speak soft words unto thee?
4 Will he make a covenant with thee? wilt thou take him for a servant forever?
5 Wilt thou play with him as with a bird? or wilt thou bind him for thy maiden?
6 Shall the companions make a banquet of him? shall they part him among the merchants?

By the shores of Gitche Gumee,
By the shining Big-Sea-Water,
Stood the wigwam of Nokomis,
Daughter of the moon, Nokomis.
Dark behind it rose the forest,
Rose the black and gloomy pine-trees,

Rose the firs with cones upon them;
Bright before it beat the water,
Beat the clear and sunny water,
Beat the shining Big-Sea Water.

I believe a leaf of grass is no less than the journey-work of the stars,
And the pismire is equally perfect, and a grain of sand, and the egg of the wren,
And the tree-toad is a chef-d'oeuvre for the highest,
And the running blackberry would adorn the parlors of heaven,
And the narrowest hinge in my hand puts to scorn all machinery,
And the cow crunching with depress'd head surpasses any statue,
And a mouse is miracle enough to stagger sextillions of infidels.

The examples are, respectively, an excerpt of biblical poetry, from Job 41:1–6, in the Authorized ('King James') Version; a passage from Henry Wadsworth Longfellow's *The Song of Hiawatha* (1855), modelled on the parallelistic form of Finnish-Karelian folk poetry in the *Kalevala*; and a passage from Walt Whitman's 'Song of Myself', from *Leaves of Grass* (1855/1892).

The play of identity and difference, repetition and variation, is manifest in all three of these examples. To recognise grammatical parallelism as the constitutive principle of such poetry is uncontroversial. Jakobson went further, however, identifying instances of grammatical parallelism in kinds of poetry that were much less obviously parallelistic: for example, in a Shakespeare sonnet (sonnet 129, 'Th'expence of Spirit in a waste of shame'), in Yeats' 'The Sorrow of Love', and in various poems by Baudelaire. In such cases, he ingeniously demonstrated that the distribution of particular grammatical categories among the formal units of the poem fell into patterns. Thus, for instance, the 'odd' stanzas of sonnet 129, the first and third, could be contrasted with the 'even' ones, the second stanza and the couplet, with respect to the distribution of certain grammatical categories. Similarly, the first two stanzas ('anterior') could be contrasted with the third and the couplet ('posterior') with the respect to the distribution of other categories, while the first stanza and couplet ('outer') could be contrasted with the second and third ('inner') stanzas with respect to yet other categories, and so on.[6]

These distributions, which Jakobson saw as manifestations of a subtle play of grammatical sameness and difference across these poems, were often invisible to the casual reader, literally subliminal, though not any less potent because of that – according to Jakobson, at least. His extension (or overextension, as some saw it) of the principle of 'projection of equivalence' provoked scepticism on the part of other theorists of poetry, who challenged Jakobson's patterns of distribution on the grounds that they were *imperceptible* and ultimately *arbitrary*.[7]

Even if Jakobson was guilty of over-ingenuity, as his critics charged, in generalising the 'projection of equivalence' principle to cases of subliminal grammatical parallelism, I do not think that invalidates the principle itself. In any case, one need not invoke subliminal patterning in connection with *Only Revolutions*, where syntactical-semantic parallelism between lines is as overt as anything in biblical poetry or *Hiawatha* or *Leaves of Grass*:

> Every **American Robin** and **Sage Thrasher** chears admurringly my tremendous blur: —*Whirrrrrrrrrrrrrrrrrrrr!*
> New **Mountain Phlox** and **Wild Strawberries** praise pleasingly my racing breeze: —*Weeeeeeeeeeeeeeeeeee!*
> Newly fidgeting **Bats, Wrens** and **Newts** by ponds and rill, **Hooknosed Snakes** tumbling over banks and logs, **Wolverines** & **Moles** grrrrring by brittle rocks, all breeeing for my impossible stir: —*Whirrrrrrrrrrrrrrrrrrrr!*
> Every simpering **Stickseed, Laurel** and **Toadstools** by pool and gush, **Brewer's Bittercress** offering up from ground and bog, **Beech** & **Spruce** whrring at clouds, all creeing my impossible rush: —*Weeeeeeeeeeeeeeeeeee!*
> And I'm allready gogone, their only On and On, shooooshing beyond these thickets and marsh by **Chorus Frogs** and **Western Turtles** with a **Gyrfalcon** circling about: —*Whirrrrrrrrrrrrrrrrrrrr!*
> And I'm allready gonegoing, their only one and on, feetbare padpadding by leaps and rounds of **Pawpaw Apple** and **Wax Currant** with abounding **Clasping Peppergrass** snippering zowns: —*Weeeeeeeeeeeeeeeeeee!*

The parallelistic structure of this catalogue of natural species (animals and plants) is manifest here, as it is in the many similarly Whitmanesque catalogues throughout *Only Revolutions*.

Readers of Danielewski's poem will have recognised that this is a fabricated example. Not only does the long-line layout here not reflect the typical spacing of the poem, but the lines themselves are drawn from different places in the text. The odd lines, the first, third and fifth, come from Sam's narrative (colour-coded green), while the even lines come from Hailey's (colour-coded gold), but they come from the *same page*, page 33, of the respective narratives. The passage from Sam's narrative (33 green) originally looked like this:

> Every **American Robin** and **Sage Thrasher** chears admurringly my tremendous blur:
> —*Whirrrrrrrrrrrrrrrrrrrr!*
> Newly fidgeting **Bats, Wrens** and **Newts** by ponds and rill, **Hooknosed Snakes** tumbling over banks and logs, **Wolverines** & **Moles** grrrrring by brittle rocks, all breeeing for my impossible stir:
> —*Whirrrrrrrrrrrrrrrrrrrr!*
> And I'm allready gogone, their only On and On, shooooshing beyond these thickets and marsh.
> by **Chorus Frogs** and **Western Turtles** with a **Gyrfalcon** circling about:
> —*Whirrrrrrrrrrrrrrrrrrrr!*

(I leave it to the reader to reconstruct the passage from Hailey's narrative.) The point of the fabrication is to demonstrate that the lines from Hailey's narrative are parallel – with variations, of course (plants substituted for animals, *Weee!* for *Whirrr!*, and so on) – to those from Sam's narrative, though the parallel lines are separated by over 150 pages of text, and appear on the page reversed in orientation, each passage upside down relative to the other. To reconstruct the parallelism, one must leaf back and forth between the two page 33s, flipping the book in the process. Of course, the catalogue of animals in Sam's narrative is *already* parallelistic in structure, though the parallelism is slightly obscured by the lineation; so too, by the same token, is the catalogue of plants in Hailey's narrative. So parallelism applies *within* each passage as well as *between* them.

In fact, the lines on *every* page of *either* of the narratives in *Only Revolutions* are parallel to the lines on the *equivalent* page of the *other* narrative. Every line, every bloc of lines, in Sam's narrative has a parallel line and bloc of lines in Hailey's, on the page with the same number (though colour-coded gold instead of green) – and vice versa, of course. Thus, for instance, the emergency-room passage from Hailey's narrative (104 gold) that I analysed above, in my account of segmentivity, is paralleled by a passage from Sam's narrative (also on 104, but green instead of gold). Retelling the same episode, but in Sam's voice and from his point of view, it begins like this:

>   Panic. DOCTORS furious for time.
> —*It's pulmonary!*   —*It's shock!*
>   Patting her face, slaps for attention.
>   Hypodermics, alcohol and gauze.
> —*It's allergic!*   —*Anaphylactic!*
> A sudden scramble for vulneraries.
>   —*Adrenaline!*
>   Losing her. Closer. Now.
>   But all I can do is hold on.
>   *Needle!*

And so on.

As it happens, this particular pair of passages, perhaps uniquely in *Only Revolutions*, parallels another pair only a few pages away. Shortly after Hailey's episode of anaphylactic shock in the New Orleans hospital, Sam, too, collapses and requires emergency assistance. The sequence of events is different – Sam is already returning to normal when the doctors begin to attend to him, for instance – but the organisation of the passage (crucially including its spacing) is parallel to the earlier passage involving Hailey's collapse. In Hailey's narrative, the new passage looks like this:

>   Relaxing. Sam's discomfort slackening.
> —*Defib him?*   —*Start CPR?*
>   But Sam's below me. Smiling.
>   I wiggle his nose. Rub his feet.
> —*Pulse evening!*   —*Pulse slowing!*
>   And The Wheel rolls on.
>   *Adenosine?*
>   Calmly, nuzzling his head back on
> the pillow. My hand squeezes Sam's.
>   —*Improving.* (112 gold)

In Sam's passage, it looks like this:

> Calm. Allready the flutters subsiding.
> —*Shock?*   —*Cardiac?*
>   But Hailey's kissing me. Smiling.

> Wiggling my toes. Petting my head.
> —*It's slowing!*   *It's evening!*
> And The Wheel rolls on.
> —*How'd that happen?*
>   Relaxing now. Head cushed on the
>   pillow. My hand mushing Hailey's.
>   —*Improvement.* (112 green)

Parallelism here is *four-fold*. Each passage has an equivalent in the *other* narrative, but it also parallels (with conspicuous variations) another passage in the *same* narrative. The effect is one of *double mirroring*, as it were: mirroring above and below the horizontal line that divides the two narratives, but also mirroring *across* each narrative, on the same plane.

Actually, this principle of double mirroring applies to *Only Revolutions* as a whole. Though I have not been able to identify another passage like the emergency-room episode that is replicated (with variations) four times over in such fine-grained detail, in general *Only Revolutions* mirrors itself not only 'vertically' but 'horizontally'. Vertically, as we have seen, each passage parallels (in microscopic detail) an equivalent passage in the *other* narrative; but also on the horizontal plane of each unfolding narrative, Sam's and Hailey's respectively, the latter half of the narrative generally mirrors its front half, though with valences reversed. In *both* narratives, Sam and Hailey begin on the heights, at the peak of their fecundity and power; they join forces and set out on their adventures; they encounter various temptations and threats along the road (notably THE CREEP, a mysterious adversary); they linger in St. Louis, near the centre of the country, bogged down. Then, after the poem's midpoint, they hit the road again, encountering temptations and threats *paralleling* those they encountered in the first half (including THE CREEP again); they deteriorate, shifting into destructive mode; they return to the heights, and part company.

Back parallels front, end parallels beginning, just as above parallels below. The entirety of *Only Revolutions* is organised as a single, complex parallelistic structure on a massive scale – an immense demonstration of the projection of the principle of equivalence from the axis of selection into the axis of combination. From the point of view of Jakobson's definition of the poetic function, *Only Revolutions* appears not merely as a *typical* poem, but something like a *hyper*-typical one, if that were possible.

The most typical poem in world literature

So whichever big tent we seek to accommodate it under, that of Jakobson's parallelism or that of DuPlessis' segmentivity, *Only Revolutions* seems comfortably at home. But surely this wouldn't be sufficient to qualify it as the most typical poem in world literature – would it?

Notes

1 See N. Katherine Hayles' chapter in this volume for further details about the formal anomalies of *Only Revolutions*.
2 The problem in *Only Revolutions* is to distinguish what is figurative from what is literally the case, but fantastic or hallucinatory. For instance, does Sam *literally* shit animals and minerals, and does Hailey *literally* shit minerals and vegetation – is this the sort of world in which such things are literally possible? Or are these just *metaphors* for Sam's and Hailey's irrepressible fecundity and creativity? (Danielewski 51 green and 51 gold; all future references will be in this form, citing page number and colour: *green* for Sam's narrative, *gold* for Hailey's).
3 There are exceptions, of course, including *Tristram Shandy* and Danielewski's own *House of Leaves*, narrative texts in which spacing is foregounded and functional. But these are, precisely, exceptions that prove the rule – sports whose very anomalousness calls attention to the norm of conventionally invisible and non-functional spacing in prose fiction.
4 For a different approach to the 'spatial form' of *Only Revolutions*, consult N. Katherine Hayles' chapter in this volume.
5 This does not exhaust the inventory of gaps potentially to be negotiated on any given page of *Only Revolutions*. Below the horizontal gutter, at the foot of every page, there appears not only an upside-down bloc of text parallel to the narrative passage at the top of the page, but also an upside-down chronology of public events parallel to the rightside-up chronology at the top of the page. Moreover, the chronology at the top of the page also parallels another such list, also rightside-up, across the spine of the book, on the facing page. In other words, if the page and the whole book are potential units, so too is the double-page *opening* that straddles the book's spine.
6 Notice that identification of these patterns of distribution depends upon the prior identification of units – lines, stanzas and groupings of stanzas – for categories to be distributed *among*. In other words, *segmentation is an unacknowledged prior condition for grammatical parallelism*. If there are no lines (or half-lines, or stanzas, etc.) there can be no parallelism *between* lines. This may be an argument for seeing DuPlessis' definition of poetry in terms of segmentivity as more basic than Jakobson's 'projection of equivalence' principle.

7 For the objection that Jakobson's patterns of distribution are imperceptible, see Riffaterre's classic article (1966). For the objection that Jakobson's grammatical categories are arbitrary, see Culler (2002: 64–86), another classic critique. 'One can produce distributional categories *ad libitum,*' Culler writes. '[I]f one wishes to discover a pattern of symmetry in a text, one can always produce some class whose members will be appropriately arranged' (67). 'Jakobson's method permits one to find in a poem any type of organization which one looks for' (73).

Works cited

Berlatsky, E. (2009) 'Lost in the gutter: within and between frames in narrative and narrative theory', *Narrative* 17(2): 162–187.

Culler, J. (2002 [1975]) *Structuralist Poetics: Structuralism, Linguistics and the Study of Literature*, London: Routledge.

Danielewski, M. Z. (2006) *Only Revolutions*, New York: Pantheon Books.

DuPlessis, R. B. (1996) 'Codicil on the definition of poetry', *Diacritics* 26(3/4): 51.

Fowler, A. (1987) *A History of English Literature*, Cambridge, MA: Harvard University Press.

Jakobson, R. (1987) *Language in Literature*, ed. Pomorska, K. and Rudy, S., Cambridge, MA: Harvard University Press.

McCloud, S. (1993) *Understanding Comics: The Invisible Art*, New York: HarperCollins.

McHale, B. (2000) 'Telling stories again: on the replenishment of narrative in the postmodernist long poem', *The Yearbook of English Studies* 30, 'Time and narrative', ed. Bradbury, N., London: The Modern Humanities Research Association.

McHale, B. (2009) 'Beginning to think about narrative in poetry', *Narrative* 17(1): 11–30.

Riffaterre, M. (1966) 'Describing poetic structures: two approaches to Baudelaire's "Les Chats"', *Yale French Studies* 36–37: 200–242.

Shklovsky, V. (1990) 'The novel as parody: Sterne's *Tristram Shandy*', in *Theory of Prose*, trans. Sher, B., Normal, IL: Dalkey Archive, pp. 147–170.

Shoptaw, J. (1995) 'The music of construction: measure and polyphony in Ashbery and Bernstein', in *The Tribe of John: Ashbery and Contemporary Poetry*, ed. Schultz, S., Tuscaloosa, AL: University of Alabama Press, pp. 211–257.

9

Mapping time, charting data: the spatial aesthetic of Mark Z. Danielewski's *Only Revolutions*

N. Katherine Hayles, Duke University

While the social, economic and political consequences of overwhelming amounts of data have been extensively researched, the *literary* implications remain under-theorised and largely unexplored (exceptions are Dannenberg 2008; Francese 1997; and Johnston 1998). The ideal test case would be a text that not only displayed the effects of data inundation at the diegetic level of the narrative but also carried out a deeper exploration on such essential literary matters as form, genre, characterisation and language. Mark Z. Danielewski's narrative poem, *Only Revolutions* (hereafter *OR*), presents such an instance. Among the transformations and deformations the text implements is a profound shift from narrative as a temporal trajectory to a topographic plane upon which a wide variety of interactions and permutations are staged. Whereas narrative temporality proceeds along a one-dimensional line whose unfolding, backtracking and foreshadowing are carried out through reading practices that typically follow line upon line, a plane has two dimensions through which interactions can take place. Stacking the two-dimensional planes adds a third dimension of depth. In *OR*, the rich dimensionality created by this topographic turn is correlated with an explosive increase in the kinds of reading practices afforded by the text. The results are a hybridisation of narrative with data, temporality with spatiality, and personal myth with collective national identity.

I. Spatial form and information multiplicity

To evaluate this topographical turn, I return to 1991, when Joseph Frank revisited his seminal 1945 essay in 'Spatial Form: Some

Further Reflections'. He rehearses the well-known semiotic model in which the paradigmatic indicates alternative word choices that define a given term through their differential relations with it, while the syntagmatic refers to the temporality of syntactic sequence. Envisioned as two perpendicular axes, the model effectively converts a temporal line into a plane of interaction. Since the paradigmatic works together with the syntagmatic, the framework implies spatiality is present in some degree in all literature. Quoting Gérard Genette, he notes that 'Saussure and his continuators have brought to the foreground a mode of language that one must call spatial, although we are dealing here, as Blanchot has written, with a spatiality "whose originality cannot be grasped in terms either of geometrical space or the space of practical life"' (Frank 1991: 124). Whereas Frank had earlier turned up his nose at Concrete, he agrees with Genette on the 'so-called visual resources of script and topographical arrangement; and of the existence of the Book as a kind of total object' (128). Again from Genette, he focuses on a passage in which the book's materiality comes almost into view: 'To read as it is necessary to read [Proust] . . . is really to reread; it is already to have reread, to have traversed a book tirelessly in all directions, in all its dimensions. One may say, then, that the space of a book, like that of a page, is not passively subject to the time of linear reading; so far as the book reveals and fulfills itself completely, it never stops diverting and reversing such a reading, and thus, in a sense, abolished it' (128).

Less than a decade later, John Johnston (1998) seems to write from a different universe when he analyses the effects of information explosion on literary texts. Although spatiality is not foregrounded as such in Johnston's analysis, it is everywhere implicit in his notion of 'information multiplicity', a vast landscape that, like the cosmos, rushes towards as it creates an ever-expanding horizon with no foreseeable limit. A phase change occurs, he suggests, when the separable (and separated) media of *Gravity's Rainbow*, *JR* and similar texts coalesce into partly connected media systems. Emerging from this de-differentiation of media come 'new behaviors and affective responses that this environment provokes as information becomes completely assimilated in a vast network of media assemblages' (4). Whereas Frank focused on the writer's subjectivity, Johnston, following Deleuze and Kittler, argues that a subject-centred view cannot account for the viral properties of exponentially expanding information: 'in the novel of information multiplicity . . . information proliferates in excess of consciousness, and attention shifts to a new space of networks and connections in which uncertainties are structural rather than thematic' (13). The aesthetic unity Frank saw as the principal feature of spatial form now dissolves in the acid bath of information multiplicity: 'Negatively defined, a novel can thus be said to become a multiplicity when its fundamental coherence derives neither from a subjective nor an objective unity; that is, when it cannot be adequately defined by the expression of an authorial subject or the totalizing representation of an objective reality' (16).

From unity to assemblage, from subjects who create/apprehend patterns to assemblages that create dispersed subjectivities, from cultural generalisations to technical media as causal agents: these transformations mark the deterritorialised spatial dynamic instantiated and reflected in novels of information multiplicity and media assemblages. 'Only a literary form that is machinic, therefore, and which takes the form of an assemblage, can fully register how various information systems, including the mass media, function as part of a larger apparatus of information production and control, while at the same time participating in processes that always exceed them. It is this aspect of information that makes it necessary to consider the novel of information multiplicity as an assemblage produced by a writing machine' (14). The writing-down system, in all its technical specificity, thus becomes the source rather than the expression of a conscious subject: 'forms of subjectivity as usually understood are displaced and redistributed through the entire machinic activity that writing and reading entails' (5).

OR simply *assumes* the information explosion that Johnston saw as a formative force on contemporary literature. Information has migrated from a foreground figure where it functioned as a causative agent to the background where it forms part of the work's texture. Whereas Johnston believed that the excess of information could never be contained or halted, *OR* puts information excess into tension with an elaborate set of constraints. It is not excess alone that determines the text's topographic form but rather the interplay between the force information exerts and the constraints that limit and contain it. Moreover, this interplay takes form not merely as a conceptual spatiality (although it has this dimension) but as visual shapes materially present on the pages.

The topographic dimensions are put into play by the configurations of page-space and constraints that govern the text's operations. The two narratives centre on the 'forever sixteen' lovers Sam and Hailey respectively, with each narrative physically placed 180 degrees and back to front to the other. The turn required to go from one to the other is accompanied by a change in the colour-coding: Sam is associated with green (green eyes flecked with gold, green ink for every letter 'o'), Hailey with gold (gold eyes flecked with green, gold ink for every letter 'o'). In the hardcover edition, the colour-coding is further emphasised by a green ribbon whose top is anchored at the top edge of Sam's narrative, while a gold ribbon is anchored at the top of Hailey's pages. These old-fashioned place markers (which turn out to be remarkably useful) reinforce visually the text's volumetric space, even when the text is closed. The publishers (ventriloquised by Danielewski) recommend that the reader perform the switching operation in units of eight pages of one narrative, then eight pages of the other. This reading practice, which I will call the octet, means that the reader is constantly performing 'revolutions' in which the physical book turns 360 degrees each time an octet cycle is completed. Reinforcing the octet are large capital letters at the beginning of each segment, which consecutively form repeating strings of SAMANDHAILEY from Hailey's beginning, and HAILEYANDSAM from Sam's, in anagrammatic fashion.

II. Narrative, database, constraint

At this point it will be useful to clarify key terms in relation to one another, especially database and narrative. In Lev Manovich's influential formulation, narrative and database are 'natural enemies' (2001: 228), with database in the ascendency as a cultural form and narrative presumably in decline. Structurally, Manovich maintains, database and narrative stand in inverse relation to one another. In narrative the syntagmatic is visible on the page and the paradigmatic is virtual; in a database, by contrast, the paradigmatic is visible and the syntagmatic is virtual. As Allen Bye Riddell (2009) points out, this formulation is seriously flawed. In semiotics, the alternative choices of the paradigm interact with the inscribed word precisely because they are absent from the page, although active in the reader's imagination as a set of related terms. Contrary to Manovich's claim, databases are *not* paradigmatic in their structures.

Mapping time, charting data 163

In a relational database configured as columns and rows, the data values of a row constitute the attributes of a given record, while the columns represent the kind of attribute itemised for many different records. In neither the rows nor columns does a logic of substitution obtain; the terms are not synonyms or sets of alternative terms but different data values. Search queries allow different kinds of attributes and data values to be concatenated. The concatenated values, although not syntagmatic in the usual sense, can be seen as a temporal process when strung together by a search query, although it is not syntax but the command's structure that determines the concatenation's order.

These corrections suggest that a more fine-grained analysis is needed rather than a simple association of narrative with the syntagmatic and database with the paradigmatic. I identify four different kinds of data arrangements relevant to *OR*, each with its own constraints and aesthetic possibilities.

1. Prohibitions on words and concepts that cannot appear in *OR*. Analogous to paradigmatic substitutions, these prohibitions function as absences that act as constraints and therefore help to define the presences in the text. Particularly important are the clusters printed on the end pages, which co-determine what and how verbal representations can appear in the text, as discussed below.
2. Collections of data, which take the form of rotations through a list of possible data elements. Particularly prominent are the lists of plants, animals and cars that the protagonists encounter (additional substitutions are the minerals associated with their lefttwist wristbands). Danielewski wrote an invitation to the visitors of the *House of Leaves* website to send him the names of 'an animal you admire', 'a plant you pause for' and 'your favorite car', so presumably many, if not most, of these rotational terms come from the data compiled from answers to his invitation.[1]
3. Chronological lists of entries, which form an assemblage in Johnston's sense. Danielewski's invitation also asked for 'a specific moment in history, over the last 100 years, which you find personally compelling, defining or at a bare minimum interesting. Necessities: exact data, a refinement of detail, along with a reference or link. An image is also welcome.' At least some of the chronological entries can be presumed to come

from reader-contributed data. As Danielewski commented in an interview with Kiki Benzon, referring to his invitation, 'It's not just my personal history, but histories that go beyond what I can perceive when I'm looking at thousands of books' (2007).
4. Terms created by permuting a set of elements (for example, letters) through the possible combinations. For example, the manager of the St. Louis café where Sam and Hailey work is variously written as Viazozopolis, Viazizopolis, Viaroropolis, etc.

To see how these data arrangements interact with the narrative, consider the topography of the page and page spread. As Danielewski remarks, *OR* activates 'a language of juxtaposition' (Benzon 2007). Technically free verse, the form is tightly constrained through an elaborate set of topographic patterns. Each page is divided into four quadrants. For the left-hand page, the upper left quadrant is the narrative n1 of that page; in the lower left and upside down is the complementary narrative n2 of the other character; in the upper right quadrant is a chronological interval headed by a date (about which more shortly); and in the lower right is the upside-down chronology accompanying n2. For right-hand pages, the same four quadrants apply but with the chronological intervals in the left upper and lower quadrants, and n1 and n2 in the right upper and lower quadrants, respectively. The left- and right-hand pages exist in mirror relation to each other, with the chronologies on both pages adjacent to one another across the spine, and the narratives on the outer edges. Thus a four-fold mirror symmetry is enacted on each page spread, with a left-right reversal along the spine and an up-down reversal along the horizontal midline. The conceptual significance of these mirror symmetries, which exist in different ways within the narrative diegeses, will become apparent shortly.

In addition to the topographic patterns, numerical and other constraints apply to layout, diction, slang and conceptualisation. On each page, there are 90 words per narrative, making 180 narrative words/page and 360 words across the page spread, enacting another variation of 'revolution'. In addition, there are 36 lines of narrative per page, counting both the right-side-up narrative (n1) and the upside-down one (n2) (the number of lines in each of the two narratives varies from a minimum of 14 to a maximum of 22, but the total always comes to 36). As one narrative grows, the complementary other shrinks, with each largest at its beginning. There are (naturally) 360 pages in each narrative, with the page numbers written upside down to one another, in green and gold respectively, encapsulated in a circle. These constraints, along with others discussed below, cage the wild yearnings of two 16-year-old lovers, who escape school, parents and authorities but remain imprisoned (as well as articulated) by the writing-down system within which they are encapsulated.

Visually this dynamic is represented by a symbol that appears before the title pages of both narratives, a circle (gold for Hailey, green for Sam) within which sit two vertical lines. The circle I take to refer to the 'revolutions' in all their diversity, while the two parallel lines represent Sam and Hailey. This may explain why the letter 'l', whenever it appears in the text, is always doubled (as in 'allso', 'allways', etc.), mimetically reproducing their duality within the revolutions performed by the narratives. The lines may also be taken to refer to the pause symbol on electronic equipment; in this sense, Sam and Hailey exist as 'pauses' (sequentially indicated by the chronological intervals) during which the text gives accounts of their actions, as well as the historical events listed under the date heading.

To see how these constraints interact with content, let us consider the chronologies. Sam's moves from 22 November 1863 (in the middle of the Civil War), whereas Hailey's starts on 22 November 1963 with John F. Kennedy's assassination, the event that the narrator of Don DeLillo's *Libra* says 'broke the back of the twentieth century' (DeLillo 1991: 181). Each moves through about a century, so that Sam's ends where Hailey's began, while Hailey's ends in our future of 19 January 2063, with the last chronological interval for which events are recorded starting with 25 May 2005. Since Sam and Hailey's chronologies do not temporally overlap, the only spacetime in which the protagonists logically can meet is in the user's reading practices as she flips the book over and over, an action juxtaposing the protagonists in her imagination. Defying temporal logic, each narrative diegesis has the character meeting his or her complement, falling in love, and re-enacting the archetypal tale of Romeo and Juliet. Their *full* story, however, is braided together through the octets. If the text were read linearly through from front to back and then back to front, it would literally be a different text than if read through the octets.

The chronological entries are written in epigrammatic style, merely gesturing towards the events they reference. Correlations with the narratives are elusive at best. On 6 January 1971, for example, we read 'Berkeley hormones. / Russian long hair. / Coco goes' (9/H/1971).² The date 6 January is that when a group of researchers from the University of Berkeley announced the first synthetic growth hormone. Hailey's corresponding narrative recounts a threesome between Sam, a woman Hailey calls a 'Warm Up Wendy's rear' who comes onto Sam, and Hailey's reluctant participation in the *ménage à trois*. Presumably the connection is hormonal: natural in the narrative, synthetic in the chronology. More opaque are 'Russian long hair' and 'Coco goes'. The latter refers to the death of Coco Chanel (10 January 1971), four days later than the header. If correlated with the narrative, this interval implies the orgy goes on for four days, illustrating how the chronologies can function to give the narratives epic scope. This strategy is even clearer for the entries that begin on 3 October 1929 (196/S/1929). 'Tuesday' undoubtedly refers to 'Black Tuesday,' 29 October 1929 (following 'Black Thursday', 24 October), when 16 million shares were sold and the US stock market collapsed completely. The popular aphorism describing the consequences of the collapse, 'When America sneezed, the rest of the world caught cold', is reflected in the narrative: 'Then little Hailey sniffs and / desnoots; / *–Ahhh Chooooooooooooo!*' (196/S/1929). The 13 'o's', with their connotation of bad luck, are followed by a scene describing Hailey upchucking, as if a world-wide cataclysm can be compressed into her vomiting, which becomes a synecdoche for the world's attempt to purge itself of the excesses of the 1920s.

A complete exploration of the connections between the narratives and entries would require researching thousands of factoids, a nearly impossible (and certainly tedious) task. In their multiplicity, the entries gesture towards a vast ocean of data, even as the text's topography puts severe constraints on the brief entries that, as a group, perform as synecdoches for an inexpressible whole. As a literary strategy, the loose correlation between the narratives and chronological entries points to a dynamic tension between coordination and contingency, epic inflation and narrative irrelevance. Neither wholly tied to the narratives nor completely untied, history wheels alongside the stories, making them more than personal accounts and less than completely allegorised correspondences. The connections that come into focus, such as the examples above, are patterns that emerge from an ocean of data, much as a Google search imparts a partial ordering on an infosphere too vast to comprehend.

More consistently correlated are the diction and slang of the narratives and the chronological dates; at every point, the characters' colloquial language is appropriate to the period. Arguably, such extensive correlations are feasible only when one has digital databases at one's command. Using Google, I was able quickly to locate many day-by-day chronologies that listed events similar to those Danielewski used. Sites such as the *Historical Dictionary of American Slang* (www.alphadictionary.com/slang) offer search tools that allow one easily to find slang equivalents for words, with usage dates indicated. In this sense as well, data permeates the text through the vocabulary used by the characters.

In addition to evoking the infosphere and establishing weak correlations with the narratives, the chronologies paint a canvas as vast as the world, in relation to which the individual desires, fulfilments and disappointments of the characters are contrasted and compared. 'Coco goes', cited above, is one entry among thousands documenting deaths around the world – from accidents, disasters, murders, wars, genocides, diseases and natural causes. The present tense 'goes', locating the particular death in the context of a certain day, month and year (thus making it distinct from the universal truth that the present tense may also connote), constitutes a 'here and now' that becomes truly present only when a reader peruses the page. Concatenated with the time of reading are the temporalities of Sam and Hailey, displaced in time relative to one another yet mysteriously interpenetrating through narrative diegesis and occupying the same page-space. Altogether, each page incorporates within its topographic dimension no less than five distinct temporalities (Sam, Hailey, their associated chronologies and the time of reading).

In addition to the spatial juxtaposition of these different temporalities, a triple pun linguistically concatenates them. Sam and Hailey denote their special bond by 'US', often in ways that portray the two of them standing against the world. In another sense, 'US' denotes the United States of America as well as all the text's readers. Thus 'US' refers at once to the exclusivity of two lovers preoccupied with each other while the world whizzes by, the national collective of America, and a transnational community of readers stretching across time and place. As a result, 'here and now' becomes a catchphrase to indicate a space and time that is anything but self-evident or self-constituted. Instead, what emerges is a spacetime within whose high dimensionality and complex topology the personal merges with the mythic in the narratives, while in the chronologies, the individual merges with the collective, and the national with the transnational.

III. What cannot be said

Along with the combinatoric possibilities constituted by the physical and conceptual configuration of page-space, an arguably even more important set of constraints is articulated by the end pages. In mirror (i.e. backward) writing, the coloured pages (gold for Hailey's end, green for Sam's) announce 'The/Now Here Found/ Concordance'.[3] The temporal and spatial markers ('Here', 'Now') are linked with a topology of great complexity. As the strikethrough indicates in its play of absence and presence (recalling Derrida's *sous rature*), this 'Concordance' is far from a straightforward listing of the text's terms. To explore its function and significance, I refer to *House of Leaves*, Danielewski's sprawling hypertext novel that preceded *OR*. Masquerading as a horror novel but with profound philosophical and psychological depth, *House of Leaves* (despite or perhaps because of its complexity) was a runaway bestseller. Danielewski, a relatively young writer virtually unknown prior to the brilliant *House of Leaves*, now faced a dilemma similar to that confronting Thomas Pynchon after *Gravity's Rainbow*: what do you do for an encore? In Pynchon's case, a 14-year hiatus hinted at the struggle of knowing that whatever he wrote would risk failing to measure up to the extraordinary achievement of *Gravity's Rainbow*. After publishing two smaller works (*The Whalestoe Letters* and *The Fifty Year Sword*), Danielewski tackled another large project. His solution to the Pynchonesque problem was ingenious: he would write the mirror text to *House of Leaves*, inverting its dynamics and flipping its conventions.

Consider the inversions. *House of Leaves* is a large prose hypertext; *OR* is a tightly constrained poem. *House of Leaves* uses footnotes to create multiple reading paths, whereas *OR* uses topographical complexity that works through concatenations rather than links. *House of Leaves* is an obsessively inward work, moving in 'centripetal' fashion (Benzon 2007) to probe the depths of the House, psychology of the characters, family tensions, cultural contexts and convoluted histories associated with the House. *OR*, by contrast, moves outward and expresses the wild desires of the 16-year-old protagonists in joyrides across the country, free of responsibilities and responsive only to their own couplings and hormonal urges.

Beyond these general mirror symmetries is the elaborate set of constraints articulated by the ovals, ellipses, circles and other 'revolutionary' patterns on the end pages. Each topographic form articulates an ideational cluster. In my parsing of the clusters, they include kinship ('Brood'), media and mediation technologies ('Write'), grammatical parts of speech and language ('Word'), seeing and looking ('Choose'), grace and condemnation ('Grace'), inwardness, interiority, 'in' words such as 'inalienable', 'inane', etc., gods and religion ('Devotion'), architectural structures and components, and colours.[4] All of these ideational groups are central to *House of Leaves*, as readers familiar with the text will recognise. In the mirror text of *OR*, they indicate what *cannot be written, cannot be said.* The mirror Concordance thus functions as a kind of anti-concordance, indicating words and concepts forbidden in *Only Revolutions*. These metonymic remnants from *House of Leaves*, relegated to the paratextual location of the end pages and further obscured by appearing as mirror writing, are the paradigmatic equivalents that define the words present in the text by their absences from it.

The play between presence and absence intrinsic to paradigmatic variation is a prominent feature of *House of Leaves*. The index to that work, for example, includes entries marked 'DNE,' which apparently stands for 'Does Not Exist'. All such entries can, however, in fact be found in the text but in unusual places, such as text in a photograph, words that when elided together form the entry, and other paratextual locations. In *OR*, the paratextual end pages provide a guide to understanding many of the odd circumlocutions and highly inventive language of the text proper, as important in their textual absence as were the many gaps, holes and elisions in *House of Leaves.*

To see how the absences inscribed on the end-page clusters help to define the textual presences, consider the relation of some of the clusters to Sam's and Hailey's narratives. Since kinship in all its forms is forbidden, extending even to the prohibition of DNA, Sam and Hailey have no kin – no parents, siblings or extended family. To all appearances, they are *sui generis*. Within the narrative, this kinless state correlates with their teenage yearning to be on their own. More constraining from a viewpoint of narrative representation are the prohibitions on interiority. With the exception of Sam's heart, no interior organs are mentioned, nor are there extended probings of their psychological states. When Sam indulges in an orgy, for example, Hailey's distress is shown by the tears she cries, not by the agony she feels. With psychological rhetoric at a minimum, the inexorable progress of their romance is often articulated through the plants and animals (and sometimes other characters) in Greek-chorus-like fashion, issuing warnings, comments and prophecies for the doomed lovers.

Relevant to the 'seeing and looking' cluster is Danielewski's comment that 'the word "light" never appears . . . Words that are about seeing, for the most part, were taken out. I've been described – not as dogmatic as Oulipo – but there's a resistance to certain things. But the resistance allows for the proliferation of other words' (Benzon 2007). In *House of Leaves*, the play between blindness (physical and psychological) and sight/insight is extensive. Zampanò, the putative main narrator, is early on revealed by Johnny Truant to be blind; Will Navidson and others strain to see in the ashen corridors of the House; and an entire chapter is devoted to the biblical twins, Jacob and Esau, and Jacob's deception of his blind father. Sam and Hailey, despite being on a riotous road-trip, never give extended descriptions of the landscape other than allusions to the mountain terrain on which they begin and end their journeys. Seizing centre stage are action terms that convey a sense of the landscape not by looking at it but by experiencing it as a three-dimensional topography manifested through movement and velocity.

The media cluster evokes the graphomania of *House of Leaves* and its obsessive interrogation of its own practices of inscription, from the ink spill that obliterates some passages to the Braille encoding, signal flag symbols, alchemical signs and myriad other writing practices that fill its pages, including references to film, video, photography, telegraphy, X-rays, radiocarbon dating, and a host of other media technologies. By contrast, technology in *OR* (with the exception of the rotating lists of automobiles in which Sam and Hailey race through the countryside) is almost entirely absent. At the same time, this is an absence that would be almost impossible to achieve without the calculative and data-searching capabilities of networked and programmable machines. As Danielewski acknowledges, 'As archaic as [*OR*] is, with its illuminated text and its ribbons, this book could not exist without technology. With my G5 and 23-inch screen, with two pages on the screen at one time' (Benzon 2007).

Moreover, the writing-down system, as Johnston calls it (à la

Kittler), includes all of the affordances of the computer, from the Photoshop 'flip horizontal' function that presumably created the mirror writing of the end pages to the word count function that was undoubtedly used to create the specified quantities of text on each quadrant, page and page spread. Because these constraints are central in defining the characters of Sam and Hailey and their expressive possibilities, it is no exaggeration to say, as Johnston anticipates in discussing the novel as media assemblage, 'forms of subjectivity as usually understood are displaced and redistributed through the entire machinic activity that writing and reading entails' (1998: 5). I would argue, however, that *OR* is finally not a narrative of media assemblage but rather a next-generation form that has gone beyond the shock and awe of first-generation internet users to bland acceptance of the infosphere as a 'natural' part of contemporary life in developed countries. Data flows, unimaginable in their totality, are rendered more or less tractable through increasingly sophisticated search algorithms, mirrored in *OR* through the constraints that partially order and contain information excess. As networked and programmable machines aggregate video, film, sound and graphics into a single platform, the interplay between text and graphics expands exponentially, as it does in *OR*. In sum, digital inscription media and the de-differentiation they are presently undergoing can be erased from *OR* precisely because they are omnipresent in its writing practices. The paradigmatic variations, along with mirror symmetries, function as the *visible* linguistic technologies made possible by digital technologies of inscription; nowhere present within the narrative diegesis, digital technologies are everywhere apparent when we consider the writing-down system as a whole.

And what, in this case, is the writing-down system? Once specified by the author, the complex set of constraints become semi-autonomous components of it, dictating to the author the spectrum of choices. Cooperating in the authorial project are the software programs, network functionalities and hardware that provide sophisticated cognitive capabilities, including access to databases and search algorithms. Networked and programmable machines are here much more than a technology the author uses to inscribe pre-existing thoughts. They actively participate in the composition process, defining a range of possibilities as well as locating specific terms that appear in the text. The author function is distributed, then, through the writing-down system that includes both human and non-human actors.

The distributed author function implies that neither the human creator nor his fictional creatures can credibly claim to be the text's sole author(s). Nowhere within *OR* is the existence of the text itself as a material document explained or inscribed, in sharp contrast to *House of Leaves*, where Johnny Truant tells the story of finding Zampanò's notes and extensively comments on his own writing process, and where the book containing the narratives paradoxically appears within the narrative diegesis. The absence of character-authors in *OR* heightens the importance of the assemblage that forms the writing-down system, visibly apparent on every page, from the historically correct slang, thousands of chronological entries, elaborate symmetries to the constrained word counts.

The last clusters I will discuss are those centring on gods and religions ('Grace', 'Devotion'). Forbidden to articulate 'Divine', 'Doctrine', 'Dogma', 'Ghost', 'Ghoul' and 'God', among other terms, the text shows Hailey and Sam at the beginnings of their narratives as near-demiurges, forces of nature that, while not divine, have exaggerated powers and actions. Sam aggrandises, 'I'll devastate the World / No big deal. New mutiny all / around. With a twist. / With a smile. A frown. / Allmighty sixteen and so freeeeee' (1/S/1863). These exaggerations function as the presences defined by the paradigmatic absences of words more directly evocative of the divine. It is worth noting that within the list of proscribed terms are many antonyms: 'Angel' and 'Demon', 'Paradise' and 'Perdition', etc. The inclusion of opposites in many clusters ('Sight' and 'Sightless' in the cluster devoted to seeing and looking, for example) indicates that the opposites are engaged in a dynamic of supplementarity, as Derrida would say, mutually defining each other within a cultural context that hierarchically privileges one term as positive, the other as negative. Attending Yale University at the height of deconstruction, Danielewski could scarcely have escaped knowing such academic discourse (Derrida appears in a cameo role in *House of Leaves*, along with other academic stars). The Yin/Yang-like inclusion of an opposite within the dominant presence of the other term is everywhere apparent, notably in the 'Gold Eyes flecked with Green' and 'Green Eyes flecked with Gold' that appear repeatedly in the text and serve as cover images for the paperback and hardcover dust jacket. The dynamic also works itself out at the level of the narratives, where the hint of death lingers even in the most exuberant expression of life. Indeed, if one is tempted (as I was) to flip the book over when arriving at the ends of the narratives and begin again, this very transformation is enacted as the octets start over in a rhythm that, as the book design hints, is an endless cycle of '*OR*'.

Brian McHale, in his chapter in this volume, explores the extent to which *OR* follows Roman Jakobson's insight that literature's 'poetic function' is characterised by a transposition of the paradigmatic onto the syntagmatic axis – that is, the overlaying of alterative choices onto the linear order of narrative, a move that de-emphasises the informative and expressive functions and gives priority to 'the message as such'. Garret Stewart (1990) makes a similar claim about literary language, arguing that its 'literarirness' comes from a nimbus of homophonic variants activated when a reader subvocalises the words actually on the page. Many of the literary strategies employed by *OR* create such variants: creative spellings, in which the words inscribed on the page differentially achieve enriched meaning through their relation with the 'correct' spellings (heart's / pumpin waaaaaay toooooooo fast (111/H/1973)); neologisms, evoking the two or more words that they differentially recall; combinatoric variations, already discussed; in a larger sense, the symmetric interplays between Sam and Hailey's narratives, which sometimes perform as paradigmatic variations of one another; and on a meta-scale, the mirror symmetries between *House of Leaves* and *OR*. The conjunction of paradigmatic variation with mirror symmetry underscores their similar dynamics, both of which operate as spatial aesthetics. Like paradigmatic variants that haunt the word actually on the page and help to define it through differential relations, mirror symmetry evokes an other at once the same and yet different (in the left-right reversal). Overlaid onto the narrative temporal trajectory, these spatial effects infuse the linear order of syntax with a dense haze of possibilities, as if the words actually on the page operated like electrons historically represented as point masses, when they actually exist as probabilistic clouds.

IV. Affect and language

Intimately related to the text's emotional charge is the emergence of the overall temporal patterns. As the two protagonists meet and become lovers, their initial self-centredness wanes and their immense egos contract to make room for the other, a process expressed visually on the page as the physical space devoted to the narrative shrinks and the other narrative/narrator comes into view as an important force. At the mid-point, each gives to the other equal consideration to the self, signified when each narrative exactly repeats the other, carrying to the extreme the anaphora characteristic of free verse. Significantly, the word at the exact middle of each narrative is 'choose', emphasising the dilemmas that the lovers already sense: leave each other and live, or continue their attachment and die. As the narratives move towards their respective ends, concern for the other supersedes that for the self. Mapping this pattern reveals an 'X' structure, in which both protagonists start out at their respective beginnings perceiving themselves as supernaturally empowered and in charge; then, as they open themselves to the other, they begin to experience vulnerability as their growing love for the other gives a hostage to fortune. In the Benzon interview (2007), Danielewski remarks, 'Freedom is ultimately the quest from anything – to be unrestrained by your circumstances, by your society, by even your own body – whereas love is all about attachment. It's all about the involvement with someone else, which is the opposite of freedom.' Yet, as he acknowledges, love (and the bond between Sam and Hailey in particular) has a 'transcendent quality. It's through love that you have the greatest amount of freedom.' As the two race towards the ending, their foretold fate moves towards tragedy and, at the same time, the momentum of the octet reading practice catapults them over the ending and into the beginning of a new cycle in yet another 'revolution'. At the mid-point of this temporal trajectory-as-circle comes their long hiatus in St. Louis, where they temporarily abandon their road-trip as they struggle with the adult responsibilities of earning a living in a hostile environment.

Correlated with this spatialised temporality is the movement of the language. In addition to the narrative slang indexed to the chronologies, neologisms and other linguistic inventions are liveliest and most prolific when the two are on the road, free to express themselves in defiance of decorum and schoolmarm correctness. Checking out a New Orleans band, Sam announces that 'I'm posalutely wild for such / Cats zesty with slide, ribbing out a / stride shufflestomping shimsham / shimmy to time. All mine! / Toetickling digs, I'm so loose for / these hands, brillo, di mi, splitticated / on reed, brass & pluck. Dance' (78/S/1922). In St. Louis their lives seem to be going nowhere, encaged in alienated labour and subject to the whims of the tyrannical manager. The language here is correspondingly replete with combinations caged within a tight unyielding frame, for example in the manager's name and the café's title. As if imitating the protagonists spinning their wheels, the language spins through tightly constrained possibilities. These enactments, while not strictly speaking paradigmatic, nevertheless evoke spatialised data arrays (for example, the alphabet envisioned as a string of letters) operating in tension with temporal trajectories.

Complementing the work that the language does in creating hooks for the reader are the symmetries of the plots as they trace the temporal trajectories. One of the ways in which the narratives interact with each other, for example, is through ironic contrast. When Sam and Hailey first meet, he announces that she is 'Ashamed she's so slow . . . / Concerning her poverty, / I resort to generosity. But / my offer's too great. She panics. / Accidentally kicks my nose' (9/S/1870). Hailey, by contrast, says that 'I'm that fast, man,' and when Sam tells her '*Okay, you can be my slave*,' 'My flying kick nicks his nose. / A warning' (9/H/1963). In other instances, their concatenations are expressed as mirror inversions. Resting in a park, for example, Hailey is approached by a lesbian 'GROUNDSLASS' (234/H/1994), while Sam converses with a gay 'GROUNDSCHAP' (243/S/1953). Other octets concatenate as similar perspectives on an event, while still others function as complementary halves that together form a whole. When Hailey confesses to Sam she cannot have an orgasm and Sam refuses to ejaculate inside Hailey, for example, their mirror choices indicate psychological reservations about total commitment and therefore limitations on their mutual vulnerabilities. After St. Louis they determine to marry, with or without official sanction. Then, for the first time, Hailey comes and Sam ejaculates inside her, opening them to reproductive possibilities and consequent entry into adult responsibilities. The only way out of this pedestrian future is for them to die, 'forever sixteen' and forever free to revel in their unsanctioned pleasures.

As the narratives approach their endings and contract physically on the page, they mimetically reflect not only the deflation of the protagonists' egos (mentioned earlier) but also the narrowing horizons of possibilities for their lives. The motifs that earlier marked the temporal trajectories move towards closure: the 12 jars of honey they ate along the way and that marked the passage of time have all been consumed; the choruses of plants and animals appear as announcements of species death, although in mirror fashion since the plants that formerly appeared in Hailey's narrative now populate Sam's and vice versa, their disappearance marked by grey (rather than black) ink; the mountain tops from which Sam and Hailey descended to begin their relationship are inversely reflected in the mountain they scale on their upward climb.

A brief return to aggrandisement has the lovers imagining universal destruction in the wake of their grief for their dead partner. 'How oceans dry. Islands drown. / And skies of salt crash to the ground. / I turn the powerful. Defy the weak. / Only **grass** grows down abandoned streets,' Sam announces (350/S/1963), judging that 'No one keeps up and everyone burns and everyone goes. / I am the big burnout. Beyond speed' (352 green). As he begins to accept 'There is no more way for US. / Here's where we no longer occur' (356/S/1963), the tone modulates as he imagines that some might be responsive to the splendour that was Hailey (no doubt the author's allusion to his hope that readers will experience her death with immersive intensity). Among the many ways in which the US that refers to the lovers is concatenated with US the nation and US the readers is to figure them as outliers who push the boundaries to make sure expansive and expressive possibilities remain for the rest of US, and it is this tone that dominates at the end. 'By you, ever sixteen, this World's preserved. / By you, this World has everything left to lose' (360/S/1963).

With this final turn, the book turns over to begin again, a renewal forecast in the burst of greenery that shoots forth from the icy mountain, foretelling spring, rebirth of young love and, last but not least, the immersive pleasures of narrative amidst the topographic dimensions of the text's spatialised aesthetic. *OR* suggests that narrative and its associated temporalities have not gone into decline as a cultural form, as Lev Manovich predicts. Rather, they have hybridised with data and spatiality to create new possibilities for novels in the age of information. As the book turns, and turns again, the title of this extraordinary work broadens its connotations to encompass the dynamic of renewal that, even as it obliterates traditional novelistic form, institutes a new typographical ordering based in digital technologies: revolutionary indeed.

Notes

1 As a registered member of the website, I received this email, from which I am quoting.
2 The notation indicates the page number, the narrator (Sam or Hailey) and, since the language is synchronised with the vocabulary current on the indicated date, the chronological date heading to provide historical context.
3 'The/Now Here Found' words are struck through because they appear in the text; they are thus in a different category than the rest of the words on the end pages. 'Concordance' is not struck through because it does not appear in the text proper; neither do all the words on the end pages other than those few in special locations.
4 The words 'Beauty', 'Brood', 'Choose', 'Devotion' and 'Grace' appear in a circle with a black background, white perimeter, and black lines striking through tiny red words, 'Found Once, Once Here' on one side, and on the other, 'Found Once, Once There.' As this cryptic message suggests, these words, in addition to naming some of the categories, are found once and only once in each narrative of Sam and Hailey, respectively (hence 'Found ... Here' and 'Found ... There').

Works cited

Benzon, K. (2007) 'Revolutions 2' [Interview with Mark Z. Danielewski]. *Electronic Book Review*, 2 March. www.electronicbookreview.com/thread/wuc/regulated.
Danielewski, M. Z. (2006) *Only Revolutions*, New York: Pantheon Books.
Dannenberg, H. (2008) *Coincidence and Counterfactuality: Plotting Time and Space in Narrative Fiction*, Lincoln: University of Nebraska Press.
DeLillo, D. (1991) *Libra*, New York: Penguin.
Francese, J. (1997) *Narrating Postmodern Time and Space*, Albany: State University of New York Press.
Frank, J. (1991) 'Spatial form: some further reflections', in *The Idea of Spatial Form*, New Brunswick: Rutgers University Press, pp. 107–132.
Johnston, J. (1998) *Information Multiplicity: American Fiction in the Age of Media Saturation*, Baltimore: The Johns Hopkins University Press.
Manovich, L. (2001) *The Language of New Media*, Cambridge, MA: MIT Press.
Riddell, A. B. (2009) Private communication, 6 April.
Stewart, G. (1990) *Reading Voices: Literature and the Phonotext*, Berkeley: University of California Press.

10

Print interface to time: *Only Revolutions* at the crossroads of narrative and history

Mark B. N. Hansen, Duke University

> You were there.
> – *Only Revolutions*

> *Only Revolutions* is about technology, partly because no technology appears in the book.
> – Mark Z. Danielewski (in Miller and Reverte 2007)

> The primal impression is something absolutely unmodified, the primal source of all further consciousness and being.
> – Edmund Husserl (1991: 70)

'More than a mode of material production . . ., digitality has become the textual condition of twenty-first century literature' (Hayles 2008: 186). This pronouncement, which culminates N. Katherine Hayles' recent survey of electronic literature, rings true for many novels and poems of our still young century, but perhaps in no case more strikingly than that of Mark Z. Danielewski's *Only Revolutions*. Published in the autumn of 2006, *Only Revolutions* is, in its own right, a revolution in literary form, composition and typography: it comprises two coupled narratives that run in opposite directions in the text and occupy opposite halves of the page; it includes a historical sidebar of 'Chronomosaics' featuring events from differing date ranges in history and akin to a vertical ticker tape; it employs several fonts for different purposes, including *Tempo* for the dates, *Myriad Pro* for the Chronomosaics and *Spectrum MT* for the characters' narratives; it uses four different letter sizes – always involving a particular coupling of two – to mark the respective progress of the two narratives as they quite literally flow against one another; it incorporates letters in four colours (yellow and green 'o's; dates and 'THE CREEP' in purple; 'house' in blue); it features mirror symmetrical covers, in both cases displaying a black pupil with either a yellow or a green iris; and it incorporates not one but two ribbon page markers (one yellow, one green) that help the reader mark his or her place as he or she unavoidably shuttles between narratives, and between the two physical orientations of the book itself (yellow cover up, green cover up). Although the main narrative was written initially in pencil on paper – a fact on which Danielewski insists[1] – it could not have been completed without a large computer screen and the internet.[2] Thus, without being in any way thematically focused on digital technology, the book is thoroughly if indirectly permeated by it, both through the history of its composition and in the infrastructure underlying its appearance.

Yet for all of these markers of its 'digital textual condition', Danielewski emphasises that *Only Revolutions* affords – and is meant to afford – an experience without equivalent in any other medium. As he did in *House of Leaves*, Danielewski here writes something that, in the words of one of his interviewers, 'does what television and film cannot do': 'That's my point,' Danielewski affirms. 'The comparison would be: what happened to painting when the camera came onto the scene? Suddenly it wasn't about figurative representational art. It was "Let's paint the way we feel." So I view my books as a success if they're offering an experience that you can't get in other media' (Benzon 2007: 7). That *Only Revolutions* makes no explicit mention of technology,[3] while eschewing all recourse to any medium other than writing, serves to specify the singular nature of *this* novel's engagement with 'the digital textual condition': in a break from its predecesssor, which, I have argued, allegorises the unrepresentable impact of digital technology on our experience (Hansen 2004), *Only Revolutions* engages its own status as a print book by affirming the print book's power not so much to absorb and imitate other (analogue *and* digital) media as to mediate for its readers a new digital world of information (Hayles 2002). Less the subject of the novel's thematisation than the vehicle of its very construction, the power of print according to *Only Revolutions* is quite literally a power to mediate. More precisely, it is the power of the print book as a singular interface to time and to history.

Danielewski recounts how, beginning from the memory of 'two kids who were about 16 years old, who were absolutely penniless and yet precocious and confident on the surface', he conceptualised the book as a three-dimensional object in his head: 'I understood how it would be his story and her story. It would be told from opposite ends. They would talk across the pages and then across the ages. I realized that they were specific and non-specific, but at the same time' (Danielewski, in Miller 2006). Similarly, it is the book's physical existence as a three-dimensional object – an existence intensified by the demands *this* book places on readers (e.g. to flip the book over at regular intervals) – that in the final instance serves to differentiate it from other media.

In my engagement with *Only Revolutions*, I want to take seriously this claim for the physicality and objectness of the book. Through its role as a stage, screen, horizon or field for actualising correlations between the two narratives, between each narrative and its 'Chronomosaics,' and ultimately, between and among all four textual components, *Only Revolutions* comprises nothing less than a physical site where temporal relationships – coincidences, divergences, parallels, anticipations, etc. – are forged for and by the reader. Of all the levels where time comes to the fore in the novel, this level of reader actualisation is without a doubt the most fundamental. Commenting on the simultaneity of voices at work on any and every given page, Danielewski characterises the effect as 'fugal', both in the standard acoustic sense of multiple, overlapping voices, but also in another sense, that is simply because 'there are four moments of history existing at the same spot on the same page' (Benzon 2007: 3). By way of amplifying Danielewski's own characterisation of the novel (again in contradistinction to *House of Leaves*) as a 'centrifugal novel' – one that is about 'getting outside', about 'addressing what the open [is]', rather than about 'interiorities and history and progeny and ancestors' – I want to explore how the print book is made to function as an interface onto time, as a technology facilitating complex correlations among markedly divergent temporalities.

More specifically still, I am interested in how *Only Revolutions* deploys the print book *qua* three-dimensional object as a medium for producing encounters between two distinct kinds of time – phenomenological, so-called A-series and objective, B-series time – that have been held by the vast majority of philosophers of time to be, quite simply, incompatible. I contend that this capacity to produce heterogeneous temporal encounters accounts for what is singular about the print book within our contemporary media ecology. Alone among today's myriad forms of media, the print book can deploy the indexicality and self-referentiality of narrative language in ways that open up to – rather than cut against or close off – the alleged objectivity or 'enunciation-independence' of the time of history and historical record. Without resolving (or in any way aiming to resolve) the long-standing philosophical debate concerning A-series and B-series time (Danielewski would surely insist here, perhaps with a nod to Stein, that his novel is (only) a novel!), *Only Revolutions* is constituted by the reader's activity of bringing these two times together, not once, but repeatedly, not whimsically, but in accord with the demands imposed by the author, which is to say, ultimately, by the book's physicality, by its very objectness. After introducing the philosophical distinction at issue here, I shall develop my argument by considering three elements of *Only Revolutions*: first, the imbrication of narrative and history as it defines and catalyses readerly concretisation; second, the function of character and its correlation with (formal, linguistic and thematic) constraint; and, third, the role of the historical sidebar of 'Chronomosaics' in relation to the informational universe of digital culture.

I. From serial time to temporalisation

The late nineteenth-century Cambridge Idealist philosopher J. M. E. McTaggart introduces A-series and B-series time in order to distinguish between phenomenological, 'past-present-future' and physicalist, 'before-after' accounts of time. The salient difference between these two series is simple: B-series events do not change with respect to their criterion (before, after) whereas A-series events do change with respect to theirs (past, present, future). This incompatibility has generated varying positions regarding the reality of time. For McTaggart, it leads to a vicious paradox that compels him simply to deny the reality of time as such: because it alone accounts for the notion of change, McTaggart reasons, the A-series must be basic; but how can A-series properties be real if any given event can be simultaneously past, present and future, depending on which other events it is evaluated against? This paradox can only be resolved at the cost of an infinite regress that ensues once one attributes non-changeable (B-series) dates to A-series events. At the other end of the philosophical spectrum is philosopher David Mellor who seeks to resolve the paradox by privileging B-series time. For Mellor, the B-series is independent from the A-series because the permanent temporal (B-series) attributes of an event have no relation whatsoever to its changing (A-series) status; put bluntly, having a date is an intrinsic property of an event which means that the B-series can *by itself* account for change.

For my purposes here, what is important is the fact that, beyond their obvious opposition, these two views ultimately *share a common foundation*: specifically, they share a debilitating dependence on an overly narrow, logicist conception of reality as coterminous with non-contradiction. Precisely this logicist conception of reality forms the target of philosopher Dominique Janicaud's criticism of McTaggart in his insightful study, *Chronos* (1997). Janicaud's criticism specifically addresses the 'philosophical sterility' of any attempt to define time independently of change: 'To maintain that "reality" is defined outside of time reveals a claim which cannot but surprise us: it is to recuperate the metaphysics of eternity by extirpating from time the very contradiction which constitutes it.' Against this claim, we must insist that 'there is no pure time, but [only] an alterity of time with respect to itself, an alterity ceaselessly reconstituted by recurrent bucklings [*boucles*]', in short, a 'chrono-logic' (Janicaud 1997: 59).

As the motor of this chrono-logic, the tension between A-series and B-series time points beyond itself – to a 'preparatory operation', a temporalisation producing an event, that makes possible the very articulation of these two (derivative) series. Both McTaggart and Mellor act as if events were preconstituted prior to the temporal horizons from which they emerge and they both assume that the process through which an event arises simply coincides with the dates of its occurrence. On both counts, the analytic philosophical tradition fails to take 'into consideration the specificity of the temporal horizon: for', reasons Janicaud, 'I do not reduce myself to a subject sliding along an axis; this type of representation always supposes my insertion into the heart of a horizon where my mobile present deploys the irremediable dissociation between past and future. *At a level more originary than the serial representation of time, a specifically temporal intentionality is deployed*: it is the event of events, temporality itself' (Janicaud 1997: 60). It is crucial to emphasise that this preparatory operation, this temporalisation that first produces an event, is preparatory *both* to the before-after and to the past-present-future accounts of time. Far from being two distinct kinds of time, A-series and B-series time turn out to be two versions of a single, though certainly not unified and homogeneous, 'chrono-logic' – a chrono-logic that forcefully affirms the priority of temporalisation.

II. The imbrication of narrative and history

This discussion allows us to specify the contribution of *Only Revolutions*: what the apparently 'objective' events collected in the historical sidebar afford is a practical context for the correlating of self-reference with dating. What underlies both of these temporalising activities is nothing less than the reader's actualisation of concrete potential correspondences between narrative and history. Far from being some rigorously non-subjective inscription of history that signifies autonomously, the historical sidebar functions by furnishing a shared 'objective' context that facilitates the concretisation of the double-barrelled narrative. Insofar as this context serves as a selectional matrix for according meaning to the narrative, it cannot remain extrinsic to the narrative, but is in fact so profoundly intertwined with it as to render dubious any attempt to demarcate the objectively historical from the intimately personal.

With this in mind, let me turn to the task of inventorying and categorising some of the correlations between the narrative and the Chronomosaics. First and most generally, there are what I can only imagine (given Danielewski's meticulous control over the construction of the novel) to be countless instances of resonance between words in the narrative and items included in the historical sidebar. One reader mentions the lines 'Turn out, turn loose and turn on' (H/78) coincident with the sidebar from 17 June 1969, a moment during the Summer of Love 'which exemplified in the culture Timothy Leary's urging that everyone "turn on, tune in, drop out"' (Comment by *Modified*, 26 May 2006, 'Chronology/Sidebar'). Another cites the lines 'Surrendering Nothing. But April does' (S/2) which coincide with an historical sidebar dated 27 September 1864 and including the phrase 'General Order', which according to this reader refers to General Lee's issuing of general order 9 calling for a surrender to the North on 9 April 1865 (Comment by *BigM*, 26 May 2006, 'Chronology/Sidebar'). To these examples involving slight temporal divergences, I can add one of my own: 'Helterskeltering' (H/79) which coincides with the date of the sidebar, 27 July 1969 and references one of its items, namely, 'Sharon Tate goes,' albeit only through a historical detour via the 1976 movie of Manson's trial entitled *Helter Skelter* (as I learned by visiting Wikipedia).

Another reader notes two further resonances:

Page: S4
The Story:
– Tranquility & Civil Authority,
The History Gutter:
June 7 1866
...
– Peace, order.
The point:
Andrew Johnson's August 20, 1866 proclamation that 'the said insurrection is at an end, and that peace, order, and tranquility, and civil authority now exist in and throughout the whole United States of America.' (via Modern History Sourcebook)

Page: S5
The Story:
– Git gone Scalwag,
The History Gutter:
April 9 1867
...
Scalawags & satraps.
The point:
The term scalawag was a derogatory term used in the Reconstruction era in the South of the United States to describe white Southerners who supported the Republican party and often but not always the effort to extend civil rights to African Americans. It made up a group of citizens who were not sympathetic to former leaders of the Confederacy in their effort to reclaim political power. (via Wikipedia)
(Comment by *Elmago*, 31 May 2006, 'Chronology/Sidebar')

I cite these last comments verbatim to draw attention to the necessary use of reference materials, including online ones like Wikipedia, in the process of deciphering the text. Mirroring Danielewski's own consultation of Wikipedia in his composition process, readers' recourse to internet archives attests to the enormity of historical record that becomes available to us in the internet age. At the same time, and for the same reason, it also foregrounds the crucial role played by selection, a role whose significance increases in direct proportion to the increase in archived information available at a given point in history.

If direct resonances between the double-barrelled narrative and the historical sidebar represent one kind of selection, revealing how narrative can constrain historical context, Danielewski's mobilisation of his fanbase to post suggestions for significant historical events online comprises another. We will never know exactly how the material thus solicited impacted upon the revisions of the narrative, nor will we ever grasp the principle of selection that guided Danielewski in his assembly of the historical sidebar. What we can know is that the opening of the text's composition to its future readers introduces a kind of torsion into the representation of B-series time: the events included are those with the most significance for a certain collectivity, namely Danielewski's readership (comprised largely of people born after the Kennedy assassination, which is to say, in the period belonging to Hailey's narrative and the second half of the novel).

More than one reader has pointed to the sense of being present that comes with temporal proximity to, if not personal experience of, historical events. Consider, for example, the following comment by *Stencil*: 'The point I was making . . . was that the Kennedy Assassination was one of those events where everyone alive at the time remembers where they were when it happened, so "You were there" serves as a reminder of this' (Comment by *Stencil*, 12 May 2006, 'Chronology/Sidebar'). Positioned at the literal middle of the text and the chronology, at the point of maximal historical intensity, the Kennedy assassination emblematises the imbrication of A-series and B-series time around which the entirety of *Only Revolutions* is constructed and which drives its concretisation through reading. We would do well to characterise it as a privileged moment of collective-personal self-reference, an event that does not so much bring a past reality into the present, in the sense of Roland Barthes' *ça a été* ('that was', the coincidence of pastness and reality (Barthes 1982)), as mark a continuity and a personal, living connection to the past – a sense that the past is not simply past, but remains part of our present. It is precisely this kind of *living* connection to the past that is at stake generally in the torsion exercised on B-series time by the selectional pressure of Danielewski's participating fanbase and, also, to the precise extent that it generates a 'You were there' feeling, by each and every reading of the text. *Stencil* makes this suggestion altogether salient in remarking on the peculiarity of encountering one's own submitted moments of history within the text: 'This also ties in with the moments of history we were asked to submit; a similar sort of identification happens when the submitters chance upon their submissions. Also, "You were there" hints at the proverbial response of Vietnam vets when telling their stories "you weren't there, man." "You were there" also suggests that the story took place somehow in our presence, that we share history in the same way Sam and Hailey share history, parallel to our own lives. Or something like that' (Comment by *Stencil*, 12 May 2006, 'Chronology/Sidebar').

The inclusion of italicised 'phrases from history' alongside historical events in the sidebar, together with the inclusion of blank sections that remain to be filled in (from 18 January 2006 to 19 January 2063), suggest how the present or being-present comprises a paradigm for the non-differentiation of phenomenological, A-series and historical, B-series time, *even when the event in question is in the past (or in the future)*. In this sense, the effect of citing actual utterances of history is to emphasise their once-presentness, a presentness that is reproduced or rather reduplicated in the register of reading/ constitution of the text. Let me focus on what may be the most famous of these inclusions: the lines '*revolution is not a dinner party*' (S/89). Spoken by Mao Tse-Tung ('A revolution is not a dinner party, or writing an essay, or painting a picture, or doing embroidery' (Wikipedia)) presumably in the context of the Cultural Revolution (1966–76), these lines appear in the sidebar for 5 November 1927, a date not long after that of the founding of the People's Liberation Army on 1 August 1927. The effect of this particular anachronism is to extend the sway of Mao's utterance backwards to the inauguration of the Red Army, as if the Cultural Revolution were somehow already contained in the earlier event, a future potentiality belonging to the broad presencing of the event of Chinese communism.

That Danielewski *intends* for the reader to negotiate between and across narrative and history, phenomenological and objective time, appears clearly from the way the history was literally extracted from the narrative during his compositional process. We are fortunate enough to have available seven versions of the first page of Sam's narrative that document its evolution from the initial handwritten version to the final published version (Danielewski 2007). What we learn from this documentation is just how complexly imbricated the narrative and historical components of *Only Revolutions* in fact are: if the compositional 'evolution' exposed here is characteristic of the entire novel, not only can we readily understand why it took

Danielewski six years to complete, but we can grasp how thoroughly the narrative is permeated by post-Civil War history – how it is, first and foremost, an allegory of this history. Danielewski's breakthrough comes in 2004, some one and a quarter years after the initial composition of the narrative, when he uses a highlighter to mark up his text and annotates his highlighting with dates and names of events in the right margin of the page (Figure 5). Three months and two versions later, this proto-separation acquires typographical materiality in the form of the two-column layout, a form that results from the literal extraction of event words and phrases from the narrative (Figure 6). This shows the extreme care Danielewski takes to imbricate the two components of his text, not by directly entangling them (as he had initially done), but precisely by separating them and making them available for the reader to re-entangle. I would surmise that the online solicitation of dates and events from his fanbase further supports this process by subjecting Danielewski's own intuitions concerning resonance to an external input, making the narrative all that much less an allegory of Danielewski's own perceived sense of history and all that more an allegory of his generation's collectively experienced and collectively selected history.[4] What Danielewski effectively accomplishes in de-coupling narrative and historical event is a re-potentialising of history on the collective matrix of his readers' rich embodiment.

III. Character between freedom and constraint

'*House of Leaves* was about plot. It was a house that sat on a "plot," and it was about stories, just like a house is supposed to have many "stories." *Only Revolutions* is about character. It is a character – literally and figuratively – "driven" book' (Danielewski, in Miller 2006). If we are to assent to this valuation – Danielewski's own – we must first insist on the peculiarity of the characters central to the twin narratives of *Only Revolutions*: Sam and Hailey are about as far as one can get from characters as we know them, that is, psychologically complex, internally rich and multiply motivated characters of the sort that populate the history of the novel from the eighteenth century onwards. Rather, these two characters are allegorical figures of sorts, and what they allegorise is the incessant movement of time itself and the universal human desire to get free from time's burden. Confronted with the objectness of *Only*

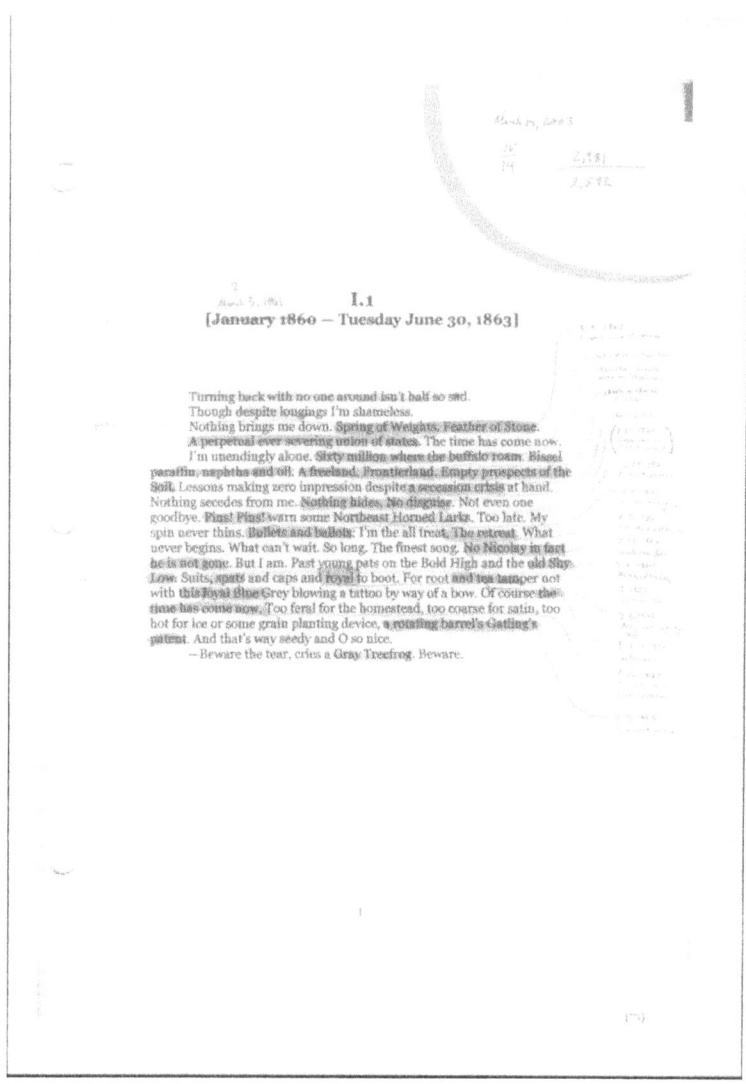

5 M. Z. Danielewski (2002) *Only Revolutions*, page 179, *Take tt7 – December 3, 2002* [471 words. Font: Hand. Black: #2 pencil. Trim size: 8.5 x 11. Software: paper]

Print interface to time

6 M. Z. Danielewski (2004) *Only Revolutions*, page 181, *Annotated Rim-Through Dailies – March 14, 2004* [210 words. Fonts: Georgia (Sam); Hand (Z). Black: 2H lead + Assorted highlighters. Trim size: 8.5 x 11. Software: Word]

Revolutions, with everything that characterises it as an experiment with the affordances of print, one quickly grasps that this allegorisation of time and the escape from time cannot remain exclusively or even primarily thematic, but must be worked through on multiple registers ranging from the pseudo-Oulipean constraints Danielewski imposes on himself (pages of exactly 180 words (or 360 words counting both narratives), with 90 (180) words of narrative and 90 (180) words of history, a total length of 360 pages, a division into 5 acts of 72 pages, and so on) to the radical formalisation of character (the evacuation of any character content or individuality other than a basic belonging to the sheer ongoingness of time itself: perpetual existence as 'allways sixteen').

What this refiguration of character facilitates is nothing less than the fundamental analogy informing the novel: the analogy between the constraints of the historical world and the constraints of the book as a form. 'The quality of the book', notes Danielewski, 'is so much about Sam and Hailey freeing themselves entirely from the constraints of the world. In a weird way, they demand being freed of the constraints of the book' (Danielewski, in Miller 2006). This analogy literally motivates Danielewski to depict Sam and Hailey in the way he does, as driven by their constraints and yet as 'unpursued' by anything other than time itself, which is also to say, by anyone other than the book's readers:

> At the heart of it are these two kids. They were two kids that I came across. They were impertinent, they were courageous, they were penniless, and most important, they were parentless. They were without anybody. They were sitting on a corner begging for change. And they loved each other. They held onto each other, they looked after each other, they lusted after each other, they protected each other. They were each other's world. And the fact that they were without anything was so inspiring. Because they were bold. Maybe they were Homeric gods in disguise. Maybe they truly were Mendicants. But there was something magical about them for me – that absolute attachment to each other. And I looked at them as a kind of American Romeo and Juliet. But later I realized that they really weren't – because they didn't have the Capulets and the Montagues out there to separate them, to chase them. There's *Bonnie and Clyde*, *Natural Born Killers*. They have the law – they have Harvey Keitel – there's someone who pursues them. These two are unpursued. So, you know, for me what became interesting was that ongoing discussion, meditation if you will, exploration about freedom and love. Because freedom is ultimately the

quest from anything – to be unrestrained by your circumstances, by your society, by even your own body – whereas love is all about attachment. It's all about the involvement with someone else, which is the opposite of freedom. And yet love allows you to transcend certain things. So, as I was working on this book – and now this is getting back to your question – I realized that I wanted to set them up in a way where they were constrained, they were limited, because their entire quest is how to free themselves. (Benzon 2007: 2–3)

What Danielewski enumerates as constraint here – circumstances, society, body – refers directly to the constraining force of history: unpursued by anyone or anything inside their narrative, Sam and Hailey are nevertheless pursued by something external to it, by the sheer force of time and by the hold that history places on the future. Paradoxically, it is their submission, in their role as surrogate for the reader, to the most extreme kind of formal constraint that generates the possibility for the hold of history to be loosened and for the force of time to become creative.

In this sense, Sam and Hailey allegorise the 'absolute power' of temporalisation as it is conceptualised in the literature of phenomenology. In Edmund Husserl's late thinking on time, undertaken in concert with his last research assistant Eugen Fink, the quest for an absolute foundation of time reaches 'rock bottom', and the realisation sets in that consciousness cannot constitute time, but rather must find its own possibility for being from time. To describe the givenness of time to consciousness (and to other temporal processes), Fink coins the term 'de-presencing' (*Entgegenwärtigung*), and he emphasises how consciousness – prior to its separation from the world and to the division of subject and object – is itself part of the ongoing worldly process of temporalisation (Fink 1966). Far from being the privileged term, the ongoing present is only possible because of the world's unceasing process of de-presencing: the present remains present precisely because worldly materiality continues to flow.

Abstracted from its phenomenological vocation, this genealogy of time-consciousness has interesting implications for our understanding of *Only Revolutions* as a technical interface onto time. In particular, it introduces a notion of self-reference (A-series time) that is not only perfectly compatible with the 'objective', enunciation-independent time of the world (B-series time), but that actually requires it as a foundation. It is only on the basis of de-presencing (the ongoing temporalisation of the world) that the experience of presencing becomes possible. Put another way, phenomenological presencing is thoroughly imbricated within worldly or 'objective' de-presencing. My contention is that the characters of Sam and Hailey are figures for this imbrication, or more precisely, they are perpetually present frames of reference that correlate directly with the ongoing temporalisation of the world and of history. In making this claim, I can solicit the aid of Danielewski himself, who comments: 'The characters are moving and are oblivious to history. History is enacted through them. They have no awareness of history. They have no memories' (Miller and Reverte 2007: 2).

There are many passages in the novel devoted to the characters' self-description in explicitly temporal terms. These occur in many different contexts, but all invariably highlight the fundamental identity of the twin narrative with the objective flux of time (history). Let me simply enumerate a few of them:

> We're solitary and yet something allways moves alongside US. Still. Hunting. (S/273)

> And though opportunities stack up around US, we stand on it, shunning the squirt brakes, leaving this tip: when the going gets slow you go. (S/284)

> By our worldturning blur (S/296)

> And I'm afraid. Quavering too while Hailey detains all she escapes. Nothing ever overtakes her freedom ride. I just hold tight. (S/303)

> Our present. Lucky world. How long will it continue? I can't dish. While we cease, it can't ever finish. But we never cease. We only jet from such an armistice. Exhausted. (S/310)

> Unpardonably slow. Still this is a way to go. And so everything else around US allso goes. (H/52)

> Hailey's my oblivion. For once. And allways. Beyond even time's front. Because now we are out of time. We are at once. (S/320)

If we contextualise these exemplary passages against Danielewski's comments on freedom and constraint, we can grasp the significance of his intervention into the road genre: the belongingness of presence to de-presencing, of self-reference to the deep temporalisation that generates historical/cosmological time, is at once a promise of freedom and a source of constraint. De-presencing or the 'objective' flow of worldly time is what burdens the present and at the same time what opens the possibility for the new to happen. What Sam and Hailey 'experience' in their respective, intertwined narratives is precisely the twin force of de-presencing: the constraint of a past beyond their making *and* the responsibility for a future that emerges from selective adoption of this past.

This, I suggest, is the deep meaning of Danielewski's claim that the novel is 'character-driven': in contrast to *House of Leaves* where enjoyment proceeded from the layering of plot, here plot is almost entirely incidental to the character's drive to keep moving. And to the extent that the reader's path into the novel, and into the historical Chronomosaics, must proceed through the narratives of Sam and Hailey,[5] the reader's job is less to concretise a pre-inscribed plot than to actualise a viable way to just keep moving. That this cannot but yield some selective actualisation of historical events attests that there cannot be a purely formal act of presencing, that any gesture of self-reference requires a content external to it, a centrifugal force coming from an outside that is the very materiality of history itself. Put more simply, Danielewski's readers come to realise something that his characters seem always already to know: that their capacity to keep moving, to continue to be present, is only made possible by some historical inheritance which remains both uncertain and open to contestation.

IV. From the pressure of history to the asymmetry of narrative

The dialectic of freedom and constraint, however, is not a zero-sum game. Simply put, there is no absolute freedom and no absolute constraint, but always some balance, some range of oscillation between them. I now want to investigate the devices Danielewski deploys to weight this balance. What does it mean that the locus for self-reference is split between a male and a female character? And how does the concentration around the year 1963 and the gradual dispersion in both directions (back to 1863 and forward to 2063) impact upon the reader's selective adoption of history, and ultimately upon the significance of the book as an interface onto time?

Danielewski defines Sam and Hailey as 'the agents or coalescents of history, what history would look like if we could get out of this computer grid we're in' (Miller 2006). More than a generic reference to digital culture or today's archival capacity, this invocation of the computer grid foregrounds the non-hierarchical, homogeneous terrain of the archival project. With Google's promises of infinite storage for libraries but also for life documentation, we are quickly entering a world where information truly has become flat, where nothing is intrinsically more important than anything else, where, in short, there need be no selection whatsoever. As characters who are the products of a selective process of historical adoption, Sam and Hailey furnish a different model – and indeed, embody a different sense – of what history can be: namely, the result of a give-and-take between the archive and some 'coalescent' that expresses the living connection of the past with the future.

Why two characters? Why these two characters? Danielewski broaches this issue indirectly when he comments on the novel's peculiar resistance to vision: 'So here [*Only Revolutions*] is something that's absolutely visual; if you look at each page, it's like a screenplay ... At the same time, it's impossible to visualize. Sam and Hailey are all races; they're all shapes and colors and clothing. How would you actually film that? You can't. But at the same time we understand who they are. Are people going to expand on that, are they going to toy with that? I don't know. It's a lot of work' (Benzon 2007: 7). All races and shapes, colours and clothing: Sam and Hailey are coterminous with the domain of sensation and the continuum of individuation, and yet they are divided by sex. We cannot but ask why. Is this simply a pretext for the scenes of sexual activity, and concomitant opportunities for creative punning, that – as a central instance of life force – form such a major investment in both narratives? Is it the necessary precondition for the operation of love, which is to say, the sole phenomenon that appears (and is cited by Danielewski as being) capable of transcending – escaping from – the constraint of time? Or, is it an indication of the inherent 'structural' partiality of any individual coalescing of history – a centrifugal call of sorts to embrace a broader scope of selection, exemplified by Danielewski's own solicitation to his fanbase? However we answer these questions, what does seem clear is that any and every reader will be able to 'understand who [Sam and Hailey] are', which is to say, to presence through them, without this understanding in any way limiting, totalising, or defining them as fixed, complete characters.

Whereas the question of sex and the sexual difference of the two characters instances a symmetrical division that literally and figuratively cleaves the novel in two, Danielewski's choice of a historical trajectory and his decision to weight it differentially introduce asymmetry – what I have above called torsion – at the level of its embrace of history. If we can unproblematically say that the selection of trajectory functions to privilege the post-civil war (and by implication or amplification, the civil rights era) within the history of America, what can we say about the text's concentration around and bidirectional dispersion out from the date of Kennedy's assassination in 1963?

While we will clearly never come to any certainty concerning the rationale for this privileging, we can perfectly well conceptualise its impact on the experience of reading and, by implication, on my claim for the novel's status as a technical interface onto time. As I see it, these decisions to weight history differentially – whether they lie with Danielewski or, as I think far more likely, involve some constraint on and centrifugal extension of his authorial agency – render the novel something less, but also something more, than a neutral platform for confronting self-reference and history, A-series and B-series time. Indeed, what the torsion exerted on the historical archive seems to yield is a scene of confrontation where the reader, following in the wake of the characters, must reckon with a particular archive or 'archaeology of knowledge', a particular set of possible historical events that in different configurations can and do continue to inform the ongoing present that is America.

With his concepts of the 'historian's code' and of 'hot and cold chronologies', structuralist anthropologist Claude Lévi-Strauss can help us understand the hermeneutic impact of Danielewski's games with historical scale. According to Lévi-Strauss, dates are the '*sine qua non*' of history (Lévi-Strauss 1966: 258) and the 'variable quantity of dates applied to periods of equal duration' comprises 'a gauge of what might be called the pressure of history'. From this conception of the density of dates comes the famous distinction between 'hot' and 'cold' chronologies: '"hot chronologies" . . . are those of periods where in the eyes of the historian numerous events appear as differential elements; others, on the contrary, where for him (though not of course for the men who lived through them) very little or nothing took place' (Lévi-Strauss 1966: 259).

Taking Danielewski's historical Chronomosaics as a historian's code in an expanded sense, we can get a sense of how *Only Revolutions* makes the density of history a function of its significance for the collective generation comprising Danielewski's readership, and thus how it redefines the 'objectivity' of history as a function of technically facilitated selectivity. By indexing the temperature of history to the perceptions of this collectivity (gathered through online solicitation), Danielewski integrates his readers' expectations as a key element in the narrative's trajectory. Accordingly, as we read the novel, we quickly come to realise that the correlation of A-series and B-series time is made to undergo a double process: proceeding chronologically, it moves from a most dispersed, cold state (with an interval of roughly ten months, from 22 November 1863 to 27 September 1864 (S/1–2)) to a most concentrated, hot state (with intervals on both sides of one day, from 21 November 1963 to 22 November 1963 (S/359–360) and 22 November 1963 to 23 November 1963 (H/1–2), respectively) and then back again to a maximally dispersed, cold state (with an interval again of roughly ten months, 17 March 2062 to 19 January 2063 (H/359–360). This torsion that the historical archive exerts on the narrative operates to constrain the correlation between the reader's (and the characters') A-series acts of self-reference and B-series objective history: the reader's capacity to temporalise Hailey's or Sam's narrative at any given moment is and can only be a function of the temporalising (or the 'temperature') of 'objective' history. At moments of extreme historical density, the temporal correlations are necessarily far more fine-grained and thus more intense and more 'local' than at periods of historical dispersion, and this differential impacts upon the meaning of the reader's (and characters') temporalising acts in ways that are indeterminate but consequential to how the collective, technically mediated historical archive informs our sense of our own history and of its significance for our living present.

In addition to introducing an asymmetry into the representation of history, this thermal selectional principle also introjects a fundamental asymmetry between the two narratives themselves. Thus, Sam's narrative starts in a dispersed state and slowly gains steam as it advances towards that date of maximal compression, while Hailey's explodes from the heat of the Kennedy assassination and gradually winds down as Hailey herself appears to die or, as Danielewski prefers to put it, to 'go'. From the standpoint of the reader's activity, what this means, first and foremost, is that the engagement with history via the confrontation of self-reference and recorded event occurs at divergent time scales depending on where he or she is in the narrative trajectory and which narrative he or she is focalising through. When beginning Hailey's narrative, the reader temporalises history on the scale of one day; when beginning Sam's, she temporalises at the scale of ten months.

Yet even the neatness of this divergence is undercut and complexified by the correlations *between* the two narratives – correlations set off by verbal correspondences between the coupled text of the two narratives on their shared pages – with the result that every act of readerly self-reference (like the characters' acts they reduplicate) occurs at two time scales. This, in turn, introduces a further asymmetry into the novel, since the correspondences that interarticulate the text at its mid-point (S/360 and H/1) correlate the exact same time scale – indeed they perfectly coincide – and proceed from there to diverge progressively until a point where they correlate events occurring at a time differential of 200 years and at time scales of ten months. How is the reader to code differentially these variant correspondences? When, for example, we discern the echoes of S/360 and H/1 – of 'I can walk away from everything' (H/1) with 'O Hailey no, I could never walk away from you'; of 'Everyone loves the Dream but I kill it' (H/1) with 'Everyone betrays the Dream but who cares for it?'; of 'I'll destroy the World. That's all' (H/1) with 'I'll destroy no World so long it keeps turning with flurry & gush . . .'; of 'Allmighty sixteen and freeeeee. Rebounding on bare feet' (H/1) with 'By you, ever sixteen, this World's preserved' – when we encounter such correspondences, how are we to inflect them with the 'meaning' of their hot temperature? And likewise, when we discern echoes at the other extreme, how should their coldness impact upon our evaluation of their significance?

As what I have called a print interface onto time, *Only Revolutions* does not resolve the philosophical paradox of time. Indeed, it does not promise any definite answers at all. What it does is afford us, its readers, an opportunity to engage with the collective, digital archive of history. More specifically, it allows us to experiment with the varying impact this archive has on our efforts to temporalise our present. Precisely because of its range across divergent scales or 'grains' of history, the print book shows itself to be an inimicable medium: more so than more recent media that incorporate the flux of time into their technicity, the print book attains its singular vocation from its capacity to stand back from the flux of time, to support both self-referential, phenomenological A-series and non-subjective B-series temporalisations, and thereby to facilitate encounters between these two divergent judgements of time. If *Only Revolutions* demonstrates that time is the result of such encounters, and indeed of their ongoing, incremental repetition, what it ultimately reveals is the power of reading itself: the reader's – each reader's – actualising of potential correspondences generates a texture of time that comprises the very materiality of the future-oriented living present.

Notes

1 See the video interview with Danielewski on the only revolutions website: www.onlyrevolutions.com, videos, video # 5.
2 As, once again, Danielewski himself suggests: 'As archaic as it is, with its illuminated text and its ribbons, this book could not exist without technology. Without my G5 and 23-inch screen, with two pages on the screen at one time.' And he makes a similar claim about the software he used: 'Adobe InDesign CS. I had – Font Pro, I think – I had like 10,000 fonts, which is also a huge deal to manage. Online resources, certain archival things. OED online so I could race through etymologies quickly, double-check words. In the old days, what do you do to find one word? You take down the two volume set, it takes you a while to find the word – with the magnifying glass' (both citations from Benzon 2007).
3 Danielewski emphasises the thematic absence of technology in his own account of how the novel engages technology: 'The thing about the Internet is it's just an extension of a capacity that was already understood when the encyclopedia was being written, when Joyce was writing *Ulysses*. These were already hypertext novels ... But now there's another type of connectivity that couldn't have been anticipated. So that's the question. The properties of hyperlinking is nothing new – even the most mundane books have a hyper-textual quality because you can go on your Apple phone and Google something if it's a recipe book, for example. At what point are we really getting at something that is useful vs. just because you can? *Only Revolutions* is about technology, partly because no technology appears in the book. Nothing. No radios, no wires, no telegraphs. All technological process has been eradicated. There are not many books where you read and ask "What's missing? What's NOT in here?"' (Miller and Reverte 2007: 4).
4 That is why Danielewski views the online solicitation as part of the 'centrifugal' nature of *Only Revolutions*: 'Addressing the online community and saying, "Hey, give me your input here: what was your favorite historical moment?" So it's not just my personal history, but histories that go beyond what I can perceive when I'm looking at thousands of books' (Benzon 2007: 4).

5 Consider the following comment on the experience of reading – and of learning how to read – the novel: 'As for the sidebar, my initial reading confused the life out of me because I was reading each page of text, followed by its sidebar and trying to extract meaning from both. I completely lost track of the story. After reading the two separately, it seems like the sidebar is there to provide a juxtaposition to the main plot. It provides dry historical context to this burning love story. It either reaffirms the meaning of human emotion, or trivializes it, depending on the reader's own experiences' (Comment by Po-M, 6 April 2006, 'Chronology/Sidebar').

Works cited

Barthes, R. (1982) *Camera Lucida*, trans. Howard, R., New York: Hill & Wang.
Benzon, K. (2007) 'Revolutions 2' [Interview with Mark Z. Danielewski]. *Electronic Book Review*. www.electronicbookreview.com/thread/wuc/regulated.
'Chronology/Sidebar' forum for *Only Revolutions* (2006). http://www.houseofleaves.com/forum/showthread.php?t=4343.
Danielewski, M. Z. (2006) *Only Revolutions*, New York: Pantheon Books.
Danielewski, M. Z. (2007) 'Only evolutions', *Gulf Coast: A Journal of Literature & Fine Arts* 19(2): 176–184.
Fink, E. (1966) *Studien zur Phänomenologie 1930–1939*, The Hague: Martinus Nijhoff.
Hansen, M. B. N. (2004) 'The digital topography of Mark Z. Danielewski's *House of Leaves*', *Contemporary Literature* 45(4): 597–636.
Hayles, N. K. (2002) 'Saving the subject: remediation in *House of Leaves*', *American Literature* 74: 777–806.
Hayles, N. K. (2008) *Electronic Literature: New Horizons for the Literary*, Notre Dame, IN: University of Notre Dame Press.
Husserl, E. (1991) *On the Phenomenology of the Consciousness of Internal Time (1893–1917)*, trans. Brough, J., Dordrecht: Kluwer Academic Publishers.
Janicaud, D. (1997) *Chronos: Pour l'intelligence du partage temporal*, Paris: Éditions Grasset & Fasquelle.
Lévi-Strauss, C. (1966) *The Savage Mind*, Chicago: University of Chicago Press.
Miller, A. (2006) 'Revolutionary roads', *Los Angeles City Beat*. lacitybeat.com/cms/story/detail/?id=4376.
Miller, C. and Reverte, M. (2007) 'LAist interview: Mark Danielewski', *LAist*, 23 October 2007. laist.com/2007/10/23/laist_interview_55.php.

11

Only Revolutions and the drug of rereading

Joe Bray, University of Sheffield

This essay considers the physical shape of Mark Z Danielewski's *Only Revolutions*, and the effects that this has on the way it is read. It argues that neither the traditional methods of book history nor those of literary criticism can fully capture all the meanings that the highly constrained form of *Only Revolutions* generates, and that fresh insights can be gained through the application of techniques associated with the emerging discipline of cognitive poetics. In particular, it shows that the emphasis in this approach on the dynamic nature of the reading experience matches up well with the way that readers are encouraged, indeed required, to read Danielewski's book. Its carefully patterned, symmetrical structure calls for a process of endless rereading, as the reader continually revolves the book and considers its narrative from different perspectives. Rereading, according to the model proposed here, is not a means to an end, but rather an instinctive, even compulsive act that reveals subtle interplays of sound and sense and compels the reader to be forever beginning interpretation anew.

I. Book history, literary criticism and cognitive poetics

In his landmark essay 'Typography and Meaning: The Case of William Congreve' (first delivered at a symposium in 1977), D. F. McKenzie draws attention to 'the integrity of Congreve's collected *Works* in all its details' (2002: 199). Noting the 'highly conscious deployment' of such features as the author's preface, the act and scene divisions, the head- and tail-pieces, the size and styles of type, the capitalisation, punctuation, italicisation and *mise-en-page*, McKenzie claims that it is 'quite impossible, in my view, to divorce the substance of the text on the one hand from the physical form of its presentation on the other.

The book itself is an expressive means' (200). He notes that in addition to uncovering its verbal and typographic meanings, 'we must learn to see that its shape in the hand also speaks to us from the past' (200). Frustrated by the 'intellectual timidity and mechanical zeal' (209) of much current 'textual criticism', McKenzie complains that 'we have at present no body of critical theory that encourages us to bring together the discrete activities which constitute the history of the book' and that 'the idea of a *text* as a complex structure of meanings which embraces every detail of its formal and physical presentation in a specific historical context is quite remote from current practice' (206). He calls for a new 'sociology of the text', which will 'marry the verbal preoccupations of literary and textual criticism, the material concerns of historical bibliography, and the economic and social dimensions of production and readership' (200).

McKenzie's call has unfortunately only patchily been met in the last 30 years, as the disciplines of 'book history' and 'literary criticism' have largely remained methodologically (and institutionally) distinct. Some recent attempts have however been made to bring the two closer together. Peter D. McDonald observes 'unexpected intersections between the apparently opposed enterprises of theory and the history of the book' (2006: 217), arguing that what he calls 'literary historiography' needs to 'make the most of the concepts, protocols, and sources both enterprises have opened up' (227). He suggests that Pierre Bourdieu's concept of the 'literary field' offers 'the most effective link between book history and theoretical reflections on literature' (225). In the same issue of *PMLA* Leah Price also attempts to forge links between the two disciplines, provocatively posing the question 'What if, instead of asking what book history can do for literary criticism, we asked what literary theory can do for book history?' (2006: 10). As she puts it, 'to pit the soaring (or flighty) ambitions of theory against the grounded (or plodding) procedures of bibliography is to understate the stakes of both. Each questions the terms that underlie our critical practice: what is an author, a reader, a work, a text?' (15).

Yet the entrenched disciplines of book history and literary criticism are not the only ones grappling with these questions. Another field has recently developed which also attempts to marry formal analysis with more theoretical considerations, and which may perhaps be able to shed light on some of the issues preoccupying both the contemporary book historian and the literary critic, and breathe new life into McKenzie's 'sociology of the text'. Emerging from a combination of cognitive linguistics and cognitive psychology on the one hand, and literary stylistics on the other, cognitive poetics lays equal emphasis on each of the three nodes of 'the triangle of "author-text-reader"' (Stockwell 2002: 5). As Stockwell elaborates, 'concerned with literary reading, and with both a psychological and a linguistic dimension, cognitive poetics offers a means of discussing interpretation whether it is an authorly version of the world or a readerly account, and how these interpretations are made manifest in textuality' (5). Crucially, cognitive poetics offers a new way of thinking about readers' physical engagement with texts, since at its core is the notion of 'embodiment', or the principle that, in Stockwell's words, 'all of our experiences, knowledge, beliefs and wishes are involved in and expressible only through patterns of language that have their roots in our material existence' (5). When combined with the groundwork of what McDonald calls 'literary historiography', cognitive poetics promises then a new perspective on, in McKenzie's words, 'the idea of a *text* as a complex structure of meanings which embraces every detail of its formal and physical presentation in a specific historical context', and a new insight into the significance of its 'shape in the hand'.

II. The book of *Only Revolutions*

This essay concerns itself with a contemporary text whose 'formal and physical presentation' is integral to its meaning. Mark Z. Danielewski's *Only Revolutions* embodies McKenzie's dictum that 'the book itself is an expressive means', and his belief that 'the substance of the text on the one hand' is inseparable from 'the physical form of its presentation on the other'. Indeed it is impossible to outline the plot of *Only Revolutions* without alluding to its form. In Danielewski's own words, 'at the heart of it are these two kids' (Benzon 2007), Sam and Hailey, whose two verse narratives start at opposing ends of the book. The two 16-year-olds become lovers and set out on a road-trip in a variety of cars across the United States. The reader is encouraged by 'the publisher' to read eight pages of one character's narrative, before rotating the book 180 degrees and taking up the other character's narrative from the opposite end of the book. He or she is thus constantly revolving the book and reading it in two opposite directions; two ribbons, a green one for Sam, who according to

Hailey has 'Green Eyes with flecks of Gold' (H7), and a gold one for Hailey, who according to Sam has 'Gold Eyes with flecks of Green' (S7), help keep the place. At the bottom of each page the reader thus sees the other character's narrative, upside down, though at a different place in the story. Both narratives diminish in font-size and number of lines as they progress, though there are always 90 words per each character's narrative on a page, thus 180 per page and 360 per double-page spread. Each character's narrative is also accompanied by a column of abbreviated historical events headed by a single date: Sam's narrative runs from 22 November 1863 (in the middle of the US Civil War) to 22 November 1963 (Kennedy's assassination), while Hailey's picks up from this latter date and runs to 19 January 2063 (though the columns are blank after 25 May 2005).

The book contains many other symmetries, which are more or less apparent to the reader, though even from this brief summary it is clear that *Only Revolutions* is very carefully and tightly structured. Its rigid form is clearly inseparable from its meaning. In his interview with Kiki Benzon, Danielewski says that he wanted to set Sam and Hailey up 'in a way where they were constrained, they were limited, because their entire quest is how to free themselves' (Benzon 2007). He describes the various symmetries of the book as 'chains that bind them, which they're constantly trying to get out of', and reveals that in the writing of the book 'structure and content' evolved 'simultaneously'. Beyond this thematic connection, though, the question remains as to what effect the highly constrained form of *Only Revolutions* has on the reader's experience of reading the book, and his or her interpretation of it. In order to begin to answer this, I believe that looking beyond the established procedures of book history on the one hand and literary criticism on the other may be helpful.

III. Reading *Only Revolutions*

First, though, some closer attention to the physical appearance of the *Only Revolutions* page is needed. As the brief summary above has indicated, the reader is encouraged to read eight pages of one character's narrative before rotating the book and reading eight pages of the other's. These short sections often retell the same story from the two different perspectives. For example, on their way up The Mississippi ('Our Mishishishi'), Sam relates how they stop to take a brief dip in the river:

> Where there's a chance,
> there's a bend. Hailey marvelling
> how I ignore the current.
> I am the current. And currently frisky.
> The currency of every risk.
> But I marvel over Hailey too,
> enjoying her then,
> however meek, fawning when
> I leap towards the adoring
> ripples to take her hand
> and her beneath broiling skies,
> on cool earth.
> (S136)

When the book is rotated, Hailey's version of the same event is as follows:

> Where there's a bend,
> there's a change. Sam admiring
> how I tear through the current.
> I am the current. And currently bare.
> The currency of every dare.
> But I admire Sam too,
> enjoying him there,
> however timid, rising when
> I stride from the fawning
> ripples to take his hand
> and him over chilly mire,
> beneath burning skies.
> (H136)

There are clearly both obvious and subtle variations here. In the first place Sam's 'Where there's a chance, / there's a bend' becomes Hailey's 'Where there's a bend, / there's a change', with the swapping of the position of 'bend' and the modulation of 'chance' to 'change' suggesting a more optimistic, carefree attitude on Sam's part. At this point in their narratives, at least, Sam is looking more for 'chances', while Hailey is more accepting of 'changes'. This subtle contrast continues throughout the rest of the two passages, as Sam 'ignore[s] the current', perhaps in a foolish act of defiance, while Hailey 'tear[s] through it'. While Sam describes himself as 'the currency of every risk', Hailey is 'the currency of every dare', with the rhyme 'bare/dare' suggesting more of a bold challenge than

The drug of rereading

the flightier 'frisky/risk'. As Hailey's swimming continues the two 'marvel/admire' each other (continuing their choice of word in the second lines), while also viewing the other as 'meek/timid'. Again a word changes position between the two passages, as 'fawning' moves down a line. While Sam describes Hailey as 'fawning when / I leap towards the adoring / ripples to take her hand', she sees him 'rising when / I stride from the fawning / ripples to take his hand'. The 'adoring' in Sam's narrative, though literally absent from Hailey's, partially echoes her two 'admirings' and is perhaps understood in the way she describes him 'rising' as she strides towards him. Finally the last two lines present a reversal: while Sam leads Hailey 'beneath broiling skies, / on cool earth', she takes him 'over chilly mire, / beneath burning skies'. While 'broiling' becomes 'burning' and 'cool earth' becomes 'chilly mire', the 'skies' and 'earth/mire' change places, suggesting the disorientating, head-over-heels effect created both by the lovers' feelings for each other and the reader's act of rotating the book, which is required to read the two passages in sequence.

No doubt there are other connections and contrasts that could be made between the two passages, and my interpretation of Sam's and Hailey's outlooks could be questioned. The important point is that these two passages work together, or rather that they play off each other. The subtle interplays of sound and sense depend on the reader either switching back and forth immediately (rotating the book 180 degrees each time), or at least having the two passages in his or her head (and ear) simultaneously. The full meaning of each passage cannot be understood without a reading of the other; the two, like Sam and Hailey (at this point at least) should not and cannot be separated from each other.

Take another example from later in their narratives, when Sam and Hailey are stuck in St. Louis, forced to work in dead-end jobs in a diner in order to get by and gradually becoming increasingly dispirited. Though their shifts mean they are now rarely together, they take separate bicycle trips to explore the local area. After one such excursion, Sam reports:

> That's how I return.
> My turn around manners
> allways flipping me back
> to my want's duty.
> (S188)

In Hailey's narrative this becomes:

> That's how I turn.
> My returning conduct
> allways heading me back
> to my want's obligation.
> (H188)

Again there are some slight, yet potentially significant, differences here: 'return' and 'turn' are exchanged in the first two lines and Sam's 'manners' becomes Hailey's 'conduct', and his 'allways flipping me back' her 'allways heading me back'. In both cases 'allways' suggests both temporal and spatial exhaustiveness, conflating 'always' and 'all ways'.[1] 'Duty' and 'obligation' are close in meaning, though 'obligation' may suggest a greater sense of binding responsibility on Hailey's part. Both reveal the constraints that the pair feel under as they endure the drudgery of their jobs in St. Louis. Again the words in the passages themselves suggest the actions the reader must perform as he or she alternates between them, turning the book around, or 'flipping' it on its head.

The reader is not however obliged solely to read from Sam's to Hailey's narrative as the note from 'the publisher' on the dust jacket recommends. For example, Hailey's narrative could be read first, in which case Sam's seems more like a playful, slangy response, with 'returning conduct' becoming 'turn around manners' and 'heading me back', 'flipping me back'. One could also read both the passages quoted above as responses to the text printed upside down on the same page. Thus Hailey's text could be read as following Sam's reasoning on why he doesn't leave his job:

> Roamings roam. Impressed by
> obligations. Embargoed by trade.
> I'm allways moved by
> conducts on going away.
> So I stay. (S173)

If the book is then directly flipped over, or turned on its head, the next words are thus Hailey's 'That's how I turn. / My returning conduct / allways heading me back / to my want's obligation.' There are a number of verbal echoes: not only are 'obligations' and 'conducts' repeated (though both become singular) but they appear, respectively, in the penultimate and second lines, and the fourth from the end and the fourth. 'Allways' is also repeated in the

The drug of rereading 207

third line from the end and the third. Sam's page 173 and Hailey's page 188 are thus to some extent mirror images of each other, and both point forwards and back to Sam's page 188 and Hailey's page 173, since the word 'manners' appears twice in each (lines 8 and 10 of S173, lines 9 and 11 of H188), recalling Sam's 'That's how I return. / My turn around manners / allways flipping me back / to my want's duty.' This passage is preceded (if the page is rotated) by Hailey's:

> Pare is pears. Working on
> duties. Organizings surrounded.
> I'm allways moved by the
> manners of going away
> So I stay. (H173)

which in turn of course responds to (or prompts) the final lines of S173 quoted above. In other words, the texts on the page containing S173 and H188, and those on that which includes H173 and S188, all interconnect and are full of repetitions and echoes. Though the two pages do not appear together in the book, there is a four-fold interplay between the passages, so that none can be read in isolation.

Each passage can also be read across to the column of historical events on the left-hand side of the page. Thus, to take just two examples, S173's 'Embargoed by trade' appears next to the column headed 'Dec 1 1941' and could relate to the US's trade embargo of Japan from 1939, which led eventually to Pearl Harbor on 7 December 1941, which is mentioned in the column, while H173's corresponding 'Organizings surrounded' is opposite the column for 'April 1 1983' and could be a reference to the crackdowns in Chile in 1983 on all those groups protesting against the Pinochet regime ('Chile & 1000 arrests' is the relevant entry). Though at times the link between the historical events listed on the left-hand margin of every page and those in Sam's and Hailey's narratives is obscure, the '*mise-en-page*' encourages the reader to look for connections and resonances, such as he or she finds abundantly between the two lovers' tales. No block of text on the page stands alone (or 'allone'), but instead each both calls out to and answers back to other texts on other pages, sometimes far removed. The book demands to be read 'allways', both in the physical and temporal sense, as its highly constrained form paradoxically dictates that the ways in which it can be read, and, crucially, reread, are without limit.

IV. Rereading

Rather than thinking of Sam's and Hailey's stories as two parallel narratives that start at opposite ends of the book and converge in the middle then, it might be more productive to think of *Only Revolutions* as composed of one multi-directional narrative, which the reader is constantly rotating, traversing and rereading. Most literary-theoretical accounts of rereading conceptualise it as a deeper, more profound experience than first-time reading. Matei Calinescu, for example, distinguishes between 'the passion for reading', which is 'in principle insatiable in regard to quantity, extension, curiosity, variety, pleasure', and 'rereading, which often springs from a deeper personal commitment, religious or otherwise' (1993: 90). He associates 'reading' with a 'quasi-hypnotic involvement' and 'rereading' with 'dedication, sustained attention, and sophisticated absorption', explaining the difference as follows: 'involvement is the effect of reading as playing a game of make-believe; absorption is the state in which we reread a text and is conceived as an invitation to play a game with rules' (164). 'Absorption' is for Calinescu 'a state of high concentration of attention', and 'more imaginatively detached and more intellectual' (164) than 'involvement'. François Roustang similarly associates rereading with a greater intellectual understanding of a text, and a deeper insight into the way it is put together. Reporting on his experience of reading Casanova's *The Story of My Life*, Roustang records how he was first 'overcome by the immeasurable complexity of the text' (1989: 123), and how it was only after several rereadings that he became aware of the relationships between 'corresponding components as I passed from one episode to another' (122). His first principle of rereading is thus as follows: 'one must reread until the text can be broken down into its basic components' (122). Rereading, for Roustang, involves a growing sense of the readerly power and mastery over the author; he claims that it 'invent[s] a strategy, adapted to the text and the author, that seeks to disarm the author in order to unmask him' (129).

Yet the notion of a first, innocent reading and a second, more sophisticated one breaks down in the face of a physical object such as *Only Revolutions*, which invites only continual, illimitable rereadings. Roland Barthes is sceptical of the belief that 'the first reading is a primary, naïve, phenomenal reading which we will only, afterwards, have to "explicate," to intellectualize', adding 'as if there were a beginning of reading, as if everything were not already read: there is no *first* reading, even if the text is concerned to give us that illusion by several operations of *suspense*, artifices more spectacular than persuasive' (1974: 16). For Barthes, rereading, 'an operation contrary to the commercial and ideological habits of society', is the suggested mode of reading for 'those of us who are trying to establish a plural' (15). He claims that 'it alone saves the text from repetition (those who fail to reread are obliged to read the same story everywhere), multiplies it in its internal chronology ("this happens *before* or *after* that") and recaptures a mythic time (without *before* or *after*)' (16). In his view if we '*immediately* reread the text, it is in order to obtain, as though under the effect of a drug (that of recommencement, of difference), not the *real* text, but a plural text: the same and new' (16).

This description of '*immediate*' rereading, a constant encounter with a 'plural' text which is both 'the same and new' captures something of the reader's experience of *Only Revolutions*, which does indeed attempt to create 'a mythic time (without *before* or *after*)'.[2] He or she is under the influence of a 'drug ... of recommencement, of difference' as he or she rotates (or 'flips') between Sam and Hailey's words. This drug is often so strong that his or her first instinct on reaching the apparent 'end', or 'ends' of the book (S360 and H360) is to begin reading again (see Hayles, this volume). This constant rereading is again encouraged by verbal connections; the final words of Sam's and Hailey's narratives 'I could never walk away from you' are echoed, in fact contradicted, in the opening third and fourth lines of each: 'I can walk away / from anything' (S1, H1). The apparent closure of the last lines is thus immediately reopened as the reader recalls that each character begins their narrative with the opposite claim.

V. Figure and ground

In cognitive-poetic terms, the reader's attention is continually engaged by a constant renewal of the figure and ground relationship. Figure and ground are concepts from gestalt psychology which explain how we differentiate visual objects from backgrounds; a figure may have a number of features which give it prominence, such as being self-contained with well-defined edges, or moving in relation to the static ground. Cognitive poetics has drawn on this basic psychological insight extensively, with figures usually being seen either as characters, who move against the background of their settings, or as dominant features of style emerging from rigorous stylistic analysis (see Stockwell 2002: 15–20). Figures attract the attention of the reader (hence are 'attractors'), while the ground is characterised by the reader's 'neglect'. This relationship is ever-changing though, as the reader's focus constantly shifts between attractors. In stylistic terms, as Stockwell notes, 'attention is paid to objects which are presented in topic position (first) in sentences, or have focus, emphasis, focalisation or viewpoint attached to them' (2002: 19).[3]

The cognitive-poetic application of figure and ground is a useful way of thinking about *Only Revolutions* because it suggests how the book manages to sustain the reader's attention as he or she becomes addicted to the 'drug . . . of recommencement, of difference'. It implies a dynamic, ever-changing conceptualisation of the reading experience, in contrast to the more static model of reading/rereading common in much literary criticism. As one figure loses its prominence and fades into the background, another becomes stylistically foregrounded and attracts the reader's attention. In the context of *Only Revolutions*, as the reader rotates the book, a different character temporarily holds the floor, with slight verbal changes standing out against the background of what he or she has just read. In each case what is new can only be judged against what is the same, and the next rotation of the book will change the prominences and the figure and ground relationship again.

Take this example from near the 'end' of the narrative, when the teenage lovers find themselves separated and caught in a snowstorm on a mountain-top. In Sam's account, he calls out for Hailey but receives no response:

> Rejected even by the prejudice of
> the Rankest Order, no longer locatable
> with even my own veerings to
> —
> her?
> Her dazzling pace? Her curving way?
> That terrible haste reeeeending a World. (S326–327)

Here the question 'her?' achieves particular prominence due to its position at the head of the next page (though enjambment between pages is relatively frequent, this is one of the few occasions on which there is just one word on the first line of a new page). Sam's call for,

The drug of rereading

and need for, Hailey is thus foregrounded, as too is his confusion concerning her whereabouts. Another attractor here is the word 'reeeeending', where the elongation suggests that Hailey's 'terrible haste' stretches the world to breaking-point.

The reader then flips the book over to encounter Hailey's version:

> Abandoning the borders of
> even the Remotest Orders, no longer locatable
> with even my own nearness to
> —
> him?
> His radiant place? His quickening race?
> That frightening pace reending a World. (H326–327)

As usual there are both similarities and differences here. Sam's 'Rejected . . . by' becomes Hailey's 'Abandoning', suggesting that she is in greater control of her fate at this point, while his 'the Rankest Order' becomes her 'the Remotest Orders', and his 'veerings' her 'nearness', with the assonance of 'veer' and 'near' reinforcing the semantic link between the two words. The page break again foregrounds the personal pronoun and question-mark at the top of the next page, with the change from 'her?' to 'him?' shifting the focus to Hailey's loss of Sam. His appreciation of her 'dazzling pace' is transposed into her acknowledgement of his 'radiant place', with the rhyme continued in 'quickening race' before the by-now-expected 'pace' itself appears in the next line. Crucially, the foregrounded 'reeeeending' changes to 'reending'. Again the unusual spelling ensures that the word is an attractor, yet the meaning has changed; though the sense of 'rending' to breaking-point remains in the background, a new lexeme, 're-ending' is brought to the fore, tying in with the notion that 'the World' of *Only Revolutions*, due to its physical form, cannot be simply 'ended', but is rather continually being begun again and 're-ended'. A cognitive-poetic perspective reveals how the reader's attention to these passages, and the book as a whole, is similarly constantly renewing itself, as new 'figures' come to prominence and others fade away.

VI. Sam and Hailey: 'allways around'

As many of the passages quoted so far suggest, Sam and Hailey are themselves aware of the formal properties of the forever 'reending

... World' they inhabit. Indeed, they frequently describe themselves as participants in the processes of rotating and revolving that the book demands. Stuck in their dead-end jobs in St. Louis, for example, they make numerous references to 'cycles', both those on which they explore the area, and in Sam's words 'The JustGettingBy / cycle of surviving' (S169), or in Hailey's 'The OnlyGettingBy / cycle of striving' (H169). Their daily work 'cycles' also mean that they are continually missing each other:

>Arriving when I leave.
>>Leaving when I arrive.
>Departing Them by drifts
>only we survive. Our cycle allways
>>putting everyone out of work. (S192)

>Leaving when I arrive.
>>Arriving when I leave.
>Departing Them with shifts
>only we survive. Our cycle allways
>>putting everyone out to work. (H192)

The rearranging of the first two lines here both suggests the continuous, frustrating nature of their shift patterns (each is continually leaving when the other arrives), and the way that each one's text is constantly being moved above and below the other's. When the page containing S192 is revolved, for example, 'Leaving' and 'Arriving' change positions again, as Hailey notes: 'Sam leaving when I arrive. / Sam arriving when I leave' (H169) (the same is obviously true in reverse of the relationship between H192 and S169). The 'allways' cyclical nature of the reading experience ensures that their words too are continually 'leaving' and 'arriving'. In both 'the World' and the book they are continually swapping places with each other. This intensifies the disorientation caused by their feelings for each other. Sam comments on how Hailey 'turns me upside down. And the World' (S246).

'Circles', as well as 'cycles', are everywhere to be found, or, as Sam and Hailey would put it, 'allways around' (see S161, H161, S193, H193). As they crash near the end of their road-trip, for example, Sam describes the tyres 'spinning US round and around, / completecircles upon this concrete cold, out of control' (S306), while Hailey's formulation is 'zinging US around and around, / fullcircles on this roadtop freeze, beyond control' (H306). Yet there is at times a difference between the kinds of 'complete' or 'full' circle that each

The drug of rereading 213

enacts. Shortly before the crash, as the car they are in 'careens' across the ice, Sam observes that:

> There's only one curve. Delicate
> with the centrifugal
>   theft of all
>   I never kept. (S305)

Hailey's words, not surprisingly, present a counter-image:

> There's only one turn. Naked
> with the centripetal
>   loan of all
>   I never owned. (H305)

The contrast between 'centripetal' and 'centrifugal' motion perhaps suggests an increasing tension between the characters; the direction of Hailey's travel is towards the centre, and the return of the 'loan of all / I never owned', while Sam's is away from the centre, and the 'theft of all / I never kept'.[4] While Hailey's 'loan' suggests a giving back to 'the World', Sam's 'theft' indicates a taking away. At other times their relationships to society, and other people, seem the reverse; Sam claims that 'to me alone everyone must cleave. / Allways' (S159), while Hailey's equivalent is 'only I allone will everyone leave. / Allways' (H159). Whether being pulled towards the centre or away from it, both are, like the book itself, in perpetual, circular motion, allways together and yet allways allone, allways circling the object they most desire: each other. As they put it in chorus: 'Whatever. Everyone circles a want' (S165, H165).

As their constant 'recirculating' (H267) appears to be nearing an end, with each trying in vain to revive the other, they are both tempted to destroy 'the World' in bitter revenge for their loss. Each declares that without the other 'I am / only revolutions of ruin' (S347, H347). Yet each rejects this path, choosing instead to let 'the World', and by implication the world of the book, continue on its circular, cyclical course:

>   I'll destroy no World
> so long it keeps turning with flurry & gush,
>   petals & stems bending and lush,
> and allways our hushes returning anew. (S360)
>
>   I'll destroy no World
> so long it keeps turning with scurry & blush,

> fledgling & charms beading with dews,
> and allways our rush returning renewed. (H360)

Again there are some subtle interplays here that link the two passages together while maintaining their distinctness; the way that the rhyme of 'gush/lush/hushes' is echoed in 'blush/rush', for example, or the chiming of 'anew' with 'dews' and 'renewed'. Both Sam and Hailey opt in the end for a lack of end, deciding to keep 'the World' 're-turning'. In this they are aligned with the reader of the book, who can also 'renew' his or her reading by starting again at the first page and beginning 'anew'.

The characters in *Only Revolutions* are thus, like the reader, travellers through the book who will never reach a destination. Sam and Hailey are aware of the way in which their own words are constantly swapping places as the reader turns their narratives 'upside down', just as they do each other. The parallels between their 'World' and the world of the reader emphasise the fluidity of the boundary between reader and book, as the former actively engages with the latter. The reader's continual, even compulsive, rotation of the book of *Only Revolutions* creates a dynamic pattern of reading in which new meanings are forever emerging from an unremittingly 'plural' text. For the reader, as for Sam and Hailey, both the demands and the pleasures of *Only Revolutions* arise from this endless process of 'allways' revolving and rereading.

Notes

1 All words beginning 'al' are consistently spelt 'all' throughout the book, the double /l/ suggesting both the lexeme 'all' and the pause symbol, which appears at the beginning of both Sam's and Hailey's narratives (and on the dust cover to the hardback edition). There is perhaps also an intertextual reference to the 'hallways' of Danielewski's earlier *House of Leaves*, and to the track '5 & ½ Minute Hallway' on his sister Poe's album *Haunted* (see Evans, this volume).
2 In his interview with Kiki Benzon, Danielewski speculates on the two kids he came across on a street corner in mythic terms: 'Maybe they were Homeric gods in disguise. Maybe they truly were Mendicants. But there was something magical about them for me - that absolute attachment to each other. And I looked at them as kind of American Romeo and Juliet. But later I realized that they really weren't - because they didn't have the Capulets and the Montagues out there to separate them, to chase them.

There's Bonnie and Clyde, Natural Born Killers.' See also Hansen (this volume).
3 For the source of the concepts of figure and ground in cognitive psychology, see Rubin (1958) and Wertheimer (1955); for their continued use in studies of attention, see Haber and Hershenson (1973); and for their application in cognitive linguistics, see Langacker (1987).
4 In the Benzon (2007) interview Danielewski argues that while *House of Leaves* concerns itself with 'interiorities and history and progeny and ancestors' and hence 'is what I would call a centripetal book', *Only Revolutions* is 'pointedly a centrifugal novel. It was about getting outside. It was about looking at landscape. It was about addressing what the open was.'

Works cited

Barthes, R. (1974 [1973]) *S/Z*, trans. Miller, R., Oxford: Basil Blackwell.
Benzon, K. (2007) 'Revolutions 2' [Interview with Mark Z. Danielewski]. *Electronic Book Review*. www.electronicbookreview.com/thread/wuc/regulated.
Calinescu, M. (1993) *Rereading*, New Haven; London: Yale University Press.
Danielewski, M. Z. (2006) *Only Revolutions*, New York: Pantheon Books.
Haber, R. N. and Hershenson, M. (1973) *The Psychology of Visual Perception*, New York; London: Holt, Rinehart and Winston.
Langacker, R. (1987) *Foundations of Cognitive Grammar; Volume I: Theoretical Prerequisites*, Stanford: Stanford University Press.
McDonald, P. (2006) 'Ideas of the book and histories of literature: after theory?', in 'Special topic: the history of the book and the idea of literature', co-ordinated by Lerer, S. and Price, L., *PMLA* 121: 214–228.
McKenzie, D. F. (2002) *Making Meaning: 'Printers of the Mind' and Other Essays*, ed. McDonald, P. D. and Suarez, M. F., Amherst; Boston: University of Massachusetts Press.
Price, L. (2006) 'Introduction: reading matter', in 'Special topic: the history of the book and the idea of literature', co-ordinated by Lerer, S. and Price, L., *PMLA* 121: 9–16.
Roustang, F. (1989) 'On reading again', in Kavanagh, T. M. (ed.) *The Limits of Theory*, Stanford: Stanford University Press, pp. 121–138.
Rubin, E. (1958 [1915]) 'Figure and ground', trans. Wertheimer, M., in Beardslee, D. C. and Wertheimer, M. (eds) *Readings in Perception*, Princeton, NJ: D. Van Nostrand, pp. 194–203.
Stockwell, P. (2002) *Cognitive Poetics: An Introduction*, London; New York: Routledge.
Wertheimer, A. (1958 [1923]) 'Principles of perceptual organization', trans. Wertheimer, M., in Beardslee, D. C. and Wertheimer, M. (eds) *Readings in Perception*, Princeton, NJ: D. Van Nostrand, pp. 115–135.

Contributors

Joe Bray is Senior Lecturer in Language and Literature at the University of Sheffield. He is the author of *The Epistolary Novel: Representations of Consciousness* (2003) and *The Female Reader in the English Novel: From Burney to Austen* (2009). His research interests include textual culture and materiality of the book, and he is co-editor of both *Ma(r)king The Text: The Presentation of Meaning on the Literary Page* (2000) and a special issue of the journal *Textual Cultures* (2.2, 2007).

Mel Evans is a Ph.D. student at the University of Sheffield. Her thesis examines the idiolect(s) of Queen Elizabeth I, combining historical sociolinguistic and stylistic methodologies. She also has research expertise in cognitive approaches to language and literature. Her essay in this volume demonstrates her interdisciplinary skills, focusing on the connections between *House of Leaves* and the music of Danielewski's sister, Poe.

Finn Fordham is a Lecturer in the Department of English at Royal Holloway University. His research centres on James Joyce and Modernism, but his interests extend into the postmodern period including contemporary author Mark Z. Danielewski. Finn has published widely in a range of journals and is the author of *Lots of Fun at Finnegans Wake: Unravelling Universals* (2007).

Alison Gibbons is a Lecturer in Stylistics, English Language and Literature at De Montfort University, Leicester. Her doctoral research (2008) applied cognitive approaches to twenty-first-century multimodal novels, and Mark Z. Danielewski was a central focus. Alison's developing work extends her interests in experimental late twentieth- and early twenty-first-century literature across media forms. Alison has had a number of articles published internationally in the following journals and collections: *Hermes: Journal of Language and Communication Studies* (2008), *New Perspectives on Narrative and Multimodality* (2009), *Electronic Book Review* (2010). She is a co-editor of the *Routledge Companion to Experimental Literature* (2011) and is the author of *Multimodality, Cognition, and Experimental Literature* (2010–11).

Mark B. N. Hansen is Professor of Literature at Duke University. He is author of *Embodying Technesis: Technology Beyond Writing* (2000), *New Philosophy for New Media* (2004) and *Bodies in Code* (2006), as well as numerous essays on cultural theory, contemporary literature and media. He has co-edited (with Taylor Carman) *The Cambridge Companion to Merleau-Ponty* and is currently co-editing two volumes: *Critical Terms for Media Studies* (with W. J. T. Mitchell) and *Neocybernetic Emergence* (with Bruce Clarke).

N. Katherine Hayles is Professor of Literature at Duke University. She has published widely and to critical acclaim. Her book *How We Became Posthuman: Virtual Bodies in Cybernetics, Literature and Informatics* (1999) won the Rene Wellek Prize for the Best Book in Literary Theory for 1998–9, and *Writing Machines* (2002) won the Suzanne Langer Award for Outstanding Scholarship. Her most recent book was *My Mother Was a Computer: Digital Subjects and Literary Texts* (2005). She is considered to be the seminal voice on Mark Z. Danielewski.

Paul McCormick is a Ph.D. student at Ohio State University who specialises in twentieth-century literature and narrative theory. His dissertation applies descriptive and analytical tools from narrative theory to study Hollywood novels and other novels that engage with cinema aesthetically and thematically. He has presented papers on authors including Dangarembga, Danielewski, Ford and Rushdie, and his first essay, "Claims of Stable Identity and (Un)reliability in Dissonant Narration", is forthcoming from *Poetics Today*.

Brian McHale is Distinguished Humanities Professor of English in the Ohio State University. He was for many years associate editor, and later co-editor, of the journal *Poetics Today*. He is a leading voice in postmodernism, having authored *Postmodernist Fiction* (1987), *Constructing Postmodernism* (1992) and *The Obligation toward the Difficult Whole* (2004), as well as articles on free indirect discourse, *mise en abyme*, narrativity, modernist and postmodernist poetics, and science fiction. He is co-editor with Randall Stevenson of *The Edinburgh Companion to Twentieth-Century Literatures in English* (2006).

Bronwen Thomas is Senior Lecturer in Linguistics and Literature at Bournemouth University, where she lectures in language and literary studies, media and communication, and creative writing. She has published a number of articles on film, hypertext fiction and fanfiction, as well as on more traditional literary forms. Her most recent book is *New Narratives: Theory and Practice* (2009) co-edited with Ruth Page.

Dirk Van Hulle is a Senior Lecturer in English Literature at the University of Antwerp, where he works at the Centre for Manuscript Genetics. He is an editor of the *Journal of Beckett Studies* and *Genetic Joyce Studies*. He is the author of *Textual Awareness* (2004) and *Manuscript Genetics, Joyce's Know-How, Beckett's Nohow* (2008). He is also co-director of the *Beckett Digital Manuscript Project,* a member of the editorial board of *Samuel Beckett Today / Aujourd'hui*.

Glyn White is a Lecturer in the School of English, Sociology, Politics and Contemporary History at the University of Salford. He has written a number of articles on the visual in literary narrative and is the author of *Reading the Graphic Surface: The Presence of the Book in Prose Fiction* (2005).

Index

A-series and B-series time 10, 181–3, 191, 196, 197
absence 20, 21, 25, 29, 168, 169
academia 12, 98–9
affordance(s) 7, 52, 56, 60–5
Amazon Kindle 1
annotations 40–1, 44–6
anti-marketing 23, 27
Apocalypse Now 34
architexture 6, 44
assemblage 160–1
Austen, Jane 12, 87
authorial audience 57, 62
Authorized ('King James') Bible 152
authorship 73–4, 77, 79, 80, 82, 83, 87–8, 95–6

Badlands 141
Baetens, Jan 63
Bakhtin, Mikhail Mikhailovich 35
Ball, Edward 123–4
Barthes, Roland 11, 116, 185, 208–9
Baudelaire, Charles 152
Beatles, The
 'A Day in the Life' 58
 Sgt. Pepper's Lonely Hearts Club Band 58
Beckett, Samuel 137–8
Benét, Stephen Vincent 143
Benzon, Kiki 8, 12, 164, 168, 203, 214n.2, 215n.4

biography 70, 79, 80, 83, 84
Blair Witch Project 54
blank space 112–15, 119
Booth, Wayne 66n.4
Borders Books and Music 54
Borges, Jorge Luis 5
Brahe, Tycho 136
Brazil 36
Buse, Peter 106–7

Calinescu, Matei 208
Calvino, Italo 29, 117
 If On a Winter's Night a Traveller 29
Carlyle, Thomas
 Sartor Resartus 134
Carson, Anne 143
Casanova, Giacomo 208
CBS 53
chronology 165–6
 hot vs cold 195–7
cinematic novel *see* film
clusters 169–72
cognition 17–32
cognitive dissonance 6, 21–5, 29
cognitive linguistics 23, 26, 144, 202
cognitive poetics 11, 17–32, 200, 202, 209–11
cognitive psychology 6, 202
cognitive reactance 6, 22–4, 27, 29

Coleridge, Samuel Taylor 36
collective intelligence 93
colour printing 105, 108–12, 119
combination, axis of 9, 150, 151, 156
conceptual metaphor 18
    TEXT AS WORLD 18
Congreve, William 200
constraint(s) 11, 161, 164–5, 169, 187–93, 203, 207
Copernicus, Nicolaus 136
Cousineau, Thomas 135
Culler, Jonathan 158n.7
Cultural Revolution, The 186

dadaism 123, 125
Danielewski, Annie 54
    see also Poe
Darwin, Charles 9, 126, 127, 131–2, 138
    On the Origin of Species 127, 132
database 162–3
Debord, Guy 124–5, 126
dedications 27–30
Deer Hunter, The 34
deixis 17, 24
    perceptual deixis 17, 24, 25, 26, 27
    see also double deixis
Delicatessen 36
DeLillo, Don 4, 5, 60
    Libra 165
    Running Dog 52, 56
    Underworld 6, 33, 41–4
de-presencing 191–3
Derrida, Jacques 8, 92, 108, 110, 113, 114, 119, 168
détournement 9, 123–6, 127, 130, 136, 138
digital technology 2–3, 10, 11, 60, 61–5, 170–1, 178–9
digital topography 1
dimension, topographic 162

direct address 17, 19, 24, 25, 30
Disney 53
Donne, John
    'The Sunne Rising' 135, 137
Dorn, Ed 143
Dos Passos, John
    Manhattan Transfer 141
    The Big Money 52
dot-com bubble 53
double deixis 24–5, 28
DuPlessis, Rachel Blau 9, 144–5, 146, 148, 149, 157, 157n.6

Easy Rider 141
Eco, Umberto 72, 73
edgework 19
Eggers, Dave 4
Eisenstein, Sergei 42
Eliade, Mircea 38
Ellis, Bret Easton 37–8
Emerson, Ralph Waldo 4
enjambment 145
epic 4, 5
    see also katabasis
equivalence, projection of 9, 150, 151, 153, 156, 157n.6
extratextual references 92, 95

Facebook 86
fan cultures 87–8
fan forums
    MZD 2, 7, 87, 88, 89–101
    Twin Peaks 92–3, 94, 95–6
Faulkner, William
    The Sound and the Fury 141
figure
    and ground 11, 209–11, 215n.3
    see also foregrounding
film
    clandestine 6, 33–4, 42
    relation to the novel 2, 7, 10, 33, 35, 36, 52, 55–6, 65, 130–1
Fink, Eugen 191

Index

Fletcher, R. 5
Fludernik, Monika 17
footnotes 6
  see also paratext
Ford, Ford Madox 131
Ford (Motor Company) 55
foregrounding 20, 21, 23, 25, 27, 29
  see also figure
Frank, Joseph 160–1
Frankel, Nick 113
Frazier, Warren 3
free verse 144
Fuentecilla, Eric 57
Full Metal Jacket 34
functions (Jakobson) 9, 149–51, 156

Gaiman, Neil 28–9
  Anansi Boys 28–9
gaps 144, 145, 146–7, 148
Gass, William H. 114
Gavins, Joanna 18, 19, 20, 21, 29
Genette, Gérard 27–30
ghost stories 105–6, 119
Gibson, James J. 7, 56, 66n.3
Gilder, George 53
Google 166, 194, 198n.3
Gray, Alasdair 118
Gregory, S. 5
ground *see* figure
gutters 147–8, 149, 157n.5

Hansen, Mark B. N. 1, 52, 68–9, 72, 78
Hayles, N. Katherine 1, 5, 10, 52, 55, 62, 70, 72, 89, 98, 157n.1, 157n.4, 178
Heidigger, Martin 50
Helter Skelter 184
Heraclitus 128
Herman, David 24–6, 28
Hidalgo Downing, Laura 20, 21

Hollywood 54, 60
Holmlund, Chris 60
Hume, Kathryn 63
Husserl, Edmund 178, 191
Hutcheon, Linda 131
hypermediation 142

iconic spacing 147
illustrations 112, 119
immersion 8, 115–17
information multiplicity 160–1
infosphere 167
intertextual competence 73, 75, 79, 81, 84
intertextuality 5, 7, 8, 28, 71, 73–84, 95, 97
  and foregrounding 74, 78
  and narrative 80–3
iPhone 1, 198n.3

Jakobson, Roman 9, 149–51, 152–3, 156, 157, 157n.6, 158n.7, 173
James, M. R. 107
Janicaud, Dominique
  Chronos 182
Jenkins, Henry 92–3, 94, 95
Johnny Truant 18
Johnson, B. S. 118
Johnston, John 160–1, 170–1
Journet, Debra 98
Joyce, James 126, 135
  A Portrait of the Artist as a Young Man 135, 136
  Finnegans Wake 5, 9, 123, 126–30, 131, 133, 135, 137, 138
  "The Dead" 135–6
  Ulysses 5
Jurassic Park 60

Kalevala 152
katabasis 6

katabasis (*cont.*)
  as epic 33, 34, 35, 43
  as initiation 38
  as narrative 44, 51
  as regression 36–8
Kennedy, John F.
  assassination of 165, 185, 195, 196, 203
Kepler, Johannes 136
Kerouac, Jack
  On the Road 141
Kinbote, Charles 5
King, Stephen 38, 137
Kubrick, Stanley
  2001: A Space Odyssey 60, 65, 80

labyrinth 6, 40, 44–6, 49–51, 75, 84
Lakoff, George 20
language
  as house 50
  as underworld 6, 34, 44, 49–51
Larsen, Reif 113–14, 117, 118
Lautréamont, Comte de 125, 126
Leary, Timothy 183
Lee, Robert E. (General) 183
Lévi-Strauss, Claude 195
Longfellow, Henry Wadsworth 152
  Song of Hiawatha, The 152, 153
Lost 98
Lynch, David 95, 96
Lynch, Deidre 11–12
lyric poetry 143

MTV 54
McCaffery, Larry 2, 5
McCloud, Scott 147
McDonald, Peter D. 201, 202
McHale, Brian 114, 116, 117, 173
McKenzie, D. F. 200–1, 202
McTaggart, J. M. E. 181, 182
Malick, Terence 141
Mallarmé, Stéphane 113

Manovich, Lev 60, 65n.1, 162, 176
Mao Tse-Tung 186
Margolin, Uri 24
Matrix III, The 36
Mauthner, Fritz 128, 138n.1
media environment 7, 10, 52–6, 59, 65, 142
Mellor, David 181–2
Melville, Herman 4
  Moby Dick 5, 65
metacommentary 5, 59, 97
Merrill, James 143
metaphor 144
metre 151
millennium bug 1
Milton, John 5
  Paradise Lost 130
Miramax 53
mise-en-page 200, 207
modernism 141, 143, 149
Morley, Catherine 4, 5
multimodality 18, 27–30
Murray, Les 143
MySpace 86

Nabokov, Vladimir
  Pale Fire 5
narrative
  and database 162–3
  and history 183–7
  layers 70, 77, 82
  poetry 9, 143
  speed 63
narrativity 5, 145
National Book Award 4
negation 6, 17, 18, 20–4, 25, 28, 29
Negroponte, Nicholas 53
networked novel 2, 52, 55

O'Hagan, Sean 4
octet 162, 165, 173–5
ontological levels 21, 30, 114, 117

Index

Orpheus
  and Eurydice 37
Ospovat, Don 131, 138n.3
Oulipo 170, 190
Ovid 92

Pantheon 54, 57
  see also Random House
paradigm/ paradigmatic 9, 150, 162, 163, 169, 173
parallelism 9, 151, 153, 154–6, 157, 157n.6
Paramount Communications 53
paranoia 44
paratext 5, 19, 27–30, 57–8, 169
pattern, temporal 173–4
Pavic, Milorad 5
  The Inner Side of the Wind 5
Percy, Marge 28
  Small Changes 28
perspectivism 141
Phelan, James 66n.4
Photoshop 60, 65
Pike, David 36–7
plane, topographic 10, 160
Platoon 34
Poe 54, 69, 78, 79, 80, 83, 84, 86
  Haunted 2, 7, 54, 55, 68, 69, 70–1, 73, 74, 75–83, 84n.1
poetic function *see* functions
Ponicsanyi, J. 39, 44
postmodernism 7, 65, 149
presence 168, 169
  see also de-presencing
Pressman, Jessica 2, 52, 55, 73, 74, 76, 79, 80, 82
Price, Leah 201
print (the printed book) 2, 11, 178–81, 197, 200–1
prohibition 163
pronouns 17–20, 24–7, 28, 29
  first-person 18
  second-person 6, 18, 19, 24–7, 29

Proust, Marcel 136
Pynchon, Thomas 60
  Gravity's Rainbow 5, 52, 168

quotation marks
  in *The Fifty Year Sword* 8, 107–12, 119

Rabinowitz, Peter 66n.4
Radcliffe, Ann 30
  The Mysteries of Udolpho 30
Rader, Ralph 66n.4
Random House 18
  see also Pantheon
récupération 9, 123–6, 137, 138
remediation 1, 3, 52, 62, 70, 86, 98
rereading 11, 200, 208–9, 214
rhetorical narrative theory 52, 66
rhyme 151
Richards, Robert J. 131
Richardson, Samuel 11
Riddell, Allen Bye 162
Riffaterre, Michael 158n.7
road movie 141
Roth, Philip 4, 5
Roustang, François 208
Rowling, J. K.
  Harry Potter novels 87
Rule, Jane 28
  This is not for you 28
Russian Formalism 142
Ryan, Marie-Laure 8, 115–17

Sacks, Sheldon 66n.4
Saussure, Ferdinand de 150
segmentivity 9, 144–5, 157, 157n.6
selection, axis of 9, 140, 156
self-reflexivity 5, 96–7
Shakespeare, William 5, 152
Sheridan Le Fanu, Joseph 107
Shklovsky, Viktor 9, 142, 143
Situationist International 123–4, 126, 136, 138

Sollers, Philippe 113
Sony Reader 1
spacing 145, 149
spatial aesthetic 10, 160
spatial form 157n.4
Spencer, Herbert 126
Sterne, Laurence
   Tristram Shandy 9, 142, 143, 157n.3
Stewart, Garret 173
Stockwell, Peter 202, 210
Stott, Andrew 106–7
Subway 36
surrealism 123, 125
Swift, Jonathan
   Battle of the Books 137
symmetry 11, 164, 169, 173, 203
syntagm/ syntagmatic 9, 150, 162, 163

Tate, Nahum 138n.5
temporality
   spatialised 174
   see also A-series and B-series time
Terminator 2 60
text
   as game 115–18
   as world 115–19
text world theory 17–27
   discourse-world 18
   negative text-world 21, 23, 27
   split discourse-world 18
   text-world 18, 19, 21, 25
Thelma and Louise 141
Time, Inc. 53
Tolkein, J. R.
   Lord of the Rings 87
trajectory, temporal 160, 175
turn, topographic 160
Tutuola, Amos 107
Twilight 38
typography 8, 63–4, 91–2, 105–15, 200–1

underworlds
   as counter-cultural 33, 36, 42–3
   structure of 40, 51
   see also katabasis
unnarratable, the 62
unnatural narration 59
Updike, John 4, 5

Van Sambeek, Peter 8, 105, 112
Viacom 53
Vico, Giambattista 129
Vietnam 34, 38, 56

Waits, Tom 36
Wallace, David Foster 4, 44, 49
   Infinite Jest 6, 33, 38–42
Warhol, Robyn 62
Warner Communications 53, 54
Werth, Paul 18, 20, 21
West, Nathaniel
   The Day of the Locust 52, 56
Whistler, James MacNeill 113
Whitman, Walt
   Leaves of Grass 152, 153
   'Song of Myself' 152
Wired magazine 53
Wolman, Gil J. 124
Woolf, Virginia 136

Yale University 4
Yeats, William Butler 152

EU authorised representative for GPSR:
Easy Access System Europe, Mustamäe tee 50,
10621 Tallinn, Estonia
gpsr.requests@easproject.com

www.ingramcontent.com/pod-product-compliance
Ingram Content Group UK Ltd.
Pitfield, Milton Keynes, MK11 3LW, UK
UKHW021832140426
5217IPUK00021B/1395